Using Fiscal Policy and Public Financial Management to Promote Gender Equality

This book examines how fiscal policy and management can promote gender equality in developing and developed countries. Providing an international look at gender budgeting, it draws on countries at different levels of development, with an emphasis on low-income developing countries. It introduces the reader to the main trends in gender equality, the key ideas and rationale of gender budgeting from a fiscal policy perspective, and where gender budgeting fits into public financial management.

It offers case studies and other empirical evidence from developing, emerging, and developed countries on what works in using fiscal policy and public financial management to narrow gender gaps in education, health care, access to infrastructure, and economic empowerment. It also provides policy recommendations appropriate to countries at different levels of development.

The reader will gain an understanding of how fiscal policy and public financial management can contribute to gender equality and women's advancement. The book provides a well-grounded set of conclusions and policy recommendations, drawn from an evaluation of the evidence. The focus is on low-income developing countries but is also combined with a well-rounded look at developing countries more generally, emerging markets, and developed countries.

This book will be a valuable resource for economists and policymakers, particularly those in developing countries still grappling with large disparities between women and men. It will also prove useful to researchers and those who provide technical assistance and aid to countries on fiscal policies and tools for gender equality.

Janet G. Stotsky is a consultant on applied public policies and on women and development. She is a retired senior staff of the International Monetary Fund, where she was a fiscal and macroeconomics expert and led a project on gender budgeting. She has worked at the U.S. Department of the Treasury and taught at Rutgers University and American University. She has a PhD in economics from Stanford University.

Routledge Studies in Gender and Economics

Using Fiscal Policy and Public Financial Management to Promote Gender Equality
International Perspectives
Janet G. Stotsky

For more information about this series, please visit: www.routledge.com/Routledge-Studies-in-Gender-and-Economics/book-series/RSGENECON

Using Fiscal Policy and Public Financial Management to Promote Gender Equality

International Perspectives

Janet G. Stotsky

Routledge
Taylor & Francis Group
LONDON AND NEW YORK

First published 2020 by Routledge

2 Park Square, Milton Park, Abingdon, Oxon OX14 4RN
605 Third Avenue, New York, NY 10017

Routledge is an imprint of the Taylor & Francis Group, an informa business

First issued in paperback 2021

Copyright © 2020 Janet G. Stotsky

The right of Janet G. Stotsky to be identified as author of this work has been asserted by her in accordance with sections 77 and 78 of the Copyright, Designs and Patents Act 1988.

All rights reserved. No part of this book may be reprinted or reproduced or utilised in any form or by any electronic, mechanical, or other means, now known or hereafter invented, including photocopying and recording, or in any information storage or retrieval system, without permission in writing from the publishers.

Notice:
Product or corporate names may be trademarks or registered trademarks, and are used only for identification and explanation without intent to infringe.

Publisher's Note

The publisher has gone to great lengths to ensure the quality of this reprint but points out that some imperfections in the original copies may be apparent.

British Library Cataloguing-in-Publication Data
A catalogue record for this book is available from the British Library

Library of Congress Cataloging-in-Publication Data
Names: Stotsky, Janet Gale, author.
Title: Using fiscal policy and public financial management to promote gender equality: international perspectives/Janet G. Stotsky.
Description: 1st Edition. | New York: Routledge, 2020. | Series: Gender economics | Includes bibliographical references and index.
Identifiers: LCCN 2019041444 (print) | LCCN 2019041445 (ebook) | ISBN 9780367278663 (hardback) | ISBN 9780429298400 (ebook)
Subjects: LCSH: Fiscal policy. | Finance, Public. | Sex discrimination in employment. | Women-Employment. | Equality.
Classification: LCC HJ192.5 .S766 2020 (print) | LCC HJ192.5 (ebook) | DDC 331.4/133—dc23
LC record available at https://lccn.loc.gov/2019041444
LC ebook record available at https://lccn.loc.gov/2019041445

ISBN: 978-0-367-27866-3 (hbk)
ISBN: 978-1-03-217541-6 (pbk)
DOI: 10.4324/9780429298400

Typeset in Bembo
by Apex CoVantage, LLC

To my mother, Sandra Stotsky, and my late father, Bernard Stotsky, for encouraging me always, their genuine intellectual passion, and serving as my role models. And to the many women and girls of the developing world, who motivated my work. I hope this book might play a small role in helping them to overcome the bigotry and discrimination they face on a day-to-day basis and to better their lives.

Contents

Figures

Tables and boxes

Tables

Boxes

Authorship

Overall Book Author: Janet G. Stotsky
Background: Consultant with international organizations, national governments, private foundations, and private consulting firms on the economics of developing countries, including applied macroeconomics and microeconomics, and the economics of women in development. She is a retired senior-level economist at the International Monetary Fund and previously worked at the U.S. Department of the Treasury and taught at Rutgers University and American University. PhD in economics, Stanford University.

Contributors

Chapters 2 and 5

Co-author: Suhaib Kebhaj
Background: Senior, Ernst and Young—quantitative economics and statistics. He was previously a research assistant at the International Monetary Fund. MA in public policy, American University.

Chapter 6

Co-author: Ellen Shnidman
Background: Medical and scientific writer for medical education and pharmaceutical industries. Experience in writing about public health programs in Ethiopia and the developing world. Currently scientific writer for Alpha Tau Medical. MS in neuroscience, Weizmann Institute, Israel.

Acknowledgments

I would like to thank the many people and institutions that were instrumental in helping to bring about this book. I am grateful to my co-authors on chapters in this book, Suhaib Kebhaj, on Chapters 2 and 5, and Ellen Shnidman, on Chapter 6, who also helped extensively with revisions to all the chapters. Manuk Gazanchyan and Li Tang ably assisted with the statistical work in Chapter 9 and Selma Osman provided capable research assistance.

I would like to express my gratitude to commenters on the book's draft or earlier versions of the chapters as International Monetary Fund working papers, including Sandra Stotsky, Tej Prakash, Saqib Rizavi, Ronen Shnidman, Rhonda Shore, and Carol Rapaport, and many former International Monetary Fund colleagues and friends, and participants in sessions at the U.S. Agency for International Development, the U.S. Department of State, and elsewhere.

I am grateful to the many government officials who provided information on their governments' gender budgeting efforts and who encouraged me to pursue this topic. They truly are on the front lines of trying to achieve gender equality. I admire their dedication, often in the face of indifference or outright opposition.

I thank the earlier participants in the International Monetary Fund gender budgeting project, which I led, including Lekha Chakraborty, Tamoya Christie, Lisa Kolovich, Lucia Pérez Fragoso, Sheila Quinn, Corina Rodríguez Enríquez, Sakina Shibuya, Dhanaraj Thakur, Asad Zaman, and my assistants, Michelle Chen, Biva Joshi, and Jing Wang.

I am indebted to Diane Elson for the intellectual leadership that she has provided on this topic and the generous assistance that she gave on my earlier project. I also thank Stephan Klasen, Mark Blackden, Caren Grown, Jingqing Chai, MariaLuz Moreno Badia, Johannes Seiwald, Virginia Alonso, Monica Costa, Carol Cohn, Victoria Perry, Andy Berg, and Cathy Pattillo, who graciously lent their time to commenting on drafts and suggesting ideas.

I am grateful to Christine Lagarde, Julie Delahanty, Mayra Buvinic, Laura Tyson, Rohini Pande, Otaviano Canuto, Phumzile Mlambo-Ngcuka, Zohra Khan, Yamini Mishra, Sylvia Tereka, Friederike Schwarzendorfer, Adil Hidane, Prakash Loungani, Rupa Duttagupta, and the International Monetary Fund's

Communications Department, whose participation, in an earlier International Monetary Fund conference on gender budgeting, helped improve this book.

I thank the International Monetary Fund, which hired me as a visiting scholar after my retirement from the staff to lead the project on gender budgeting, during which I conducted some of the initial research for this book. I am indebted to the United Kingdom's Department for International Development, which supported my work at the International Monetary Fund on this topic. However, none of the views in this book necessarily represent those of either of these institutions.

Executive summary

Since its inception about 30 years ago in Australia, gender budgeting has spread to over 80 countries. Gender budgeting is an approach to budgeting that uses fiscal policy and public financial management to promote gender equality and women's and girls' development. It has been recognized as an important, if inadequately implemented, tool for improving access to education, health care, and the labor force for women and girls and for empowering them economically and politically. Gender budgeting also calls attention to the role that fiscal policies and public financial management can play in promoting gender equality, even when ingrained cultural influences and traditional practices present countervailing pressures.

Early interest in gender budgeting arose mostly in developed countries. But the evidence that we present in this book shows clearly that the greater need to elevate equality for women is in the developing world where gender disparities in fundamental areas such as education, health care access, paid workforce participation, and legal inheritance, still prevail in a large number of countries.

Developing regions of the world with pronounced gender inequality, such as the Middle East, South Asia, and sub-Saharan Africa, have experienced a significant increase in female political participation in recent decades but usually without comparable gains in economic equality. Both increased political participation *and* economic equality are needed to significantly improve the welfare of women and their societies as a whole. Figure 2.1 in Chapter 2 shows that as GDP increases, typically the Gender Development Index (GDI), a well-accepted composite index of gender equality, rises. However, the results of our econometric analysis in Chapter 9 demonstrate that modest rises in income in a developing country like India do not necessarily translate into sufficient increases in school enrollment to close all gender gaps. Specific government policies are needed to promote increased gender equality as a complement to economic growth. Our case studies in Chapters 5–8 highlight many of these policies.

There are very wealthy countries in the Middle East where women have high income (as part of household income) but few political and social rights. There are also low-income developing countries like Rwanda and Ethiopia in which women are now gaining more equal political rights compared to men but have not achieved wage parity or equivalent economic opportunities. Gender budgeting efforts should be focused on both of these dimensions—the economic and the political or social. In a model program, such as that in Rwanda, this is happening.

Without government leadership promoting passage of laws and implementing policies and programs, progress will be slow in many of these countries, and economic development will remain stymied. The focus of this book, therefore, is on the regions of the world that are low income and developing, where the need for gender equality is greatest. In countries of these regions, education and instruction in gender budgeting can be valuable both for its potential to bring about competent implementation of programs that reduce inequality, and also for its capacity to inculcate a gender equality consciousness in the national political and lay leadership, which should contribute to progress in the future.

Our introductory chapter highlights main themes in the book. Then we provide, in Chapter 2, a statistical overview of key indicators of gender equality and women's development, and trends in the GDI. We also discuss the derivation of the GDI and compare its value as a tool for policy purposes with that of individual indicators.

We then follow this overview by Chapters 3 and 4, in which we review the economic principles and fiscal policies underlying gender budgeting, as it has evolved in the past 30–40 years. In Chapter 3, we discuss how the broader rationale for gender budgeting comes from a desire to improve economic efficiency and productivity. A better educated female adult population with fewer work limitations will contribute more to economic productivity and to the education of the next generation, producing gains for women but also for their broader societies. However, the benefits of increased gender equality also include a concern for equity. Producing stable societies in the developing world requires *both* increased income levels *and* increased equity for women and men. We also provide examples of fiscal policies, programs, and tax reforms that have been adopted in various countries to reduce gender inequality. Some of these programs have rarely been included in gender budgeting initiatives and we encourage policymakers to incorporate them more frequently in their initiatives. For example, cash transfer programs that encourage families to send their children (or sometimes specifically their daughters) to school in exchange for a small cash subsidy, in particular, have proven to be quite successful in improving school attendance and retention in various regions of the world. We also present evidence that some programs that are gender neutral ended up benefiting women and girls more than men and boys. These, too, should be considered part of a gender budgeting program, supplemented by specific targets for women and girls.

In Chapter 4, we review details about how government budgets are actually constructed and key entry points for gender budgeting, which includes gender budget statements, budget circulars, and gender-related audits and benefit incidence analysis. Also, critically, we discuss which key stakeholders must be involved in creating, designing, and supporting gender budgeting. This includes such figures as a minister of finance, senior officials in the spending ministries, parliamentary committees, and women's advocacy groups. Gender budgeting has been most successful and has produced a measurable impact in countries where the minister of finance and often the president of the country have openly promoted its importance and have played a role in enforcing compliance with its directives.

In Chapters 5 through 8, we offer overviews of gender budgeting efforts in Africa, Asia, and selected emerging market and developing countries, and developed countries, respectively. We have noted where such efforts seem to have produced positive results, and where they have not made much of an impact or have not been seriously implemented. In the chapters on Africa and Asia, we focus on two key success stories—Rwanda and the Indian state of Kerala. In particular, we conclude that the success of these two sovereign entities in achieving improvements in many dimensions of gender equality shows that low income levels need not prevent significant improvements in the status of women, in a relatively short period of time.

In Chapter 9, we have used data from Indian states to build an econometric model testing the hypothesis that the presence of gender budgeting and grant money transferred from the national government to state governments, contributes positively to increasing gender equality. We use the ratio of females to males enrolled in primary and secondary school as our surrogate dependent variables for gender equality. The results of our statistical analysis suggest that rising income levels improve gender equality, but not by enough to close gender gaps, and that gender budgeting can have an impact on enrollment, too. This analysis is presented partly as an example of how econometrics can be used to sift through correlations between factors that influence gender equality versus those that do not, when many variables are thought to have influence.

In our concluding Chapter 10, we provide checklists of key findings and recommendations regarding the implementation of gender budgeting, with the goal of producing positive results in both the developing and developed regions of the world. We emphasize that low-income developing countries have needs of a different sort from developed countries, and therefore separate recommendations have been made for each type of country.

Evaluating the evidence we collected from a group of low-income developing countries in Africa and Asia, and a selection of emerging market and developing countries and developed countries, from around the world, most of which we thought had better structured gender budgeting programs, we conclude that gender budgeting or gender-related reforms can have a positive role in increasing gender equality. However, this will only be true if these goals are pursued with a level of seriousness and follow-through, and when the political leadership of a country has been convinced that the development of the country requires reform of inherited traditions and conditions of gender inequality. Full implementation and refinement of programs to produce positive outcomes are the key factors determining success and failure, plus support from leading political and public figures. In addition, we should point out that the entities that have been among the most successful with their gender budgeting efforts (Kerala and Rwanda) have legislative requirements for a mandated number of female representatives in public life. This also seems to make a difference, though we do not explore this issue in detail in this book.

Changing the mindset and outlook of ordinary men and women at all levels of the society is a necessity for gender-based reforms to be adopted and sustained in a comprehensive way over several generations. This is never an easy task for a political leadership and requires determination and courage as well as managerial competency for successful passage of laws and execution of policies and programs. Gender budgeting may be necessary in the developing world until the cultural and economic conditions change so as to create a society-wide consensus on the value of gender equality for the society as a whole.

1 Introduction

Gender budgeting is an approach to budgeting that uses fiscal policy and public financial management to promote gender equality, and women's and girls' development. Gender budgeting is a worldwide phenomenon. Since its inception in Australia more than 30 years ago, over 80 countries in the world have embraced some version of gender budgeting. The question arises: Why would scholars interested in gender inequality write a book focused on *budgeting*? The answer is that budgets are the main instrument of governance that reflects the priorities and values of a government. This is all the more critical in developing countries where gender gaps in education, health care, and economic opportunities are still large and the influence of women's voices at the policy level is still small.

Much of the focus on gender budgeting has been in developed countries, where gender-related reforms have been substantive and longstanding. However, many of the most needed and innovative efforts are in the emerging market and developing countries, including some low-income developing countries where gender inequality is still pervasive. This book adds to the growing literature on gender budgeting by focusing mainly on initiatives in the developing world. We have also highlighted some key efforts in the developed countries, which we feel might offer ideas to developing countries in shaping their own programs and avoiding pitfalls in the future.

A unique feature of this book is that we evaluate the success of past efforts in promoting gender equality and women's and girls' advancement, either through gender budgeting or other mechanisms. We discuss, in Chapters 5–8, progress made in different regions of the world. We carefully note the key government agencies and advocacy groups that have institutionalized gender budgeting in various countries, and the resulting policy or programmatic outcomes.

Although fiscal policies for gender equality and gender budgeting efforts have largely focused on the needs of women and girls, these efforts are not intended to detract from the important development needs of men and boys. In fact, a few gender budgeting efforts have focused on male-specific needs as well, such as the example of Austria (Chapter 8). In this book, though, we have focused our attention on gender inequality and its effects on women and girls because this is the overwhelming need in countries of the developing world, and the object of almost all of the research and policymaking.

We present important trends in gender equality and women's and girls' advancement, grouping countries by their region in the world and by their level of income and development. This sets the stage for focus on key fiscal policy and public financial management practices that support gender budgeting efforts in promoting international goals in equality of education, health care, economic and political opportunities, and quality of life. Next, we survey and evaluate the success of efforts in sub-Saharan Africa, Asia, a selection of middle-income countries, and lastly, a selection of developed countries. We then present econometric evidence, drawn from a study of Indian states, on the efficacy of gender budgeting and other fiscal variables in improving female enrollment in primary and secondary education. We conclude by drawing together key policy and practice implications of gender budgeting efforts with an eye toward the future.

Incorporation of gender budgeting into budget laws and public financial management practices is important to ensure that gender equality efforts are sustained and lead to substantive changes in policies and outcomes. Nonetheless, even a strong legislative framework is not enough, by itself to guarantee success. A few countries have successfully incorporated gender budgeting into performance or program-based budgeting, which is a natural fit because of the thematic and cross-cutting nature of gender budgeting; almost all areas of government spending, including education, health care, and infrastructure, contain room for gender-specific remedies to inequalities and biases against women. Two positive examples in this regard are Rwanda and the Indian state of Kerala, which we highlight in Chapters 5 and 6 on Africa and Asia, respectively. Even without performance or program-based budgeting, government should strive to integrate gender budgeting as a theme across government programs and policies.

Effective gender budgeting efforts rely on the ability of governments to improve their policies and programs over time, and to monitor the results throughout the agencies and departments of government. Unfortunately, only a few developing countries have elevated the monitoring function to the level expected of government oversight or audit offices. Nongovernmental organizations, academic scholarship, and advocacy groups, therefore, must often play an essential role in gender budgeting efforts as do parliaments and their committees, in keeping political leaders and civil servants focused on these tasks, even when they are out of the spotlight. In most countries, subnational governments play a critical role in the provision of essential public services, such as education, health care, and infrastructure, and therefore gender budgeting efforts should extend to these levels of governments as well.

Low-income developing countries face a unique set of challenges, both from a policy and administrative point of view, because of the large gaps in education, health care, and work-related opportunities between females and males in these countries. Thus, gender-related goals should fit appropriately into a budget whose priorities are those related to the United Nations' Sustainable Development Goals. Cash transfers have been shown in many developing countries to be an effective means to improve girls' access to education and female access to health care at all ages, as a complement to essential state services. Key public or publicly subsidized infrastructure, such as the supply of electricity and water to households as well as cooking technologies, reduce girls' and women's time demands for domestic work, and contribute to gender equality by giving women time to engage in educational and paid work pursuits. It is necessary to identify the ongoing constraints to women's participation in political and economic life and to develop fiscal policies to help address these constraints, including subsidized lending, tax incentives, and encouragement of female representation in parliamentary government.

Emerging markets and other middle-income developing and developed countries also face challenges of gender inequality, but largely of a different nature. The problems for women in developed countries often relate to a desire to balance workforce participation with rearing of children, and insufficient pensions for aging female populations. Fiscal incentives or public spending to support child and dependent care can ease the burden of unpaid labor in the home, including dependent care, which still falls disproportionately on women. Income security for elderly women is an important challenge going forward, as populations age and women's more limited participation in the labor market in the past means that they are inadequately covered by existing social security programs. Countries can also encourage female labor force participation by building into their gender budgeting efforts a way to reduce the higher effective tax rate on secondary workers in the household.

It is hard to assess what explicit contribution gender budgeting reforms have made to the positive trends in gender equality in every region of the world over the last 30 years (shown in Chapter 2 figures). Nevertheless, it is clear there is room for more work in reducing persistent gender inequalities. Thus, it is critical to learn from past and existing gender budgeting efforts, which policies and programs actually produced positive outcomes, which did not, and how the successful initiatives can be enlarged and extended. We attempt to address this challenge in this book.

2 Trends in gender equality and women's development[1]

I. Introduction

In the past several decades, all regions of the world have witnessed movement toward greater gender equality and the advancement of women measured by a wide range of economic, social, and political indicators. Nonetheless, in many regions of the world, women remain at a disadvantage compared to men in key areas of economic, social, and political life. Goal 5 of the Sustainable Development Goals, adopted by the United Nations in 2015, calls for gender equality and the empowerment of women and girls over the next 15 years.[2]

This chapter briefly examines trends in indicators of gender equality and the advancement of women, using evidence derived both from individual indicators and a gender equality index, which aggregates a number of critical indicators. We use our own version of the gender equality index created by the United Nations Development Programme (UNDP), namely, the Gender Development Index (GDI), which assesses gender equality and women's advancement in terms of components for education, health, and income (UNDP, 1995). We calculate values using this index, going backward in time in a consistent manner, to examine trends over several decades.

Gender equality and women's advancement in access to education and health care, and in their ability to earn income or participate in the labor market are all commonly accepted indicators of economic and social well-being. In the political realm, women's participation in elected office and other key political positions are ways of measuring their empowerment. Gender equality indices aggregate a number of indicators and vary in their composition, which explains why different countries have varying measures of equality, depending on the index.

Similar to a number of other recent studies, we find that the trends in individual indicators and the GDI point toward improvement in women's education, health, economic opportunities, and political empowerment. Nonetheless, progress across the world is uneven.[3] When grouped by geographic regions, we observe that South Asia, the Middle East and Central Asia, and sub-Saharan Africa lag behind other regions, even though these regions have all recorded significant improvement in key indicators. When grouped by level of economic development, we see that countries at all levels of development have generally made progress, though there were certain periods during which progress was more rapid. Generally, we observe that developing countries tend to lag behind the developed countries in gender equality and women's advancement. The gaps between the developed countries and emerging market and developing countries are surprisingly small on some indicators, suggesting that considerable progress is possible even while sizeable income gaps remain.

The remainder of this chapter is as follows. Section II is an overview of the methodology underlying our analysis contrasting individual indicators and composite indices characterizing gender equality. It also discusses some data-related issues. Section III examines trends in key indicators. Section IV explains the derivation of the GDI. Section V explains our time-consistent version of the GDI. Section VI examines the challenges of using indicators and indices to guide policy analysis. Section VII concludes.

II. Methodology: the value of individual indicators versus composite indices, and other data issues

Two ways to capture trends in women's development and gender equality are through individual indicators and composite indices. Both approaches have distinct advantages and disadvantages.

Gender-specific individual indicators provide information regarding one aspect of women's development or gender equality. They provide a readily accessible basis for assessing progress and offer guidance to policymakers who want to follow specific development targets. On the other hand, the risk in relying on single indicators is that various related indicators may not always move in parallel in response to specific developments and sometimes may even move in different or inconsistent directions. Thus, for a more comprehensive view, it is useful to create composite indices.

The UNDP was a pioneer in constructing an index to measure women's development. Its Human Development Index (HDI) is a widely used composite index that aggregates measures of education, health, and income to assess relative human development levels among countries. The GDI was constructed from the HDI to assess the gap between men's development and women's development. In recent years, the UNDP has revised the GDI to be a stand-alone index and also created a new index, called the Gender Inequality Index (GII).

The main advantage of gender equality indices such as the GDI and GII is their ability to provide a broader perspective than is possible with individual indicators. However, the different combination of indicators, the weighting of each indicator, and methods of aggregation have all led to a certain degree of arbitrariness in the formulation of the indices. This has led to an ongoing debate regarding the merits of each index.[4]

Analyzing trends in gender equality is also challenging because it requires some value judgments as to what is meant by equality between men and women.[5] We present trends, rather than levels, to avoid making judgments as to what the precise differences between women and men should be for a particular indicator. We also use relative measures, such as female-to-male ratios, which is the most common approach in the literature, rather than absolute differences between women and men.

We believe that it is reasonable to assume that for variables such as primary or secondary education enrollment and completion rates, equivalence between men and women is a desirable goal. Likewise, for political empowerment, equality between men and women is a reasonable goal. In the area of health, on the other hand, women's average life expectancy is about five years longer than men's average life expectancy.[6] Therefore, it is reasonable to assume that gender equality should aim to achieve this biological norm.

Women's labor force participation rate is lower than men's in most countries. There is, nonetheless, considerable variation in the relative rates of participation, and in some countries, the women's participation rate has come close to men's rate, as the men's rate has plateaued or fallen. There is an extensive literature on the determinants of women's labor force participation (e.g., Bertrand, 2011; Fernandez and Fogli, 2009; Goldin, 1995). When differences in participation rates are influenced by social customs that prevent women from working—when there is evidence that they would prefer to do so—this suggests the presence of gender biases that should be addressed by policymakers.

Robust indicators must satisfy a number of properties, including relevance to many countries across different cultures. They must also be available in the scholarly literature over long periods of time, allowing for an evaluation of improvement or deterioration. These indicators should also be constructed in similar ways across countries and over time. In reality, data classified by gender suffer from spotty coverage across time and countries. While this is a constraint in our analysis, it is not one that fundamentally undermines the ability to track trends in key variables. In our analysis, we have used gender-relevant indicators available in the World Bank's World Development Indicators database. We note that there are a number of international initiatives underway to improve these indicators.[7]

Most microeconomic data on individual economic and household behavior from developing countries are derived from household surveys. Only some of these data are available disaggregated by gender, such as labor force participation. Klasen (2004) points to the lack of data on intra-household resource allocation, which limits analyzing how well men's and women's different household needs are met. For example, data on income, consumption, and assets may be available only at the level of the household, and access to power, clean water, sanitation, and cooking fuels may be available only at the level of the household or even the community.[8]

Folbre (2006) notes the importance of including time-use data as another source of information, though this information can be difficult to obtain on a consistent basis. Women have traditionally borne a disproportionate burden of unpaid work, and thus, improved information on time use provides a better understanding of men's and women's well-being, supplementing economic and other socioeconomic measures.

III. Trends in selected indicators and the GDI

Relationship between income and the time-consistent GDI

To start, we present in Figure 2.1 the simple relationship between the natural log of per capita income and our time-consistent GDI, using 2016 data for each country. It shows a clear, direct relationship, in accordance with the observation that more-developed countries tend to have higher levels of gender equality and women's development. However, we note that there is considerable variation around a line drawn through the data. Clearly, some countries are well below where we would predict them to be on the basis of income, in terms of the gender equality index, and some above, as the simple relationship shows.

We next highlight trends using indicators from the areas of education, health, and economic and political opportunities. Table 2.1 defines these indicators in more detail. For education, we use the GDI education sub-index, which is a good measure of the ability of boys and girls to acquire an education. Educational attainment is a key measure of human capability and the ability to lead a rewarding life, engage in civic activities, and improve one's living standards.

For health, we use the GDI health sub-index, which is based on life expectancy, because it is one of the most widely used summary indicators of health status and captures many variables that affect health and well-being. One advantage of using life expectancy is that it is available in a wide cross-section of

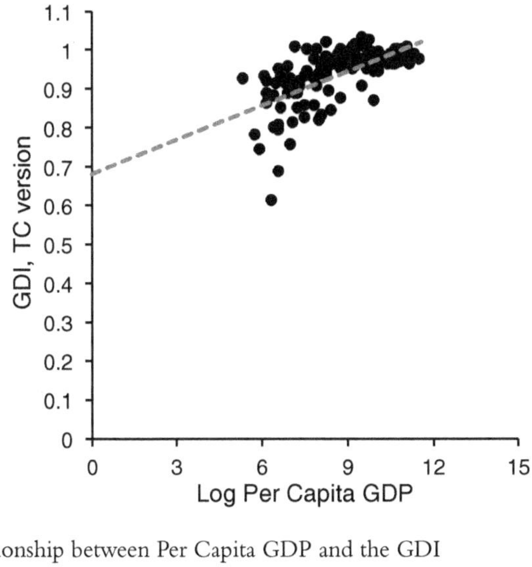

Figure 2.1 Relationship between Per Capita GDP and the GDI

Source: Authors' estimates.

Table 2.1 Definitions of Selected Gender Indicators and the Gender Development Index

Indicator	*Definition*
GDI index	The GDI index consists of education, health, and income components, combined into an aggregate index. See later in this chapter for a fuller description.
GDI education sub-index	The GDI education sub-index consists of two variables, combined into an index: mean years of schooling and expected years of schooling.
GDI health sub-index	The GDI health sub-index consists of life expectancy at birth, constructed as an index. Life expectancy at birth indicates the number of years a newborn infant is expected to live if prevailing patterns of mortality at the time of their birth were to stay the same throughout their life.
Maternal mortality ratio	The maternal mortality ratio is the number of women who die from pregnancy-related causes while pregnant or within 42 days of pregnancy termination per 100,000 live births. The data are estimated with a regression model using information on the incidence of non-AIDS maternal deaths in women aged 15–49, plus data on fertility, birth attendants, and GDP.
Labor force participation rate, ages 15–64	The labor force participation rate for ages 15–64 is the proportion of the population aged 15–64 that is considered economically active.
Mean nominal monthly earnings of employees	Monthly earnings is defined as gross remuneration in cash and in kind paid to employees. Earnings are assumed to occur at regular intervals, for time worked or work completed, combined with remuneration for time not worked, such as annual vacation or other types of paid leave or holidays. This indicator is presented in terms of the average monthly earnings per employee, in local currency.
Seats held by women in national parliaments	Seats held by women in parliaments is the percentage of parliamentary seats in a single or lower chamber held by women relative to total seats.

Sources: World Bank, World Development Indicators database (World Bank, various years); International Labor Organization (ILO), ILOSTAT (ILO, various years); and authors' estimates for the GDI and its education and health sub-indices. GDI=Gender Development Index.

countries on an annual basis making it useful for comparative analysis. Because our focus is developing countries, we also use a single indicator, maternal mortality. Maternal mortality is a critical indicator of women's advancement and well-being, and it is incorporated in some gender equality indices, even though no comparison of women and men is possible. Maternal mortality has one significant drawback in that few developing countries collect the information necessary to measure it accurately, and thus it is an estimated variable and likely to be measured with some error.

To capture trends in economic opportunity, we select the labor force participation rate because it is an informative indicator of women's economic role and has been a focus of policymakers. In addition, it has the best data quality and availability compared to other economic indicators available on a sex-disaggregated basis. Nonetheless, this variable has limitations in that it does not take fully into account the complexity of the job market, especially in countries where the informal labor market and subsistence agriculture comprise a significant part of the labor force. Notwithstanding the more limited data, we also present trends in wages by sex using mean monthly earnings of employees. One unavoidable limitation of this variable is that it mixes two separate factors: hours of work and pay per hour.

Although we concentrate mainly on trends in economic and socioeconomic variables, we also include an analysis of political opportunity because, as a measure of empowerment, it helps to characterize the status of women in society and is complementary to the economic measures. For political opportunity, the only indicator with reasonably comprehensive data coverage is the proportion of seats held by women in national parliaments. However, we note that this indicator alone does not necessarily give a full picture of women's political empowerment.

World trends by region and income group

This section presents world trends for selected indicators, broken down both by region and by income level, between 1995 and the last year available, usually 2016.[9] To group countries by region, we use the five categories created by the International Monetary Fund (IMF) for reporting purposes: sub-Saharan Africa; the Americas and Caribbean; Asia and the Pacific; Europe; and the Middle East and Central Asia. Newly formed countries, such as Timor-Leste, South Sudan, and the former Soviet republics, enter the sample in the year they came into being. Countries are classified using the IMF's three descriptive categories for economic development or income: low-income developing countries, emerging market and developing countries, and developed economies (IMF, 2014). For example, China and India are considered emerging market and developing countries, as are many Middle Eastern countries. In contrast, almost all African countries are classified as low-income developing countries.

Some countries may have switched income classification over time but were held in the same category over the entire period of the sample. For calculation of the specific gender indicators listed in Table 2.1, we used unweighted country averages to produce regional data points. Weighted averages, using population shares, provide similar trends.

Educational differences between females and males

Figure 2.2 presents trends in the female-to-male ratio of the GDI education sub-index from 1995–2016 for countries grouped by region and level of development. All regions saw progress in equalizing female and male educational attainment over the sample period. Pronounced gender gaps persist

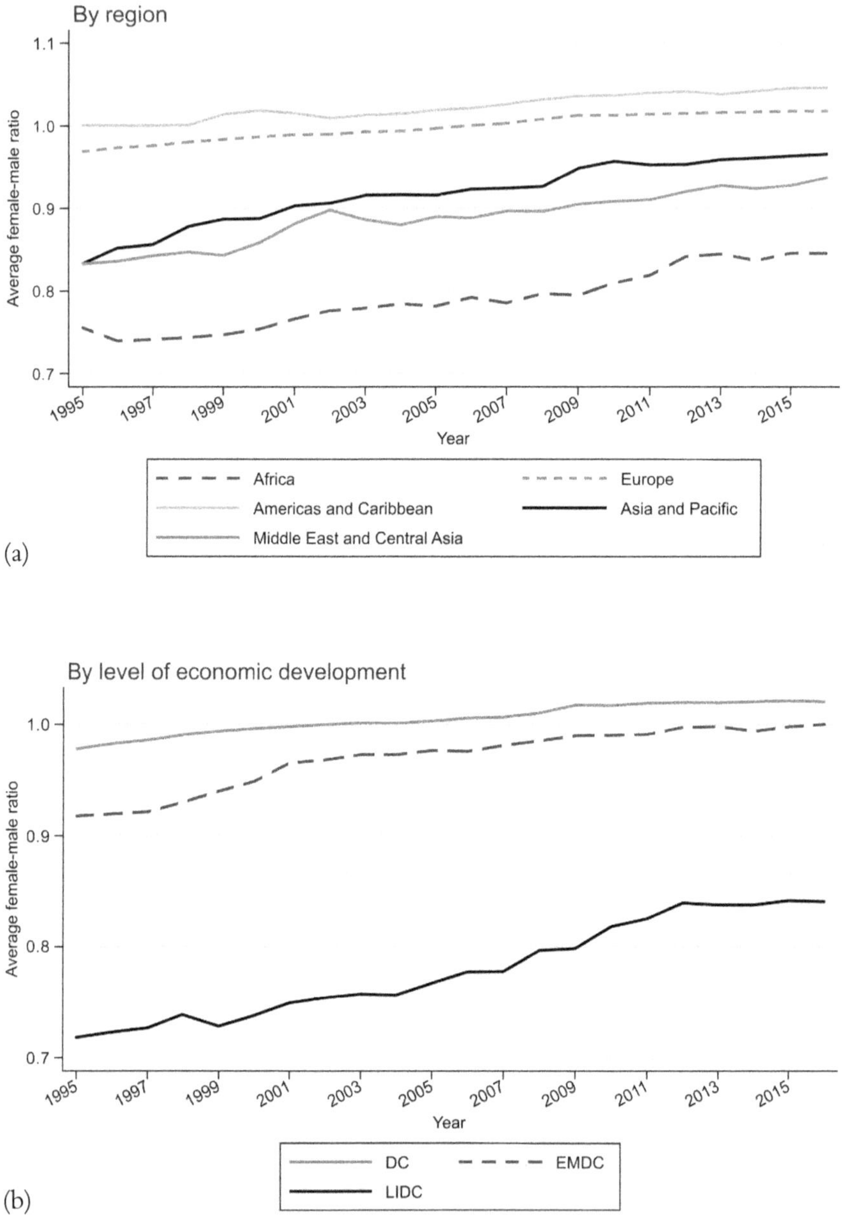

Figure 2.2 GDI Education Sub-Index (female-to-male ratio)

Sources: World Bank, World Development Indicators database; Barro and Lee (2014); and authors' calculations.

Note: DC = developed countries; EMDC = emerging markets and developing countries; and LIDC = low-income developing countries in three regions: sub-Saharan Africa, the Middle East and Central Asia, and Asia and the Pacific. Substantial progress was observed over the sample period in the latter two regions, while more modest progress was observed in the former. Improvements in the education sub-index were modest in the two more developed regions: Americas and Caribbean, and Europe. However, this is not surprising given the high baseline levels in these regions in 1995. Interestingly, during the entire 1995–2016 period, the ratio in the Americas and Caribbean was higher than one, demonstrating higher educational attainment for women than men. In Europe, the ratio was steadily approaching one during this time period.

The trends in female educational attainment by economic development or income level show that all income groups were steadily improving between 1995–2016. The most persistent gap is found in the low-income developing countries compared to the developed and emerging market and developing countries. In spite of substantial improvement in female education by the low-income developing countries, the gap stopped narrowing at the end of the sample period. In contrast, while in 1995, the emerging market and developing countries were approximately 25 percent lower in female-to-male educational achievement than in developed countries, by 2016 the gap had shrunk to a less than 10 percent difference.

Health differences between females and males

Figure 2.3 presents regional trends in the GDI sub-index for health, from 1995–2016, based on life expectancy at birth. Women normally have a longer average life expectancy than men, thus it is expected that this ratio should be greater than 1. In all regions other than Europe and the Americas and Caribbean, the female-to-male ratio trends upward, reflecting the relatively faster improvement in female health relative to male health, as gaps in access to health care were narrowing.

The recent pattern of a declining advantage in female-to-male life expectancy noted particularly in Europe has been observed for developed countries elsewhere (Liu, Arai, Kanda, Lee, Glasser, and Tamashiro, 2012; Thorslund, Wastesson, Agahi, Lagergren, and Parker, 2013). This reflects a reversal of the pattern from earlier in the 20th century of female life expectancy rising faster than male life expectancy. This may be the result of any number of factors, including increased smoking among females, or the success in reducing cardiovascular disease among men.

The marked declines in Africa early in the sample period, may reflect the impact of HIV/AIDS, which had a disproportionately harmful effect on female life expectancy in Africa. The rising ratio later in the sample period reflects life expectancy rising toward the biological norm after the impact of the AIDS epidemic was blunted. Only the Asia and Pacific region shows a consistent, steady increase in the gender ratio, reflecting women's very disadvantaged position diminishing gradually over time.

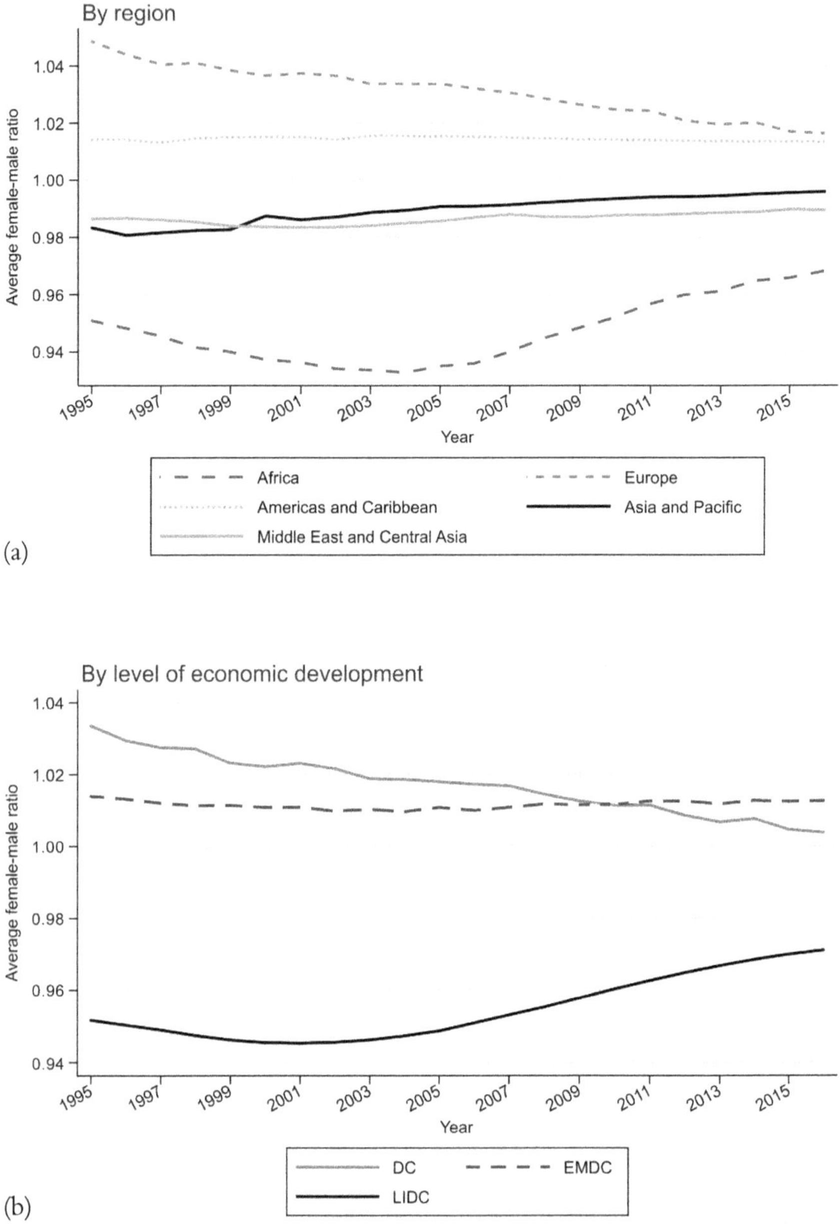

Figure 2.3 GDI Health Sub-Index (female-to-male ratio)

Sources: World Bank, World Development Indicators database; and authors' calculations.

Note: DC = developed countries; EMDC = emerging market and developing countries; and LIDC = low-income developing countries

The health trends by level of economic development also show a diminishing female-to-male ratio in developed countries similar to what was seen in Europe in the first chart of Figure 2.3. A relatively stable ratio appeared in the emerging market and developing countries, perhaps reflecting offsetting trends among some of the more and less developed of these economies. After an initial decline (perhaps explainable by the impact of AIDS), the low-income developing markets show a sharply improving ratio in recent years.

Figure 2.4 presents trends in maternal mortality ratios from 1997 to 2015. All regions of the world achieved a decline in maternal mortality. Sub-Saharan Africa has the highest rate of mortality, but this rate almost halved over the sample period. Asia and the Pacific, and the Middle East and Central Asia also achieved a significant decline. The decline in the Americas and Caribbean was minimal; this ratio remains slightly higher than that of Europe. Emerging market and developing countries and low-income developing countries achieved a large reduction.

Labor force participation differences between females and males

Figure 2.5 presents regional trends in economic opportunity, measured by the female-to-male ratio of labor force participation, among people aged 15 to 64. This age group is considered prime age workers. In general, countries throughout the world are heading toward greater gender parity in labor force participation but this pattern is not uniform.

There are several interesting points to note about female labor supply. One is the pattern where there is a high female-to-male ratio in the highest income and lowest income countries in the world, with middle-income countries having the lowest female-to-male ratio. Goldin (1995) and others have discussed this phenomenon. In low-income, predominantly agricultural countries, women's work is largely in subsistence agriculture and is largely inseparable from their household. As a country's income level rises, the labor market becomes more formalized and work is separated from the home, leading to a lower rate of labor force participation for women in these countries, especially among married women. In developed countries, women have attained high educational levels and have low fertility rates, thus facilitating greater labor force attachment.

Another interesting point is the strikingly large gap in the Middle East and Central Asia region compared to other regions in the world in the labor force participation ratio (Mithra and Farid, 2013). This feature of the Middle East and Central Asia region is related in part to the influence of cultural mores and higher fertility rates, not just economic development per se. Asia and the Pacific has shown a flat female-to-male ratio in recent years, even while the education gap has closed. The trend is driven by declining female labor force participation in India and, to a lesser extent, China, and rising female labor force participation elsewhere. International Labor Organization (2013) and Klasen and Pieters (2015) discuss the factors contributing to this anomalous trend.

In Figure 2.6, we look at the trends for males and females separately, to parse out the separate effects. We can see that female labor force participation is

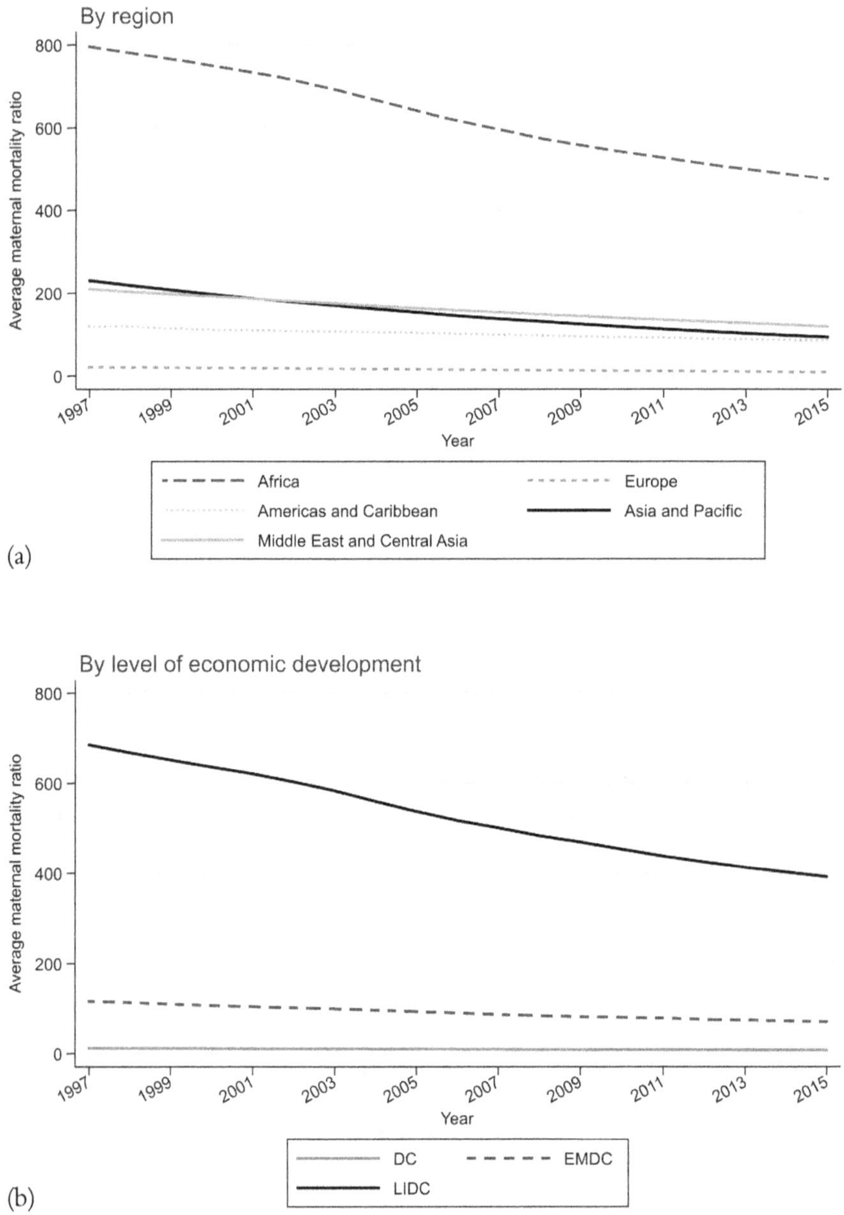

Figure 2.4 Maternal Mortality Ratio (modeled estimate, per 100,000 live births)

Sources: World Bank, World Development Indicators database; and authors' calculations.

Note: DC = developed countries; EMDC = emerging market and developing countries; and LIDC = low-income developing countries

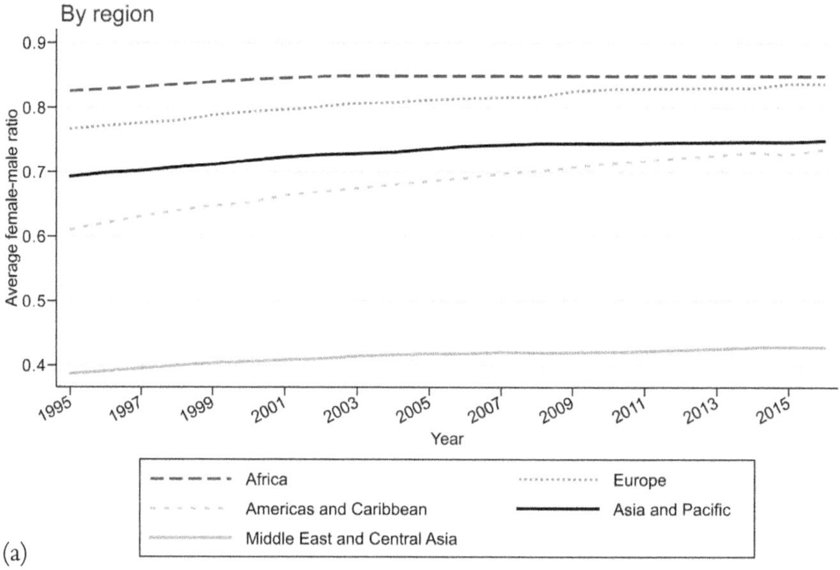

(a)

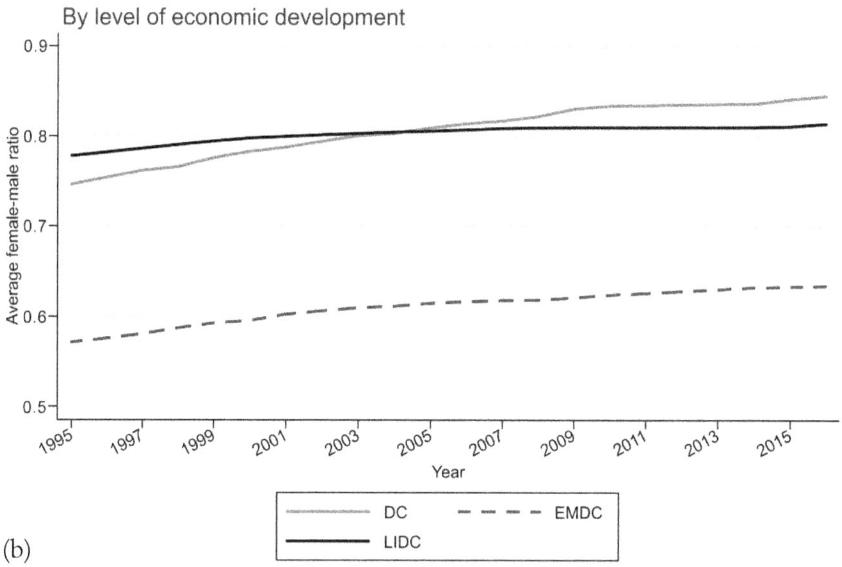

(b)

Figure 2.5 Labor Force Participation Rate, Ages 15–64 (female-to-male ratio)

Sources: World Bank, World Development Indicators database; and authors' calculations.

Note: DC = developed countries; EMDC = emerging market and developing countries; and LIDC = low-income developing countries

(a)

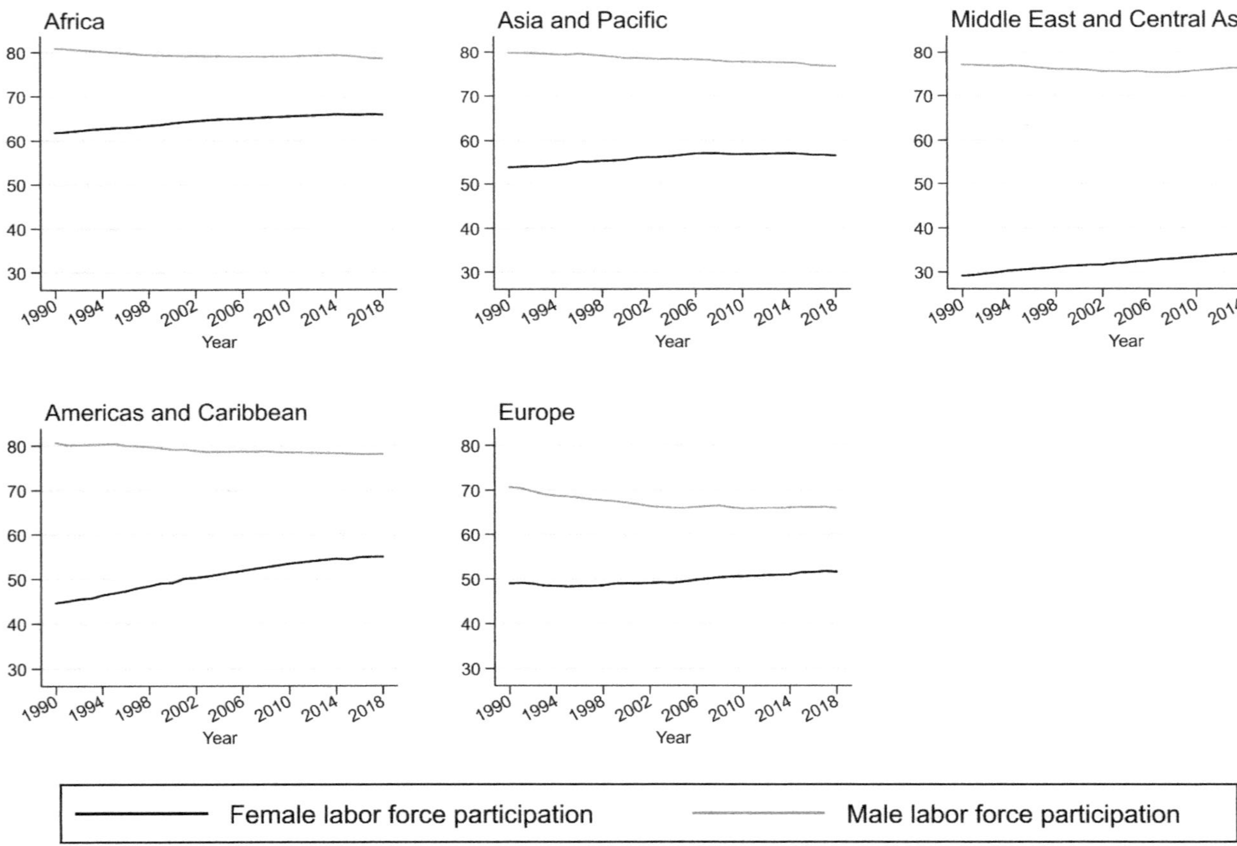

Figure 2.6 Labor Force Participation Rate, Ages 15–64 (percent)

Sources: World Bank, World Development Indicators database; and authors' calculations.

Note: DC = developed countries; EMDC = emerging market and developing countries; and LIDC = low-income developing countries

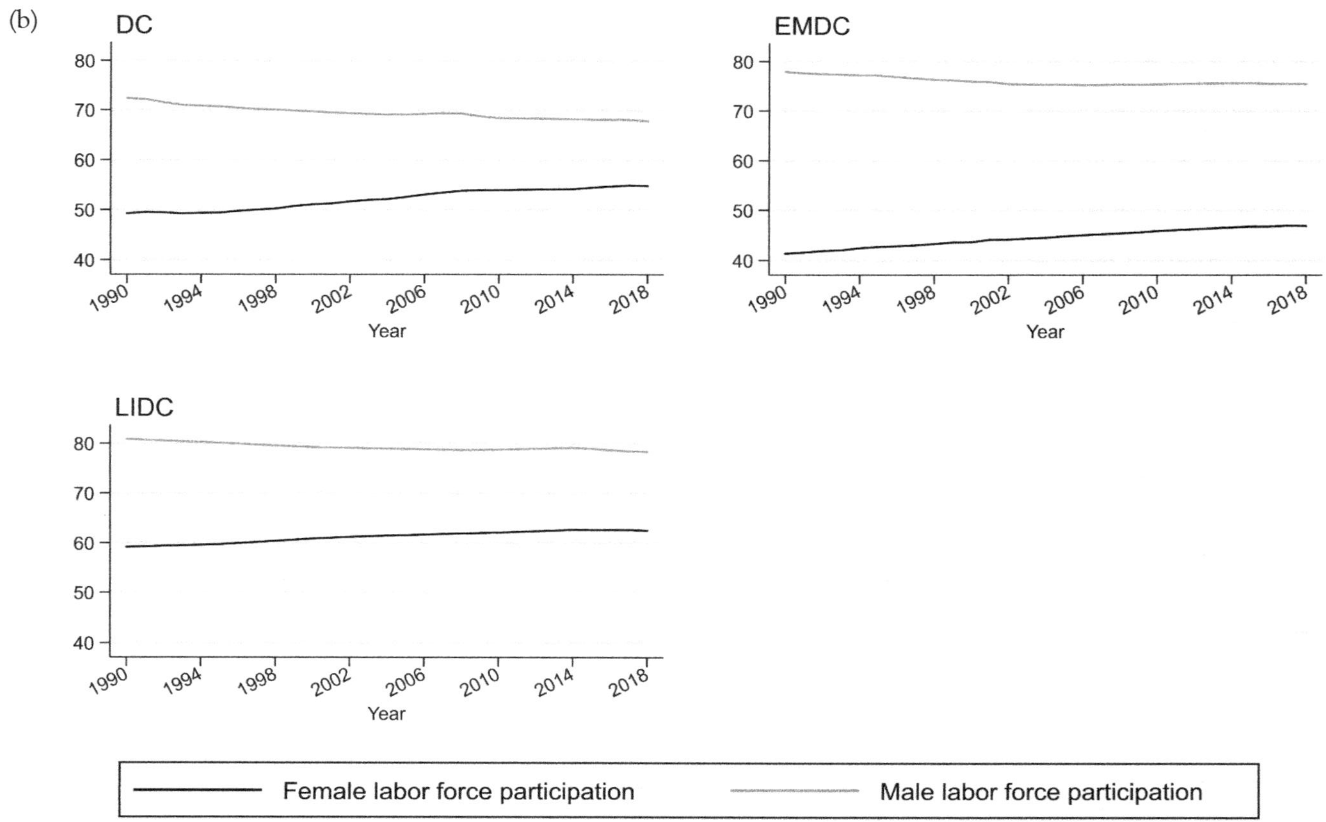

Figure 2.6 (Continued)

rising throughout the world, while male labor participation is slowly declining, except in the Middle East and Central Asia region.

As an alternative, we explore wage differences between males and females. We have many sources of data from developed countries with which to draw conclusions, especially where workers earning wages encompass the majority of the labor market (as opposed to small family businesses or informal labor). Data from emerging market and developing countries are more modest, and data from low-income developing countries are limited to a few countries, thus we have excluded these countries from the analysis.

Using only the countries for which data were available over the 1995–2018 period, Figure 2.7 shows that wage gaps between females and males diminished during the 1995–2014 period and then stabilized at the end of the sample period, in both developed and emerging market and developing countries, for reasons which may just reflect the small sample. This suggests that barriers to women persist in terms of flexible work hours, lack of access to day care, discrimination, and other factors, as well as systematic occupational and educational differences (e.g., certain low paying professions have mostly female employees). These barriers continue to leave females at a disadvantage in wages.

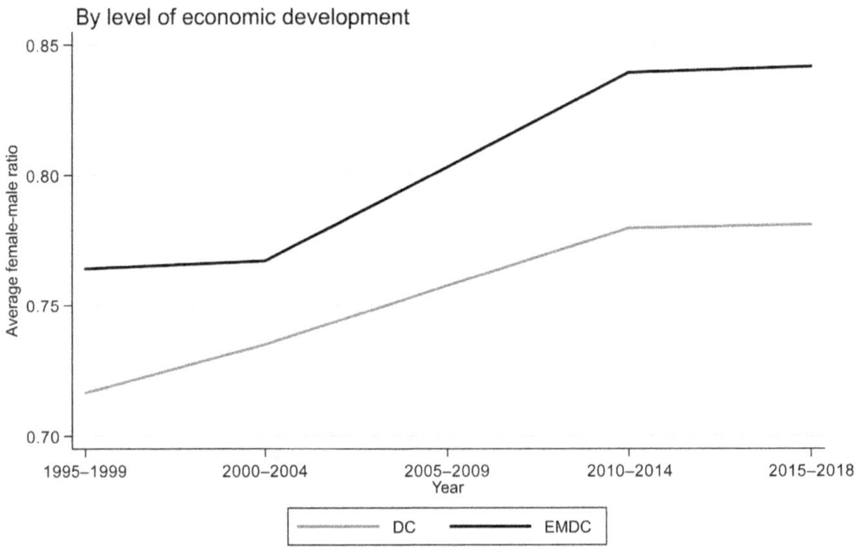

Figure 2.7 Mean Monthly Earnings of Employees (female-to-male ratio)

Sources: ILO, ILOSTAT; and authors' calculations.

Note: DC = developed countries and EMDC = emerging market and developing countries. Using 38 countries, whose data encompassed the relevant period of analysis.

Political representation differences between females and males

For a final individual indicator, we look at political empowerment. Figure 2.8 presents the trends for the proportion of seats held by women in national parliaments. Overall, the data show that in all regions of the world, women have made substantial progress in improving their share of legislative representation. Nonetheless, women's representation remains well below 50 percent in every region. Two countries, Rwanda and Bolivia, achieved the milestone of over half of the legislative body being women in 2015. Strikingly, despite the relative lack of economic progress for women in the Middle East and Central Asia, they have made sizeable gains in increasing political representation. Also notable is the improvement in women's political representation in sub-Saharan Africa, surpassing that of the Americas and Caribbean by the end of the study period.

The trends by level of income show the same underlying developments. Countries at all levels of income made progress in increasing women's political representation. Perhaps surprisingly, the low-income developing countries surpassed the emerging and developing countries by sample end. The interesting shifts in women's political participation across regions and levels of economic development, shown in both charts in Figure 2.8, highlight two important conclusions that can be drawn from these data. The first is that the status of women regarding political participation can be improved in spite of persistent poverty and lack of economic opportunity. The second is that cultural factors and changes often outweigh economic factors in supporting improvements or continued stagnation (or deterioration) in women's status.

IV. Measuring gender equality with a gender equality index, old and new

In 1995, the UNDP introduced the GDI ("old GDI"). The old GDI was the first widely used index to analyze the extent of gender equality and women's development in several key areas (education, health, and income) relative to that of men. The index, though, was subject to several criticisms. For instance, Klasen (2006b) and Schüler (2006) note that it was not a measure of gender equality but instead a measure of how the HDI score was reduced for women due to gender inequalities. In response to these criticisms, the UNDP introduced in 2014 a revised GDI (UNDP, 2014a). Aside from a change in the way the index was computed, the UNDP did not change the component indicators of the GDI. These indicators still comprise the education, health, and income variables of the HDI (UNDP, 2014b).

Stotsky, Shibuya, Kolovich, and Kebhaj (2016) presented the methodology involved in calculating of the old and revised GDIs and summarized the evolution of the indices over time. The old GDI, like the HDI, employed three

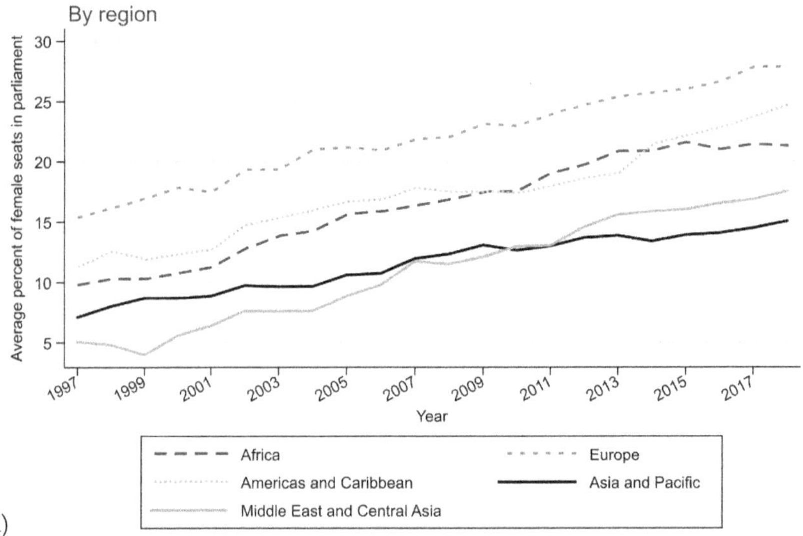

(a)

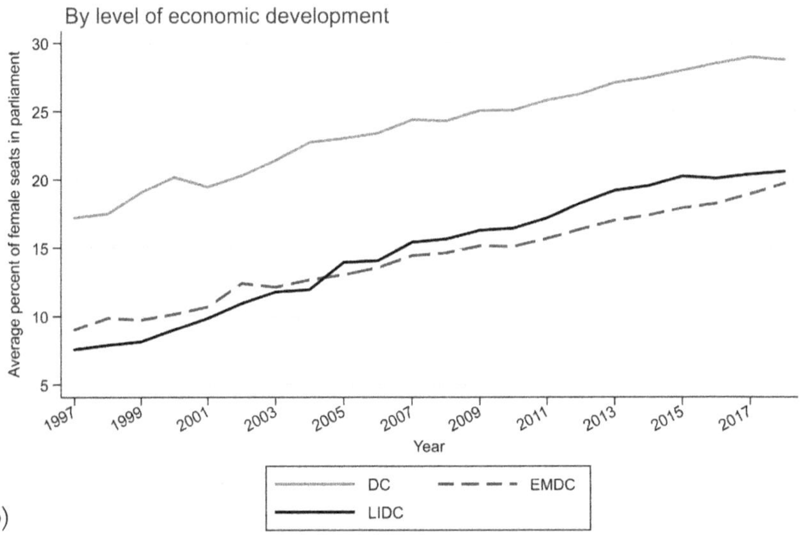

(b)

Figure 2.8 Seats Held by Women in National Parliaments (percent of total)

Sources: World Bank, World Development Indicators database; and authors' calculations.

Note: DC = developed countries; EMDC = emerging market and developing countries; and LIDC = low-income developing countries

sub-indices with variables reflecting educational attainment, health status, and income. These indicators were initially calculated without regard to gender. A gender-equity-sensitive indicator was then calculated for each of these gender-neutral indicators. The GDI was then calculated as the simple average of the sub-indices. Hawken and Munck (2013) commended the GDI for its clear overarching concept of human development, while noting that it made use of relatively few indicators, in part reflecting the availability of data at the time the index was introduced.[10]

A series of articles in a special issue of the *Journal of Human Development*, edited by Klasen (2006b), Bardhan and Klasen (1999, 2000), and Klasen and Schüler (2011), highlighted a number of conceptual and empirical problems with the old GDI. Klasen (2006a, 2006b) observed that the biggest problem with the old GDI derived from the income variable, which is problematic in its measurement. Folbre (2006) suggested that some account should be taken of women's greater time devoted to unpaid or home activities, which are ignored by a measure based on cash income alone. Moreover, Chant (2006) noted that earned income may not be the most meaningful measure of equality given that pooling of income takes place in the home and because it cannot be assumed that women control their own earnings. Klasen (2006a) suggested replacing non-agricultural wages by economy-wide wages and seeking more complete data coverage of the earned income component. Dijkstra (2002) recommended replacing earned income with labor force participation.

In contrast, the revised GDI (referred to hereafter as the GDI) allows a direct measure of the gender gap between males and females, using the components of the HDI (which were also substantially revised in 2010), with gender-specific data (UNDP, 2014b). The health variable remains life expectancy, with an adjustment for an average female biological advantage over males of five years. The education variables are mean years of schooling and expected schooling. The estimation methodology for income is based on gross national income (GNI) per capita in purchasing power parity dollars at 2011 constant prices, and the ratio of female-to-male wages is calculated in all sectors, not just non-agricultural sectors. Where countries do not have wage data disaggregated by sex, the UNDP uses a presumed global average of female to male wages of 0.8.[11]

The basic comparison between females and males relies on the simple ratio of the HDI for females to males, following recommendations in Klasen (2006a) and Klasen and Schüler (2011). Thus, while the index typically ranges from 0 to 1, it may be above 1 when females are deemed to be more advantaged than males. Numbers closer to 1 imply gender parity. Countries are ranked based on the absolute value of the deviation of the GDI from 1 (gender parity), which gives a different ranking than on the basis of the GDI value alone because some countries have a ratio exceeding 1.

UNDP (2014b) reported that the world average GDI value was 0.920, indicating a gap of 8 percent in the HDI for females relative to males, based on a calculation for 148 countries in 2013. The OECD countries average was 0.964, the Latin American and Caribbean region was 0.963, South Asia was 0.860, the Arab countries were 0.866, and the sub-Saharan African region was 0.867. A number of countries have scores higher than 1 because of some combination of higher female than male education achievement, and female life expectancy exceeding that of males by more than five years.

The UNDP also developed another measure of gender inequality, the GII, which is based on three components: female reproductive health, women's empowerment, and labor market variables (Gaye, Klugman, Kovacevic, Twigg, and Zambrano, 2010; UNDP, 2014b). Stotsky, Shibuya, Kolovich, and Kebhaj (2016) discussed the advantages and disadvantages of using this measure in place of the GDI.

V. Extension of the UNDP's gender equality indices consistently over time

Because the UNDP's GDI is not constructed consistently over time, it may be misleading to look at the evolution of a country's rating without taking into account how the construction of the index or data has changed. Consequently, we have constructed a time-consistent version of the UNDP's GDI.[12] Stotsky, Shibuya, Kolovich, and Kebhaj (2016) provide more details on the construction of the index and how it differs from the UNDP's own calculations. We have updated the calculations with data until 2016, the latest available.

Figure 2.9 shows the evolution of the time-consistent GDI, over time (1995–2016) and by region, amplifying the results shown in Figure 2.1. Each of the regions shows a trend toward greater gender equality during the study period, which is consistent with the trends for the individual indicators and the sub-indices. Gender equality in the sub-Saharan Africa, Asia and Pacific, and Middle East and Central Asia regions considerably lag behind the Americas and Caribbean, and Europe regions. All three of the lagging regions, nonetheless, demonstrate a steady improvement in gender equality over time. When broken down by income level, countries in all categories of development show improvements, though significant gaps remain when comparing the developed countries to the emerging market and developing countries, and the latter relative to the low-income developing countries.

In summary, inserting the data into this time-consistent GDI over the sample period shows virtually nonoverlapping (with a partial exception for the Middle East and Central Asia versus Africa for a period) stable or upward trends toward gender equality in each of the five regions and three levels of economic development. We may therefore conclude that each region or income category seems to be pursuing its own path toward gender equality in terms of the evolution of government policies and cultural shifts.

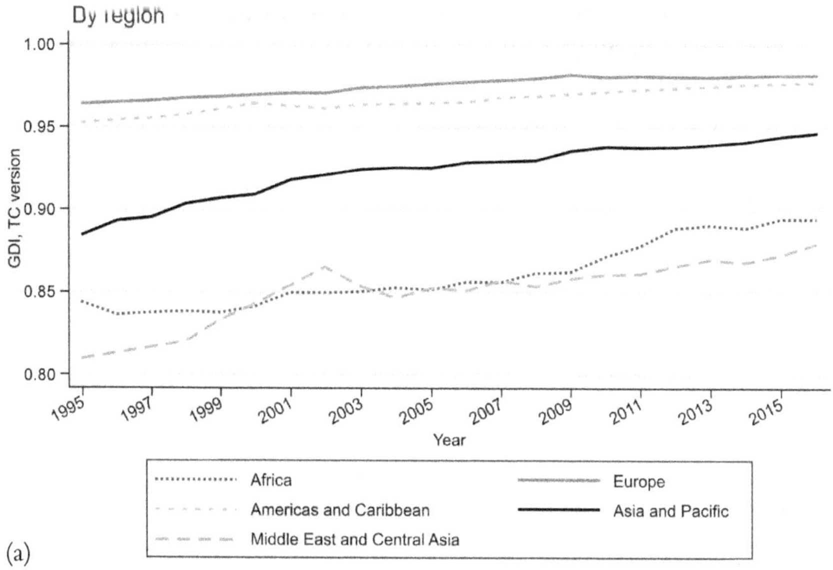

(a)

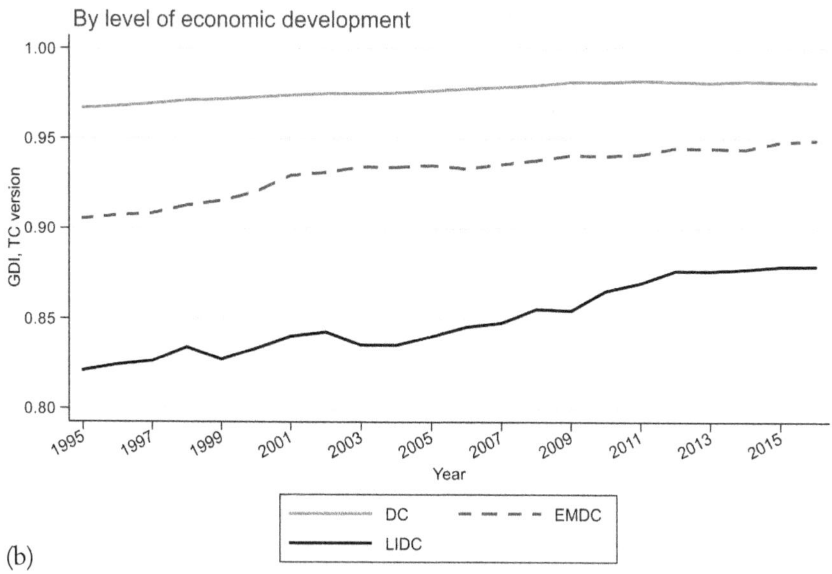

(b)

Figure 2.9 GDI Time-Consistent Version (index ranges from 0 to 1)

Sources: ILO, ILOSTAT; World Bank, World Development Indicators database; Barro and Lee (2014); and authors' calculations.

Note: DC = developed countries; EMDC = emerging market and developing countries; and LIDC = low-income developing countries

VI. Distinct benefits of using individual indicators versus composite indices, for policy analysis and decision-making

Both individual indicators and composite indices of gender equality and women's advancement play important roles in providing information on trends across countries and over time. Individual indicators seem to be more useful when the analysis focuses on a specific, limited area to which the indicator directly relates. Although some individual indicators have data deficiencies, they have the distinct advantage of being straightforward to understand and interpret. International initiatives are working to improve and expand the coverage of key indicators on education, health, and economic and political opportunities and outcomes, which will be critical in improving their information content.

In contrast, an index that contains a variety of summary statistics regarding different facets of gender equality, such as the GDI, has limitations in that the numerical results are dependent on the particular choice of variables, and weighting and aggregation schemes, that go into the construction of the index. The absence of consistent time series of data limits their use for trend analysis. We share the view of Klasen (2014) that a good index should be relatively simple and transparent and that the UNDP's revised GDI is a step forward. Klasen laid out some useful proposed modifications of the GDI by suggesting that an index is stronger when it does not mix measures of well-being with empowerment. An index should also demonstrate stability in the face of minor changes in the variables included in the aggregation, or in the weighting and aggregation methodology, in order to be viewed as credible.

The explicit incorporation of gender equality goals in the newly adopted Sustainable Development Goals suggests that governments should make greater use of gender equality indicators and indices to guide their decision-making regarding economic, social, and political matters, all of which are influenced by gender concerns. The ability to measure important social and economic outcomes by means of these indicators will allow policymakers to provide input to budget and other decision-making processes. The use of gender equality indicators also allows formulation of public policies that will help close the gender gap and advance women's and girls' well-being worldwide.

VII. Conclusion

This chapter surveys trends in key gender-related indicators and how these indicators are used to construct a practical and useful index of gender equality. It presents trends in indicators on education, health, labor force participation, and political representation, disaggregated by region and level of development. These trends suggest that all of the world's regions are making progress in gender equality and women's development. Although gender inequalities remain, women have made significant progress in closing education gaps and in key areas of health, including those unique to women such as maternal mortality.

Women are making progress in closing economic and political gaps, as well, though they remain significant.

Certain regions of the world continue to lag in indicators of gender equality and women's advancement, especially South Asia, sub-Saharan Africa, and the Middle East and Central Asia. Developed economies tend to present better outcomes, though emerging market and developing countries have made significant strides in key education and health outcomes, and in some areas, such as labor force or political participation, low-income developing economies have achieved reasonable success. One important conclusion is that countries can make significant progress in closing gender gaps and women's development, even while lagging in economic development.

Both individual indicators and composite indices serve a useful purpose for policymakers in that they provide an objective view of how countries are doing in gender-related social changes connected to education, health, and labor force participation. Policymakers can make use of the information contained in individual indicators and composite indices by tracking their evolution over time. This should enable government policymakers to evaluate the success of government policies that are linked to gains in gender equality and women's conditions of life.

Both gender-related indicators and indices have their advantages and disadvantages as a source of information informing government policy. While individual indicators can be tied to specific policies more easily, they represent only one facet of any economic, political, or social issue being addressed. Composite indices can have a complementary value in presenting a broader picture across additional measurable variables.

Notes

1 Suhaib Kebhaj co-authored this chapter.
2 See United Nations (2015).
3 See Morrison, Sabarwal, and Sjoblom (2008), World Bank (2011), Clinton Foundation and Gates Foundation (2015), and UN Women (2015).
4 See Stotsky et al. (2016), Klasen (2006a), Klasen and Schüler (2011), Hawken and Munck (2013), Permanyer (2013), and Van Staveren (2013).
5 See Klasen (2004) and Casarico and Profeta (2015) for further discussion.
6 The United Nations uses this metric in its construction of the GDI.
7 See Buvinic, Furst-Nichols, and Koolwal (2014).
8 Agenor and Canuto (2015) incorporate into a model of growth how a lack of infrastructure affects women's allocation of time to formal labor markets.
9 Details on this and other data issues are provided in Stotsky et al. (2016). End dates other than 2016 are maternal mortality (2015), mean monthly earnings (2018), and women in parliament (2018).
10 Table 1 of their paper provides a useful summary of the methodological framework for the evaluation of indices.
11 Our calculation suggests that this estimate is high.
12 Dilli, Rijpma, and Carmichael (2015) and Gonzales et al. (2015) also replicate gender indices backward in time in a consistent manner. We term our replications *time-consistent* or *TC* to signify that they are time-consistent and to distinguish them from the UNDP's own indices.

References

Agenor, Pierre-Richard, and Otaviano Canuto, 2015, "Gender Equality and Economic Growth in Brazil: A Long-Run Analysis," *Journal of Macroeconomics*, Vol. 43, pp. 155–172.

Bardhan, Kalpana, and Stephan Klasen, 1999, "UNDP's Gender-Related Indices: A Critical Review," *World Development*, Vol. 27, pp. 985–1010.

Bardhan, Kalpana, and Stephan Klasen, 2000, "On UNDP's Revisions to the Gender-Related Development Index," *Journal of Human Development*, Vol. 1, pp. 191–195.

Barro, Robert, and Jong-Wha Lee, 2014, Educational Attainment Dataset (Seoul: Korea University).

Bertrand, Marianne, 2011, "New Perspectives on Gender," in *Handbook of Labor Economics*, Orley Ashenfelter and David Card, editors (Amsterdam: Elsevier), pp. 1543–1590.

Buvinic, Mayra, Rebecca Furst-Nichols, and Gayatri Koolwal, 2014, *Data2X: Mapping Gender Data Gaps* (Washington, DC: United Nations Foundation).

Casarico, Alessandra, and Paola Profeta, 2015, "Introduction to the Special Issue 'The Determinants of Gender Gaps,'" *CESifo Economic Studies*, Vol. 61, pp. 1–6.

Chant, Sylvia, 2006, "Re-thinking the 'Feminization of Poverty' in Relation to Aggregate Gender Indices," *Journal of Human Development*, Vol. 7, pp. 201–220.

Clinton Foundation and Gates Foundation, 2015, *No Ceilings: The Full Participation Report* (New York: Clinton Foundation).

Dijkstra, A. Geske, 2002, "Revisiting UNDP's GDI and GEM: Towards an Alternative," *Social Indicators Research*, Vol. 57, pp. 301–338.

Dilli, Selin, Auke Rijpma, and Sarah G. Carmichael, 2015, "Achieving Gender Equality: Development versus Historical Legacies," *CESifo Economic Studies*, Vol. 61, pp. 301–334.

Fernandez, Raquel, and Alessandra Fogli, 2009, "Culture: An Empirical Investigation of Beliefs, Work, and Fertility," *American Economic Journal: Macroeconomics*, Vol. 1, pp. 146–177.

Folbre, Nancy, 2006, "Measuring Care: Gender, Empowerment, and the Care Economy," *Journal of Human Development*, Vol. 7, pp. 183–199.

Gaye, Amie, Jeni Klugman, Milorad Kovacevic, Sarah Twigg, and Eduardo Zambrano, 2010, *Measuring Key Disparities in Human Development: The Gender Inequality Index*, Human Development Reports Research Paper 2010/46 (New York: UNDP).

Goldin, Claudia, 1995, "The U-Shaped Female Labor Force Function in Economic Development and Economic History," in Investment in Women's Human *Capital* and Economic Development, Theodore P. Schultz, editor (Chicago: University of Chicago Press), pp. 61–90.

Gonzales, Christian, Sonali Jain-Chandra, Kalpana Kochhar, Monique Newiak, and Tlek Zeinullayev, 2015, "Catalyst for Change: Empowering Women and Tackling Income Inequality," International Monetary Fund Staff Discussion Note 15/20 (Washington, DC: IMF).

Hawken, Angela, and Gerardo L. Munck, 2013 "Cross-National Indices with Gender-Differentiated Data: What Do They Measure? How Valid Are They?" *Social Indicators Research*, Vol. 111, pp. 801–838.

International Labor Organization (ILO), various years, ILOSTAT Database (Geneva: ILO).

International Labor Organization (ILO), 2013, "India: Why Is Women's Labour Force Participation Dropping?" ILO News, February 13; downloaded May 14, 2015.

International Monetary Fund (IMF), 2014, *Proposed New Grouping in WEO Country Classifications: Low-income Developing Countries*, International Monetary Fund Policy Paper (Washington, DC: IMF).

Klasen, Stephan, 2004, "Gender-Related Indicators of Well-Being," Working Paper No. 102, Discussion Papers, Universitat Gottingen, Ibero-Amerika-Institute für Wirtschaftsforschung.

Klasen, Stephan, 2006a, "UNDP's Gender-Related Measures: Some Conceptual Problems and Possible Solutions," *Journal of Human Development*, Vol. 7, pp. 243–274.

Klasen, Stephan, 2006b, "Guest Editor's Introduction," *Journal of Human Development*, Vol. 7, pp. 145–159.

Klasen, Stephan, and Dana Schüler, 2011, "Reforming the Gender-Related Development Index and the Gender Empowerment Measure: Implementing Some Specific Proposals," *Feminist Economics*, Vol. 17, pp. 1–30.

Klasen, Stephan, 2014, "UNDP's Gender-Related Measures: Current Problems and Proposals for Fixing Them," unpublished manuscript.

Klasen, Stephan, and Janneke Pieters, 2015, "What Explains the Stagnation of Female Labor Force Participation in Urban India," *World Bank Economic Review*, Vol. 29, pp. 1–30.

Liu, Yan, Asuna Arai, Koji Kanda, Romeo B. Lee, Jay Glasser, Hiko Tamashiro, 2012, "Gender Gaps in Life Expectancy: Generalized Trends and Negative Associations with Development Indices in OECD Countries," *European Journal of Public Health*, Vol. 23, pp. 563–568.

Mithra, Pratha, and Sanaa Farid, 2013, "Female Labor Force Participation in MENAP," *Regional Economic Outlook, Middle East and Central Asia* (Washington, DC: International Monetary Fund), Box 1.3, p. 29.

Morrison, Andrew R., Shwetlena Sabarwal, and Mirja Sjoblom, 2008, "The State of World Progress, 1990–2007," in *Equality for Women: Where Do We Stand on Millennium Development Goal 3?* Mayra Buvinic, Andrew R. Morrison, A. Waafas Ofosu-Amaah, and Mirja Sob-lom, editors (Washington DC: World Bank), pp. 33–92.

Permanyer, Iñaki, 2013, "A Critical Assessment of the UNDP's Gender Inequality Index," *Feminist Economics*, Vol. 19, pp. 1–32.

Schüler, Dana, 2006, "The Uses and Misuses of the Gender-Related Development Index and Gender Empowerment Measure: A Review of the Literature," *Journal of Human Development*, Vol. 7, pp. 161–181.

Stotsky, Janet G., Sakina Shibuya, Lisa Kolovich, and Suhaib Kebhaj, 2016, "Trends in Gender Equality and Women's Advancement," International Monetary Fund Working Paper, 16/21 (Washington, DC: IMF).

Thorslund, Mats, Jonas W. Wastesson, Neda Agahi, Marten Lagergren, and Marti G. Parker, 2013, "The Rise and Fall of Women's Advantage: a Comparison of National Trends in Life Expectancy at Age 65 Years," *European Journal of Aging*, Vol. 10, pp. 271–277.

United Nations Development Programme (UNDP), 1995, *Human Development Report* (New York: Oxford University Press).

United Nations Development Programme (UNDP), 2014a, *FAQ Gender Development Index* (New York: United Nations).

United Nations Development Programme (UNDP), 2014b, *Technical Notes: Calculating the Human Development Indices—Graphical Presentation* (New York: United Nations).

United Nations (UN), 2015, *Transforming our World: The 2030 Agenda for Sustainable Development*, A/RES/70/1 (New York: United Nations).

UN Women, 2015, *Progress of the World's Women 2015–2016: Transforming Economies, Realizing Rights* (New York: United Nations).

Van Staveren, Irene, 2013, "To Measure Is to Know? A Comparative Analysis of Gender Indices," *Review of Social Economy*, Vol. 71, pp. 339–372.

World Bank, various years, World Development Indicators (Washington, DC: World Bank).

World Bank, 2011, *World Development Report 2012: Gender Equality and Development* (Washington, DC: World Bank).

3 Gender budgeting and improved fiscal policies to promote gender equality and women's advancement

I. Introduction

As Chapter 2 showed, gender disparities are still prevalent throughout the world regarding access to education, health care, paid employment, and political participation. They are particularly pronounced in parts of the developing world, even though many countries have made significant progress in recent decades in reducing and, in some cases, eliminating the gaps women face compared to men.

A growing body of evidence suggests that eliminating gender disparities and promoting women's and girls' development are economically beneficial to societies. World Bank (2011) and Duflo (2012) present evidence on the many ways in which women's development and the reduction of gender inequality lead to more rapid economic growth, improved labor productivity, healthier children, and more responsive government.[1]

Elson (2002), a pioneer in integrating fiscal policy and gender equality considerations, observed that fiscal policies and practices that are seemingly neutral in their effects on gender equality may still be biased against equality. Consequently, governments need to ensure that they take explicit account of gender equality in fiscal policymaking and public financial management. Once governments have set goals for different aspects of gender equality, such as ensuring that women have equivalent opportunities for education and health care and in labor markets, these goals can be met, in part, through appropriately designed fiscal policies and practices.

The status of women varies commensurately in countries across the world based on their differing stages of economic and political development. There are countries where women enjoy equality in most areas of life, even while their economic and political role is still limited compared to that of men. However, there are also countries where women's most fundamental rights, such as access to education and appropriate health care, along with freedom from domestic violence, are still under threat. Given these differences, it is not surprising that there are country-specific approaches recommended for countries in structuring fiscal policies and practices to achieve gender equality.

Gender budgeting is an approach to budgeting that uses fiscal policy and public financial management to promote gender equality, and women's and girls' development.[2] Gender budgeting takes many different forms. For example, some countries focus on fiscal policy measures that alter budgetary allocations. Other countries focus mainly on managerial or administrative changes to track and monitor expenditures aimed at gender equality. The most successful efforts combine both policy and managerial/administrative measures.

However, most gender budgeting efforts seem to have not gone very far. This seems to be the result of several factors: a lack of commitment on the part of fiscal policymakers and governmental bureaucracies, and weaknesses in the structure and implementation of the program initiatives.

This chapter discusses how gender budgeting can improve fiscal policies to produce beneficial economic and social outcomes. Section II lays out an economic framework for addressing gender equality through fiscal policies. Section III examines fiscal policies that have been adopted to achieve gender equality objectives.[3]

II. Economic rationale for gender budgeting

Fiscal policies influence economic and social outcomes and general well-being

The economic rationale for using fiscal policies to address gender equality is that these policies influence economic and social outcomes such as economic growth, the distribution of income, and general well-being. For developed and developing countries, sound fiscal policies play an essential role in contributing to the high and sustainable economic growth that supports the achievement of many of the Sustainable Development Goals.

There are many channels through which fiscal policies influence economic growth (Elborgh-Woytek et al., 2013; International Monetary Fund, 2015). Sound fiscal policies help ensure that debt burdens are manageable and economic conditions remain conducive to investment and saving. Fiscal policies also determine the composition of expenditures and revenues, and the benefits and costs of government spending programs and revenue policies. Fiscal policies influence human capital and physical capital accumulation, and create incentives that affect labor supply, investment, and risk-taking behavior, among other economic activities.

Because of the theoretical and practical difficulties in determining the effect of fiscal policies and programs on women and men separately and because women traditionally have had a weaker voice than men in political discussions and governmental bureaucracies, women's and girls' developmental concerns are unlikely to be taken fully into account in public budgeting. Fiscal policies that promote gender equality and women's and girls' development are intended to commit public budgeting to formulating and implementing programs that benefit the development of women's and girls' potential and participation in society.

The proportion of public expenditure dedicated specifically to gender equality objectives is limited. However, the proportion of expenditure that actually contributes to gender equality and women's advancement is much larger because it encompasses spending across many areas of the budget (e.g., general health care expenditure affects women, etc.). Any attempt to disaggregate public spending into these different gender-specific categories requires some degree of arbitrariness (UN-WIDER, 2014). This has been an important consideration in setting up monitoring of government efforts to achieve gender equality goals under Goal 5 of the Sustainable Development Goals. But devising an adequate system is challenging given the inherent ambiguities.

Economic principles underlying gender budgeting

There are several important economic principles underlying a well-functioning budget process.[4] From the perspective of using public funds efficiently, the budget process should weigh competing benefits from public spending against their costs, and expand programs for which, at the margin, the net benefits are positive and have a higher net social return than other competing priorities for the budget. From the perspective of equity, the budget process should consider whether the benefits of government spending programs, and the burden of taxes and other revenues, is distributed in accordance with a society's notion of fairness. Where market processes are not efficient and equitable, well-designed fiscal policies can contribute to better economic outcomes and higher social welfare.

The scope and need for fiscal policies that promote gender equality, or gender budgeting, arises when public budgeting does not adequately bring about the full economic and social benefits of gender equality and women's and girls' development.[5] Gender budgeting rests on the view that government budgets are not "gender neutral" and either neglect the benefits of women's development and gender equality or prevent it (Elson, 2002).[6] Advocates of gender budgeting seek to incorporate as a matter of course attention to women's needs into fiscal policies and administration, and to promote greater accountability for governments' commitment to addressing them. Examples of how gender-related considerations can influence fiscal policy are found in virtually all areas of public policy formulation and public financial management and administration.

We provide just a few examples. In the most gender unequal countries, illiteracy among adult women tends to be widespread. Thus, an important component of a strategy that seeks to both reduce gender inequality and generate faster overall economic growth could be designing literacy programs that focus on reaching adult women. These programs would be created for women who can no longer benefit from traditional school environments and whose time for classroom study may be limited. Another example concerns female labor force participation. In countries seeking to raise women's labor force participation, such as countries with aging labor forces or relatively low women's participation, a strategy might entail ensuring that the income tax system is structured to avoid penalizing secondary earners (typically assumed to be women). Tax incentives for workers or employers could also be used to encourage hiring of female workers.

On the administrative side, a system of accounting for and reporting on government budget execution could track whether spending for gender-related goals was actually taking place. Sometimes allocations may remain unspent because programs could not be executed adequately, or donor requirements were not met.

Gender budgeting addresses positive externalities

The concept of externalities also provides an economic rationale for gender budgeting. Externalities are the costs and benefits of activities that spill over to other markets but are not accounted for in prices. For example, providing a child with a high-quality education produces positive externalities through the improved health of the child and his or her useful civic participation and employment. There are sound economic reasons for addressing the issue of externalities.[7] Activities that result in positive externalities are often not sufficiently undertaken while those that result in negative externalities are undertaken in excess.

The persistent inadequacy of government budgets to address women's and girls' development needs in education, health, and other services suggests that the budget process, as currently practiced, is inherently unable to recognize fully the positive externalities that stem from meeting these needs. Where positive externalities exist, governments can use various fiscal and regulatory instruments to achieve the socially optimal outcome. Usually, the instruments used are taxes and subsidies, but may also include regulatory changes that encourage the desired activity.

To illustrate the above point, assume that in a low-income developing country, the government pays for primary education, but mainly boys attend school because girls are needed to perform household chores (and assume there are no compulsory education laws, or they are not enforced). Both girls and the broader society would gain from promoting girls' attendance, because society benefits from allowing all individuals to achieve their productive potential instead of relegating some to low-level jobs or the inability to work outside the home. In making the schooling decisions of their children, parents weigh the benefits of their daughters becoming better educated against the cost to the household of the loss of their labor. Parents would tend to ignore the benefits to society of having better educated girls and women, which shows up in reduced fertility and child mortality, and in a host of other ways. Even today, the differential rates of literacy of women and men in the poorest countries of the world speak to the relative deprivation of girls in education. The gain to the girls, in this example, is considered a private benefit, while the gain to society, exclusive of the private gain, is considered the external benefit.

Using the concept of gender budgeting, the government might expand its own budgetary allocations for schooling to enable all children (boys and girls) to attend school for minimal or no cost and might seek ways to overcome the reluctance of parents to educate their girls. Some of the gender budgeting initiatives have been undertaken to ensure that girls are better able to attend school. For example, India, Rwanda, Uganda, and other low-income countries have undertaken efforts to provide appropriate toilet facilities for adolescent girls because this was viewed as critical to their remaining in school. Other countries have instituted subsidies in cash or in kind, to induce parents to keep their daughters in school. For example, Bangladesh adopted a program where parents were given food if they sent their children to school, which had a disproportionately positive effect on girls' attendance. Or more recently, the Indian state of Bihar now provides free bicycles for girls to commute to school. Many countries, including all developed countries, have passed laws that require children to attend school until they reach a minimum age and forbid employment outside of the home through child labor laws. However, in many developing countries, the problem of inadequate schooling persists.

A social cost-benefit analysis could be done to calculate the benefits to the girls, the economic cost to the parents, and the benefits to society beyond those benefits that the girls themselves capture through higher earnings or some other measure of their well-being. The total benefits would be compared to the monetary costs of the program. Were budget-makers to ignore the social benefits from better-educated girls and women, they might underestimate the benefit to society of programs to educate females and therefore not provide a sufficient allocation for them in the budget. In this case, females would receive a lower than socially optimal amount of education absolutely and compared to males.[8]

The example above highlights an important dimension to gender budgeting: the role of unpaid labor of women and girls in the household and for care of dependent household members. If there were greater social awareness and appreciation of the importance of this labor, it might alter public decisions about the role of women in economic and social life. Women and girls remain responsible for a disproportionate share of this unpaid labor (Floro, Grown, and Elson, 2011; Bertrand, Kamenica, and Pan, 2015; Burda, Hamermesh, and Weil, 2013). This distribution of labor within the household produces a positive externality to others in the household or society at large in that women and girls take on activities that would otherwise fall upon other members of the household, the government (Palmer, 1995), or not be done at all. Economic analysis has, in recent years, incorporated time spent on non-market activities into modeling.[9] Non-market time spent on care and other domestic work can be integrated into models as a productive factor. With this understanding, it is possible to incorporate formally into public policy the recognition that unpaid work in the home is an important part of the economy. Such considerations can then be built into public spending and investment decisions.

Time-use studies providing data on how women and men spend their time are now more frequently available in Asia and Africa. These data can help policymakers use the reality of separate roles for women and men in the social and economic spheres to promote the equalizing of opportunities for both. For example, time-use data allow analysts to assess how the expansion of key public services, such as water and energy or electrical infrastructure, can contribute to reducing the unpaid labor of women and girls, which inhibits their participation in the work force and in school. Until now, the benefits of public services have generally been viewed as flowing to households or communities, not to individual women and men, and thus their impact on women has not been properly understood.

This discussion highlights the good budgeting principles that should underlie gender budgeting. It also offers examples of how it is possible, through fiscal policymaking and budgetary considerations, to promote gender equality. Governments should weigh the benefits and costs of gender policies and programs, both those that they have and those they could develop and choose those that produce the highest return—measured in strictly monetary and nonmonetary ways, as discussed above.

When considering competing priorities, spending should be increased for programs which produce the greatest additional benefits. These benefits include both direct benefits to individuals and positive externalities (or social benefits). It is important that governments recognize the positive and negative externalities associated with individual decisions, when considering the size and structure of government programs. The improvement of female education and health and provision of certain forms of infrastructure in developing countries has many positive externalities that have not been considered adequately in the past.

As our examples suggest, ***gender budgeting is not a special approach to budgeting***, or even an add-on to budgeting. Rather, gender budgeting is an approach that improves the social and economic outcomes of regular budgeting by structuring fiscal policies and procedures to address gender inequality and women's and girls' development needs. When properly done, gender ***budgeting is good budgeting***. Therefore, it is important to emphasize that gender budgeting is also not an approach to budgeting that benefits only women and girls. In its most general conception, ***gender budgeting improves economic and social welfare outcomes for entire families and the general society***.

Gender budgeting can increase income and social equity

So far, we have emphasized the efficiency-enhancing aspects of incorporating gender considerations into the public budgeting process. However, equity is also an important dimension to public budgeting. Thurow (1971) extends the concept of externalities to encompass notions of equity, where more equitable societies generate benefits that individuals do not fully capture. Equity is often undervalued in the public sphere. Fiscal policies that are redistributive in nature can move a society closer to its own notion of equality, and thus raise aggregate well-being. This is true even though there is considerable variation in what each society regards as an ideal degree of redistribution.[10] For instance, almost all countries in the world have adopted a personal income tax structure that is progressive in that the average tax rate rises as taxpayer income rises. Value added taxes and other forms of sales taxes often build in progressive features by applying reduced rates of tax or exemptions to goods and services that are considered necessities. On the spending side, most governments have programs to bolster the income or consumption of low-income households through various forms of cash transfers or subsidies.

Gender budgeting that involves redistributive policies can produce an improved social outcome, even if these policies come with some loss of efficiency. The Convention on the Elimination of all Forms of Discrimination Against Women (CEDAW) principles and the Sustainable Development Goals explicitly and implicitly recognize that ***there are both efficiency and equity benefits to government actions that promote gender equality.*** Evidence suggests that economies that are more income-equitable grow faster than those that are less equitable (Ostry, Berg, and Tsangarides, 2014).

Elson (2006) notes that the CEDAW principles call explicitly in Articles 3 and 5 for governments to take "appropriate measures" to ensure the equality of women with men, and to support women's development, but governments do not allocate money for these measures in their budgets.[11] It is thus left to gender budgeting initiatives to ensure that this linkage is created, and that budgets ensure that programs and policies designed to address gender equality have adequate funding. Article 7 indicates that women should participate equally with men in budget decision-making and the exercise of related powers at all stages of the budget process.[12]

Conclusion: gender budgeting addresses positive externalities and improves equity

The concept of gender budgeting is firmly grounded in public finance principles. If the goal of fiscal decision-making is to improve efficiency and equity in a society, gender budgeting that promotes gender equality and women's development should be a factor in determining public budgeting decisions. Gender budgeting can ensure that social benefits from gender equality are taken into account in public decisions. Value should be attached not just to time spent in the formal labor force, but also in caregiving within the household. Externalities, including those from caregiving, should be considered as important factors in assessing the benefits and costs of government programs that affect women.

III. Examples of fiscal policies to achieve gender equality objectives

This section examines the nature of fiscal policies used and adapted to gender equality objectives from two perspectives. First, we look at policies typically found within gender budgeting efforts. Then we look briefly at cash transfers that have only occasionally been incorporated into gender budgeting efforts and could be effective in addressing gender- and poverty-related objectives. A better marriage of fiscal policies that have been shown to be effective with gender budgeting efforts should be one of the key steps in strengthening future gender budgeting initiatives.

Gender budgeting involves adopting policies and programs that affect women

Education programs

For developing countries, where females still face significant disparities in access to primary and secondary education, fiscal policies are key to addressing gender gaps. An essential component of addressing educational disparities is to ensure that public budgets have sufficient resources to meet essential public education needs, for both boys and girls, and that schools have sufficient space for both. This result can be achieved by governments through specific fiscal incentive programs. An example is Bangladesh's food for education program (Chapter 6; Chakraborty, 2016). This program encouraged parents to keep their daughters in school in exchange for increased food allotments, to achieve gender-related goals. Clearly, though, these limited food transfer programs cannot fully compensate for lack of adequate public services.

For secondary schooling, a lack of appropriate hygienic facilities remains a critical constraint on keeping girls in school in low-income developing countries. Other reasons contributing to girls dropping out of school include economic pressures from the home that induce early marriage and pregnancy, and safety concerns, all of which can be addressed, at least in part, by fiscal measures. For example, in Rwanda, the Ministry of Education expanded funding to address a lack of sanitary and hygienic facilities for girls that caused them to drop out of school in disproportionate numbers, resulting in better school attendance and retention of girls (Chapter 5; Stotsky, Kolovich, and Kebhaj, 2016). In Uganda, gender budgeting also led to increased allocations in the budget for monitoring efforts designed to increase participation and retention of girls in school (Chapter 5; Stotsky, Kolovich, and Kebhaj, 2016).[13]

Evans and Yuan (2019) recently published a paper looking at strategies to improve girls' education in the developing countries of Asia and Africa. They discovered from analysis of empirical data that programs to increase school enrollment that were gender-neutral (in other words, targeted at all children regardless of gender) on average achieved the same results as those that were directed specifically at girls. In some gender-neutral programs, in fact, girls outperformed boys in increased enrollment. Gender-neutral programs often are able to get broader support from political leaders than female-specific ones, and thus should be considered as a comparable alternative to explicit gender budgeting initiatives in countries where this may be relevant.

Although in low-income developing countries, females remain at a disadvantage in access to tertiary education, in many middle income and higher income countries, girls now graduate from secondary and tertiary education at a higher rate than boys, raising concerns about how to address boys' relative lack of interest in more advanced education (Chapter 8; OECD, 2012). However, looking at what subjects girls and boys study globally, the relative lack of women's representation in science, technology, engineering, and mathematics fields remains a hindrance to their access to high-paying jobs (OECD, 2012).

Health programs

With respect to health, the problems that countries face differ widely across levels of development and different regions of the globe. Low-income countries continue to grapple with ensuring basic funding for primary health and maternity needs. Even while maternal death rates have declined worldwide, the United Nations' Millennium Development Goal target on maternal death rates was missed in many low-income developing countries. And in sub-Saharan Africa and some other countries, HIV/AIDS remains a critical problem. In Mexico, the primary focus of federal gender budgeting efforts concerns the health needs of women and specific risks they face. An analysis of whether government programs met women's health needs and, if not, how they could meet those needs, was also carried out, including an estimation of resources needed to execute the program (Chapter 7; Pérez Fragoso and Rodríguez Enríquez, 2016). The government also developed indicators to ensure that its goals to improve women's health were being met.

Women's economic empowerment programs

A body of evidence suggests that various types of women's empowerment programs and policies can be beneficial. Buvinic, Furst-Nichols, and Courey Pryor (2015) provide a comprehensive overview of what works in promoting women's economic empowerment. Governments can provide a variety of job-related services to raise employability and earnings of women. On the supply side, governments can provide skills training and job search assistance, internships, and wage-related subsidies or tax benefits. On the demand side, governments can provide incentives to employers in the form of subsidies or tax abatements to increase the labor demand for women. Governments can also provide fiscal incentives to help women start and expand businesses, including by improving their ability to collateralize assets and borrow money. Governments can use incentives to encourage businesses to make loans to women for entrepreneurial activities. For example, government programs that encourage the use of mobile phones or provide capital in-kind can help women to retain control of their finances.

In countries where the personal income tax is a significant part of the tax base, this tax can be restructured to minimize the higher effective tax on secondary earners (or "marriage tax"). Such reforms can also create incentives for secondary workers in a household or single parents (most frequently women), and can facilitate increased work effort by women, thus raising the net tax income to the government brought about by work.[14] Bick and Fuchs-Schundeln (2017) concluded that the higher effective tax on secondary earners creates a significant disincentive for female labor supply in developed countries.

Accompanying these efforts, fiscal incentives for child and dependent care can help ease the burden of unpaid labor in the home and facilitate increased women's workforce participation. In Organization for Economic Co-operation and Development countries, the main factor influencing a mother's decision to return to work after having children is the availability of affordable, flexible, good quality child care (OECD, 2012). In some Organization for Economic Co-operation and Development countries, child and dependent care is taken on as the explicit financial responsibility of the government. In other countries, fiscal incentives partially reduce the cost of child care to parents through direct spending or tax preferences (OECD, 2016).

In much of Europe, as in other developed countries, increasing women's labor force participation and work effort is an important consideration in gender budgeting efforts (Chapter 8; OECD, 2016; Quinn, 2016). One outgrowth of the focus on gender in Austria was reform of the income tax to reduce the higher effective tax rate on second earners.

Improving public infrastructure to increase female access to services

Public spending can also address infrastructure needs that enhance women's and girls' ability to gain access to education and health care, and participate in market work (Chapters 5, 6, and 7; UN Women, 2016; Mishra and Sinha, 2017). Public safety in transportation and public spaces and greater freedom from violence against women are considered priorities by many working women and are often essential to their fuller participation in economic and political life. In Mexico City, one tangible outcome of gender budgeting efforts was changes in public transportation to provide safer options for women (Chapter 7). In Ethiopia and elsewhere in sub-Saharan Africa, women play an essential role in subsistence agriculture. Addressing the constraints on their ability to achieve greater farm productivity and bring their product to market is essential to improving their work efficiency (Chapter 5; Mogues, 2013).

Strengthening the social safety net

For some countries, especially in the developed world, an element of the gender budgeting agenda has focused on how well low-income assistance programs aid such families, especially those with dependent children. These types of families are disproportionately headed by single women, and government interventions can help ensure a more equitable treatment of such families relative to two-parent households. The rate of single women-headed households is increasing throughout the world, highlighting the importance of the issue for gender budgeting efforts.

In developed countries, with more extensive social safety nets, especially for the elderly, gender budgeting can also work to ensure that social insurance programs, typically designed to cover those who have worked throughout their adult life, don't leave a gap for older women who have had more limited work histories. Argentina is an example of a middle-income country grappling with ensuring equitable treatment of older women, outside of its formal gender budgeting efforts (Chapter 7).

The United Kingdom is an example of a high-income country where public pensions were restructured to ensure a fairer pension for elderly women (United Kingdom, 2014). Restructuring measures include reducing the number of qualifying years, introducing a caregiver's credit to build up entitlement to a full pension, uplifting the pension for the poorest pensioners, and introducing a single-tier pension for new retirees after April 2016, bringing forward the point at which women will have an equivalent state pension outcome to men (to the early 2040s instead of the early 2050s). Additional reforms will support residential care for elderly, which predominantly benefits women.

Programs to prevent violence against women

Finally, across the world, an important focus of gender budgeting is to ensure that there are adequate laws, regulations, and administrative structures in place to address domestic violence against women, including those who may live in marginal circumstances, such as immigrants or women who are victims of sex trafficking. Generally, these programs include a combination of efforts to enhance police training to address violence against women, prevention strategies among men, and remediation and treatment options, including safe houses and health services for women and their children. In several gender budgeting efforts, such as those in Bolivia and Timor Leste, addressing violence against women was a critical component of gender budgeting initiatives (Christie and Thakur, 2016; Pérez Fragoso and Rodríguez Enríquez, 2016).

Cash transfers to households, which influence decisions affecting women and girls

A set of fiscal policies that encompass conditional cash transfer programs have also been shown to influence many different types of household decisions such as: plans for education and health care, the workforce participation of women and men, other household economic decisions, and the strength of women's decision-making power in the household.[15] Research shows that use of cash transfers in gender budgeting efforts until now has been negligible. This is surprising given that a growing body of research demonstrates that cash transfers can significantly influence government policy outcomes. They can also be designed in a cost-effective manner. Thus, conditional cash transfers should be considered an important fiscal policy tool for gender budgeting efforts. We survey some recent illustrative studies here.

Benhassine, Devoto, Duflo, Dupas, and Pouliquen (2015) examined the impact of a conditional cash transfer to fathers of school-aged children in poor rural communities in Morocco, to encourage participation of their children in formal education. They found that these transfers produced large gains in school participation. The authors concluded that adding conditionality and targeting mothers as the recipient of the transfer made almost no difference to the results. The program increased parents' belief that education was a worthwhile investment from the parents' point of view. It is important to stress here that targeting recipients who are genuinely needy is critical to making the cost of such initiatives affordable to governments.

The above results suggest that conditional cash transfers can boost enrollment, not only of boys but also of girls in traditional societies where girls' enrollment lags. In societies with strong cultural bias against girls' education, where girls' enrollment lags boys', use of a gender-neutral cash transfer may not be enough to increase girls' enrollment to levels comparable with boys. In such cases it should be possible to build further incentives to increasing girls' enrollment into the design of such a gender budgeting policy.

Attanasio, Meghir, and Santiago (2011) examined the impact of a Mexican conditional cash transfer program called PROGRESA (now discontinued). This program, introduced in 1998, provided cash transfers to poor, rural families conditional on specific behaviors, targeting improved nutrition, health, and education. In a set of targeted villages, mothers in the poorest households were given grants to keep their children in school. The authors found that the program had a positive effect on enrollment of children, especially after primary school. The design drew on the specific culture of Mexico, where mothers were viewed as likely to make the best decisions with regard to spending on children. This is an example of a fiscal policy taking advantage of a prevailing cultural norm.

De Brauw, Gilligan, Hoddinott, and Roy (2014) examined the effect of Bolsa Familia, a Brazilian variant of a conditional cash transfer program, on women's decision-making power. Influencing decisions made by women in households is another important lever through which fiscal policies can effect change. Bolsa Familia is interesting in that unlike the program in Morocco, it was specifically designed with women as the recipient. Poor families received a combination of unconditional and conditional transfers related to the following conditions: that pregnant women receive timely prenatal care, children 0–5 years of age receive timely vaccinations and growth monitoring, and all children 6–15 years of age attend school. The authors found that Bolsa Familia had significant impacts on women's decision-making. However, there were heterogeneous effects across households, and the main positive effects were in urban areas only. It was concluded that where the program led to benefits, both in spheres related to child rearing and women's own welfare, it led to greater equity.

The widespread use of similar cash transfer programs suggests that they are effective in helping achieve fiscal policy goals of improving education and health care access and influencing work force participation. Their effects vary based on a number of factors such as: whether they are structured as conditional or unconditional transfers, how much cash is transferred, how substantial the transfers are relative to family or per capita income, how recipients may qualify for the transfer, who is the recipient of the transfer, and whether recipients are urban or rural residents.

Tax reform efforts

Gender budgeting in developing countries has largely been concerned with government spending on programs that affect women, and cash transfers to households whose decisions affect girls and women. However, there have also been a few cases of tax reforms motivated by gender-related concerns. In South Africa, in 1995, the government undertook a comprehensive reform of the tax system, one of whose goals was to equalize tax rates on all taxpayers, addressing explicit bias in the income tax (Stotsky, 1997). Previously, married women were taxed at a higher rate than men or single women. In another instance, South Africa reduced the value-added tax on paraffin (e.g., kerosene), an important household fuel in poor households, which are predominantly female-headed in that country (Stotsky, Kolovich, and Kebhaj, 2016).

Notes

1 Several other studies also surveyed the evidence on the relationship between gender equality, women's advancement, and growth (e.g., Bandiera and Natraj, 2013; Berik, Rodgers, and Seguino, 2009; Cuberes and Teignier, 2014; Elborgh-Woytek et al., 2013; Kabeer and Natali, 2013; and Organization for Economic Co-operation and Development (OECD), 2012).
2 OECD (2016) provides a similar definition.
3 This chapter and the subsequent analysis of gender budgeting efforts draws in part on an IMF-led survey of governments throughout the world on their gender budgeting efforts. The results of this survey are summarized in the Appendix, where we highlight 23 efforts that we considered noteworthy or "prominent." Stotsky (2016) provides more details. See also Kolovich (2018).
4 See Rosen and Gayer (2013).
5 This includes both the private and external (or social) benefits.
6 An example is government neglect in school budgets in developing countries to provide adequate toilet facilities for teenage girls to stay in school.
7 See Rosen and Gayer (2013).
8 In many countries in developed countries and emerging markets today, girls attend secondary and post-secondary school at rates higher than boys, leading to new issues to be addressed by public policies.
9 See, for instance, Agenor and Canuto (2015), Blackden and Bhanu (1999), and Ilkkaracan, Kim, and Kaya (2015).
10 In formal economic modeling, social welfare functions aggregate the interests of individuals and one can weigh an individual's contribution to social welfare differently, in accordance with society's notion of fairness.
11 Elson (2006, pp. 31–32).
12 Elson (2006, p. 33).

13 Additional details on these programs can be found in these governments' reports as part of the five-year "Beijing" process.

14 Feenberg and Rosen (1995) discuss basic issues surrounding the idea of the "marriage tax," the higher effective taxation of secondary earners resulting from a progressive marginal rate structure of the personal income tax.

15 See Parker and Todd (2017) and Fizbein et al. (2009) for surveys; see also United Nations (2013).

References

Agenor, Pierre-Richard, and Otaviano Canuto, 2015, "Gender Equality and Economic Growth in Brazil: A Long-Run Analysis," *Journal of Macroeconomics*, Vol. 43, pp. 155–172.

Attanasio, Orazio P., Costas Meghir, and Ana Santiago, 2011, "Education Choice in Mexico: Using a Structural Model and a Randomized Experiment to Evaluate PROGRESA," *Review of Economic Studies*, Vol. 79, pp. 37–66.

Bandiera, Oriana, and Ashwini Natraj, 2013, "Does Gender Inequality Hinder Development and Economic Growth? Evidence and Policy Implications," *The World Bank Research Observer*, Vol. 28, pp. 2–21.

Benhassine, Najy, Florencia Devoto, Esther Duflo, Pascaline Dupas, and Victor Pouliquen, 2015, Turning a Shove into A Nudge? A "Labeled Cash Transfer" for Education," *American Economic Journal: Economic Policy*, Vol. 7, pp. 86–125.

Berik, Gunseli, Yana van der Meulen Rodgers, and Stephanie Seguino, 2009, "Feminist Economics of Inequality, Development, and Growth," *Feminist Economics*, Vol. 15, pp. 1–33.

Bertrand, Marianne, Emir Kamenica, and Jessica Pan, 2015, "Gender Identity and Relative Income within Households," *Quarterly Journal of Economics*, Vol. 130, Part 2, pp. 571–614.

Bick, Alexander, and Nicola Fuchs-Schundeln, 2017, "Quantifying the Disincentive Effects of Joint Taxation on Married Women's Labor Supply," *American Economic Association: Papers and Proceedings, 2017*, Vol. 107, pp. 100–104.

Blackden, C. Mark, and Chitra Bhanu, 1999, "Gender, Growth, and Poverty Reduction," World Bank Technical Paper No. 428 (Washington, DC: World Bank).

Burda, Michael, Daniel S. Hamermesh, and Philippe Weil, 2013, "Total Work and Gender: Facts and Possible Explanations," *Journal of Population Economics*, Vol. 26, pp. 239–261.

Buvinic, Mayra, Rebecca Furst-Nichols, and Emily Courey Pryor, 2015, *A Roadmap for Promoting Women's Economic Empowerment* (Washington, DC: United Nations Foundation and Exxon Mobil Foundation).

Chakraborty, Lekha, 2016, "Asia: A Survey of Gender Budgeting Efforts," IMF Working Paper 16/150 (Washington, DC: IMF).

Christie, Tamoya A. L., and Dhanaraj Thakur, 2016, "Caribbean and Pacific Islands: A Survey of Gender Budgeting Efforts," IMF Working Paper 16/154 (Washington, DC: IMF).

Cuberes, David, and Marc Teignier, 2014, "Gender Inequality and Economic Growth: A Critical Review," *Journal of International Development*, Vol. 26, pp. 260–276.

de Brauw, Alan, Daniel O. Gilligan, John Hoddinott, and Shalini Roy, 2014, "The Impact of Bolsa Familia on Women's Decision-Making Power," *World Development*, Vol. 59, pp. 487–504.

Duflo, Esther, 2012, "Women Empowerment and Economic Development," *Journal of Economic Literature*, Vol. 50, pp. 1051–1079.

Elborgh-Woytek, Kristin, Monique Newiak, Stefania Fabrizio, Kalpana Kochhar, Kangni Kpodar, Philippe Wingender, Benedict J. Clements, and Gerd Schwartz, 2013, "Women,

Work, and the Economy: Macroeconomic Gains from Gender Equity," IMF Staff Discussion Note 13/10 (Washington, DC: IMF).

Elson, Diane, 2002, "Integrating Gender into Government Budgets within a Context of Economic Reform," in Debbie Budlender, Diane Elson, Guy Hewitt, and Tanni Mukhopadhyay, eds., *Gender Budgets Make Cents: Understanding Gender-Responsive Budgets* (London: Commonwealth Secretariat), pp. 23–47.

Elson, Diane, 2006, *Budgeting for Women's Rights: Monitoring Government Budgets for Compliance with CEDAW* (New York: UNIFEM).

Evans, David K., and Fei Yuan, 2019, *What We Learn About Girls' Education From Interventions That Do Not Focus on Girls*, Center for Global Development Working Paper 513 (Washington, DC: Center for Global Development).

Feenberg, Daniel R., and Harvey S. Rosen, 1995, "Recent Developments in the Marriage Tax," *National Tax Journal*, Vol. 48, pp. 91–101.

Fizbein, Ariel, Norbert Schady, Francisco H. G. Gerreira, Margaret Grosh, Niall Keleher, Pedro Olinto, Emmanuel Skoufias, 2009, *Conditional Cash Transfers: Reduce Present and Future Poverty* (Washington, DC: World Bank).

Floro, Maria S., Caren Grown, and Diane Elson, 2011, "Guest Editors' Note," *Feminist Economics*, Vol. 17, pp. 1–4.

Ilkkaracan, Ipek, Kijong Kim, and Tolga Kaya, 2015, *The Impact of Public Investment in Social Care Services on Employment, Gender Equality, and Poverty: The Turkish Case* (Istanbul: Istanbul Technical University and Levy Economics Institute).

International Monetary Fund (IMF), 2015, Fiscal Policy and Long-Term Growth, IMF Policy Paper (Washington, DC: IMF).

Kabeer, Naila, and Luisa Natali, 2013, "Gender Equality and Economic Growth: Is There a Win-Win?" *IDS Working Paper*, Volume 2013, No. 417 (Brighton: Institute of Development Studies).

Kolovich, Lisa, editor, 2018, *Fiscal Policies and Gender Equality* (Washington, DC: International Monetary Fund).

Mishra, Yamini, and Navanita Sinha, 2017, "Gender Incursions in the Domain of Budgets: The Practice of GRB in Asia Pacific," in Zohra Khan and Nalini Burn, eds., *Financing for Gender Equity: Realising Women's Rights through Gender Responsive Budgeting* (London: Palgrave Macmillan), pp. 141–175.

Mogues, Tewodaj, 2013, "The Reach of Rural Services in Ethiopia: An Asset and Gender-Based Public Expenditure Benefit Incidence Analysis," *European Journal of Development Research*, Vol. 25, pp. 230–251.

Organization for Economic Co-operation and Development (OECD), 2012, *Closing the Gender Gap: Act Now* (Paris: OECD).

Organization for Economic Co-operation and Development (OECD), 2016, *Gender Budgeting in OECD Countries* (Paris: OECD).

Ostry, Jonathan D., Andrew Berg, and Charalambos G. Tsangarides, 2014, "Redistribution, Inequality, and Growth," IMF Staff Discussion Note 14/02 (Washington, DC: IMF).

Palmer, Ingrid, 1995, "Public Finance from a Gender Perspective," *World Development*, Vol. 23, pp. 1981–1986.

Parker, Susan W., and Petra E. Todd, 2017, "Conditional Cash Transfers: The Cash of *Progresa/Oportunidades*," Journal of Economic Literature, Vol. 55, pp. 866–915.

Pérez Fragoso, Lucia, and Corina Rodríguez Enríquez, 2016, "Western Hemisphere: A Survey of Gender Budgeting Efforts," IMF Working Paper 16/153 (Washington, DC: IMF).

Quinn, Sheila, 2016, "Europe: A Survey of Gender Budgeting Efforts," IMF Working Paper 16/155 (Washington, DC: IMF).

Rosen, Harvey S., and Ted Gayer, 2013, *Public Finance* (New York: McGraw-Hill/Irwin).

Stotsky, Janet G., 1997, "Gender Bias in Tax Systems," *Tax Notes International*, pp. 1913–1923, June 9.

Stotsky, Janet G., 2016, "Gender Budgeting: Fiscal Context and Current Outcomes," IMF Working Paper 16/149 (Washington, DC: IMF).

Stotsky, Janet G., Lisa Kolovich, and Suhaib Kebhaj, 2016, "Sub-Saharan Africa: A Survey of Gender Budgeting Efforts," IMF Working Paper 16/152 (Washington, DC: IMF).

Thurow, Lester C., 1971, "The Income Distribution as a Pure Public Good," *Quarterly Journal of Economics*, Vol. 85, pp. 327–336.

United Kingdom, 2014, *Response of the Government of the United Kingdom and its Devolved Administrations to the UNECE Questionnaire on the implementation of the Beijing Declaration and Platform for Action (1995) and the Outcome of the Twenty-Third Special Session of the General Assembly (2000)* (London).

United Nations (UN), 2013, *Women in Development: Report of the Secretary General* A/68/271 (New York: United Nations)

UN-WIDER, 2014, *Position Paper-Aid and Gender Equality* (Helsinki: UNU Wider Institute for Development Economics Research).

UN Women, 2016, *Gender-responsive Budgeting in the Asia-Pacific Region: A Status Report* (New York: UN Women).

World Bank, 2011, *World Development Report 2012: Gender Equality and Development* (Washington, DC: World Bank).

Appendix

Survey of practices across the globe

A survey of practices on gender budgeting for 23 countries with prominent gender budgeting efforts is summarized in Appendix Table 3.1, taken from Stotsky (2016).

Table 3.1A Key Components of 23 Prominent Gender Budgeting Efforts (number of countries in which the gender budgeting efforts had the characteristic below)

	Total
Origins	
Supported by international organizations or bilateral aid agencies	13
Tied to Millennium Development Goals or national development plan or gender equality strategy	18
Selected components of fiscal policy	
Focus on spending	23
Spending focus on key human development (education and health)	22
Spending focus on physical infrastructure (transport, water, electricity, and energy)	18
Spending focus on justice and security (violence against women, judicial assistance)	22
Spending focus on jobs, entrepreneurship, wages, etc.	21
Structural reforms in spending (subsidies, transfers, incentives, or distributional objectives)	15
Focus on revenue	5
Focus on personal income tax	3
Other tax focus, including general or selective sales and trade	2
Indicators to place gender budgeting in the fiscal process	
Broad statement of goals of Minister of Finance	15
Gender budgeting statement in budget documentation	19
Gender budgeting circular or related to instruct the bureaucracy	18
Gender budgeting in planning and programming	21
Gender budgeting outcome report or audit	12
Explicit reporting on gender equality spending	17
Legal basis	
Gender budgeting has constitutional standing	4
Gender budgeting is incorporated in organic budget or other finance laws	13

Role of government	
Ministry of Finance is lead entity	17
Other ministries play consequential role	23
Subnational government is involved	16
Role of civil society	
Significant encouragement or participation of civil society	18

Source: Stotsky (2016).

4 Incorporating gender budgeting into good public financial management

I. How gender budgeting fits into the government budget

A variety of considerations influence government financial decision-making, and public budgets reflect the outcomes of political and social considerations, not just economic ones. The technical requirements of good budgeting, measuring the costs and benefits of each decision, are challenging because political and social costs are subjective, and short-term costs are not always indicative of long-term ones. Figure 4.1 provides an overview of the stages of public budgeting. The budget process starts with formulation, then moves to legislative discussion and enactment, followed by implementation. One cycle of an effective budget process should terminate with an audit of the program results and an evaluation for future planning.

There are several key phases in the formulation of a governmental budget. At the outset, a budget is developed within the broad macroeconomic framework, where the intended fiscal stance is decided on, revenues under existing laws are calculated, and spending objectives are established. Spending objectives are generally related to existing policies and programs of the government. Spending is typically divided into those areas which are mandatory (e.g., debt service, pensions to civil servants, and entitlements, such as social security) and those that are discretionary (e.g., spending for goods and services and discretionary subsidies, transfers, and capital investments).

Gender budgeting programs are most likely to be incorporated into the expenditure side of the budget, usually under discretionary spending. Over the medium term, they may be included under entitlement spending, such as social security or social safety net programs or built into wages and pensions, if they entail hiring objectives. Gender budgeting considerations can also be incorporated into the revenue side of the budget under various forms of taxation, such as the personal income tax, the value added tax, or selective sales taxes, such as excises. Figure 4.2 depicts graphically where gender budgeting initiatives may be placed on the expenditure side of a typical government budget.

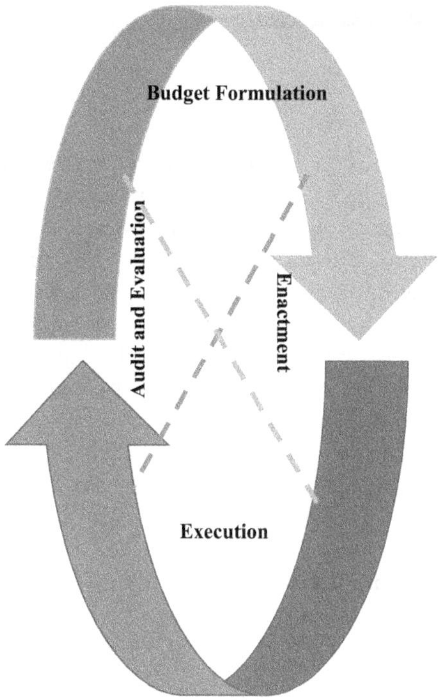

Figure 4.1 Stages of the Budget Process

Source: Adapted from Sharp (2003).

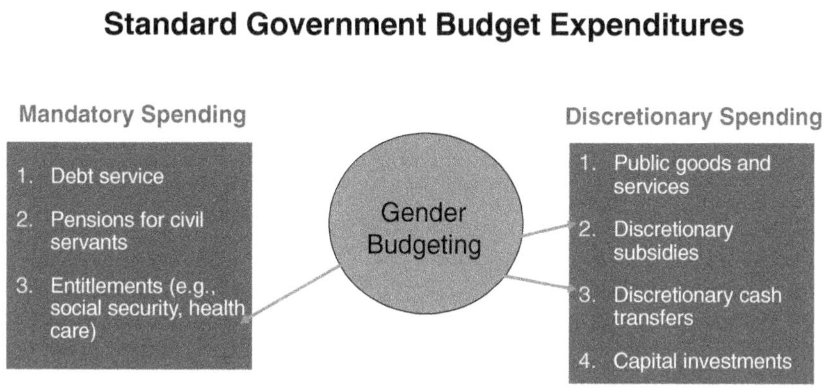

Figure 4.2 How to Incorporate Gender Budgeting into the Expenditure Side of a Standard Government Budget

Source: Author.

II. How gender budgeting can be incorporated into the budget process

Formulation and enactment

Government budgets are underpinned by laws and regulations set out in a country's constitution, organic budget laws, or administrative rules (OECD, 2016). The laws and regulations for gender budgeting may be found in any of these government documents or may simply rely on practices that have developed over time within a government. A clear legislative basis for gender budgeting is likely to provide the firmest basis for gender budgeting efforts to become a formal and substantive part of the budget process. Nevertheless, legislation mandating gender budgeting or gender equality spending cannot by itself guarantee that any substantive reforms in policy or managerial practices actually lead to meaningful results.

Austria presents an interesting case, where as part of recent constitutional reforms, it introduced gender equality as a clear governmental objective, and required gender budgeting at all levels of government. Taking this a step further, the government then introduced gender equality in the context of public management reform in 2013, which put in place a framework for performance budgeting (Chapter 8; Quinn, 2016; OECD, 2016; IMF, 2017). This initiative mandated that every federal government ministry set at least one gender-related objective out of a required set of performance objectives, which are then related to specific government tasks.

In 2007, the Belgian parliament passed a law that required the integration of a gender dimension into all federal policies, including budgeting (Chapter 8; Quinn, 2016). The law requires each government ministry to identify gender equality objectives and then to link these objectives to their budget programs. For instance, the Ministry of Civil Service commits to integrate a gender perspective into its consideration of more flexible work terms for civil service employees. The Ministry of Justice commits to examine gender-related goals with respect to prison policies. Further, the Belgian law requires the discussion of the budget in parliament to include gender equality actions, and for all government policies and laws to be subject to an assessment in terms of the potential differential impact on women and men. Another important part of the law is to mandate the collection and use of gender-specific data.

Sweden does not formally have gender budgeting but considers itself a "feminist government" and makes use of gender equality analysis throughout the budget process (Chapter 8; Quinn, 2016). Similarly, in Germany, the federal government has not adopted gender budgeting, even though it considers gender equality issues at a ministry level (Quinn, 2016). Some German states, including Berlin, have introduced substantive gender budgeting measures. Spain also has made use of elements of gender budgeting tools, including a gender impact statement, while Andalusia has introduced the most notable efforts at the provincial level.

Among sub-Saharan Africa countries, Rwanda adopted an organic budget law that included gender budgeting as a fundamental principle, echoing the same commitment found in budgetary reforms in Austria (Chapter 5; Stotsky, Kolovich, and Kebhaj, 2016). Uganda also demonstrates a strong commitment to gender budgeting, which it strengthened in 2015 with the introduction of a certificate of compliance with gender budgeting that ministries must meet (Ibid.).

Among the Middle Eastern and North African countries, Morocco has been a leader in trying to put in place a gender budgeting initiative (Chapter 7; Kolovich and Shibuya, 2016). In 2014, changes to the organic budget law required gender equality to be considered when defining performance objectives, results, and indicators, in all parts of the budget. In addition, a gender report must be included as part of each year's finance bill.

There are also examples of provisions for gender budgeting in laws in Asia and Latin America. India, Nepal, the Philippines, and the Republic of Korea all present examples of Asian countries where gender budgeting is embedded in national and in some cases state or local laws (Chapters 6 and 8; Chakraborty, 2016; Pérez Fragoso and Rodríguez Enríquez, 2016). Korea has enacted gender budgeting provisions into several national financial acts, which require preparation of a gender budget statement (Chapter 8; UN Women, 2016). Other legislation supports accounting, local extensions, and gender impact analysis. Similarly, in Latin America, Mexico, among other countries in the region, has formally incorporated gender budgeting into budget acts at both the federal and state levels (Chapter 7; Pérez Fragoso and Rodríguez Enríquez, 2016).

Alongside the enactment of laws and rules underpinning gender budgeting, there are two other key activities that help incorporate a "gender consciousness" into the budget process: preparing gender budget statements and budget circulars. Gender budget statements serve to lay out clearly the objectives of the government with respect to its gender-related goals. Budget circulars ensure that the ministries and agencies of government responsible for the formulation of specific aspects of the budget incorporate these goals into proposed programs and policies.

Gender budget statements

As a practical matter, governments must decide where to include gender-related goals as a theme or category in budget making. Typically, once the macroeconomic goals of the budget are established, the ministry of finance is charged with developing and delivering to parliament (and public) a statement of principles that will underlie the budget to be proposed for the coming fiscal year. The incorporation of gender-related goals into the basic statement of principles of the budget, in the form of a gender budget statement, is a strong signal that this issue is to be of critical importance. It also increases the likelihood that gender-related goals will be integrated into the budget process and receive budget allocations. Budget statements may be quantitative or qualitative in nature or a combination of both. Budlender (2015) surveyed practices with respect to gender budget statements. In the developing world, countries typically lay out gender-related goals in a development strategy or national development plan, often drawn up in conjunction with their budget targets under international agreements.

Budget circulars

Budgets normally rely on transmission of instructions from the ministry of finance to spending ministries through a budget circular or related communication informing about the new fiscal policies and programs to be incorporated into the budget for the fiscal year. Gender budgeting may be integrated into the budget circular in a variety of ways. For example, the circular may require that ministries include measurements of gender-relevant indicators in their program requests. It may also require data that measures progress in achieving these indicators. Budlender (2015) also surveyed existing practices regarding budget circulars in developing countries.

In Austria, the central budget authority has developed guidelines for applying gender budgeting, complemented by an annual budget circular with details and instructions to civil servants (OECD, 2016). In Korea, the budget circular requires ministries to report on budget allocations intended to promote gender equality and provides a format based on the existing national financial reporting (UN Women, 2016).

Parliamentary discussion and enactment

Governments vary in the specific processes related to discussion and enactment of the budget. Where gender budgeting is a part of the budget process by law, the role of parliament may be one of ensuring that the governmental bureaucracy has translated accurately the policies of the government into actual programs to address gender-related objectives, and that their funding is adequate. Where gender budgeting is a matter of tradition rather than law, parliament may still play the same role, but may have little formal recourse if the executive branch fails to take its gender budgeting responsibilities seriously.

Execution, audit, and evaluation of the budget

The responsibility for execution of the budget falls to the ministries and other agencies of the government. A critical element for effective public financial management and accountability is fiscal transparency. This refers to the comprehensiveness, clarity, reliability, timeliness, and relevance of public reporting on public finances. Another key building block of fiscal transparency is having an effective system of budget classification that allows for the monitoring and tracking of budget execution (Figure 4.3). Countries develop over time a

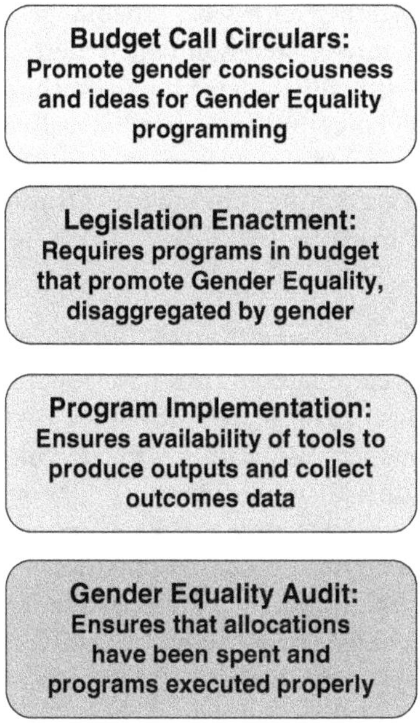

Figure 4.3 Entry Points for Including Gender Equality Interventions in the Budget Process

Source: Author.

structure for budget classification, with an accompanying chart of accounts, that become the basis for fiscal reporting and documentation.

For gender budgeting, it is useful to adapt fiscal reporting and documentation to identify spending programs of the government that are related to key gender-related objectives. To assess whether gender budgeting efforts are succeeding and are cost effective, fiscal reporting on these programs must be separated from the rest of the budget. Some governments, including several in Latin America such as Ecuador and El Salvador, built gender disaggregation into the budget classification scheme (Pérez Fragoso and Rodríguez Enríquez, 2016). This was done specifically to help identify, quantify, and track spending for gender-related objectives. Such gender-specific reporting can help policymakers to measure the cost of these programs relative to their effectiveness in achieving their goals. To execute this type of analysis properly, however, it is important that gender programming be incorporated as an expenditure item in all existing sections of the budget, such as health, education, etc. rather than as a separate expenditure category with programs scattered through various areas of the budget. This latter type of budgeting scheme can cause problems in evaluation, as was discussed by Barba and Coello (2017) in the case of Ecuador.

Another key issue is the availability of gender-specific data, which can be used to evaluate government programs and policies. Most governments collect some sex-disaggregated data, for instance, on births or deaths, or number of students. Gender budgeting efforts can encourage greater use of gender-specific data and help identify programs in which there is a shortage of this type of reporting, making it difficult to determine whether gender-programming goals are being met. Several countries have specifically sought to improve the availability of sex-disaggregated data as part of their gender budgeting efforts, including Uganda and several other sub-Saharan African countries (Chapter 5; Stotsky, Kolovich, and Kebhaj, 2016).

Program-based budgeting

Some developed and developing countries have sought, in recent decades, to restructure public financial management toward a program-based budgeting framework, where the budget classification is divided into programs rather than administrative units.[1] Rather than just focusing on the inputs (or cost of inputs) within administrative units, governments focus on programs and their associated performance objectives, outputs, and outcomes.[2]

For example, in education, under a traditional administrative unit-based line item approach, the government might set its education spending goals in terms of hiring a certain number of teachers at a certain cost of salaries. Under a program budgeting approach, the government might set the program goals in terms of the performance objective of having a fully literate adult population. The inputs would be teachers and schools, the activities would be teaching, the outputs would be seats in the classroom and time spent in instruction, the desired outcome would be the full enrollment of the school age population of both girls and boys (Figure 4.4). Program budgeting tends to lend itself better than traditional line item budgeting to incorporating themes, such as achieving gender-related objectives, into the budget process. Sharp (2003) observed the potential of program or performance budgeting to further gender budgeting goals.

Traditional Line-Item Budgeting

Budget Inputs	Costs per Administrative Unit
Administrative Unit #1	
Inputs	
# Teachers	$X1
# Schools	$Y1
Educational materials	$Z1
Administrative Unit #2	
Inputs	
# Teachers	$X2
# Schools	$Y2
Educational materials	$Z2

Program-Based Budgeting

Budget Inputs	Activities	Outputs	Outcomes
# Teachers **# Schools**	**Teaching**	**# Seats occupied** **Time spent in instruction**	**Percent full enrollment for boys and girls**

Figure 4.4 Comparisons of Traditional Budgeting versus Program-Based Budgeting

Source: Author.

Austria and Rwanda are two examples of countries that made a point of ensuring that the gender budgeting efforts accompanied implementation of a program-based budgeting approach (Chapters 5 and 8; Quinn, 2016; Stotsky, Kolovich, and Kebhaj, 2016). In contrast, in the Philippines, the original form of the gender budgeting effort entailed requiring government departments to allocate five percent of their funds to gender-related goals (Chapter 6; Chakraborty, 2016). However, this focus on an input-based and across-the-board allocation of resources, without specific objectives, led to what was regarded as wasteful spending.

Evaluation tools to assess gender equality programs and policies

Benefit incidence analysis, ex-ante (before) and ex-post (after) gender equality impact assessments and gender equality audits are all tools of evaluation that governments and researchers use to influence the design of programs and policies (Figure 4.5). They are also used to assess how well gender-related objectives of government are being met. Benefits incidence analysis looks at the benefits or burdens of a particular government program or policy. This type of analysis in the gender-related context is typically undertaken with the beneficiaries categorized by gender.

Gender equality impact assessments are a similar but broader exercise in that they cover a wider range of issues or impacts. For example, it is common for an impact analysis to examine the impact of programs and policies on women's and men's labor supply, time use, and spending patterns. Nowadays, the differential impact of climate change on women and men is a topic of growing concern and provides a useful intersecting point for themes of gender and climate in budget policy. Both incidence and impact analysis can be used to examine legislation, programs, policies, concepts, strategies, and any other facet of government policymaking.

Gender equality audit analysis is similar to a gender equality impact assessment in that it focuses on the impacts of programs and policies, from a gender angle. But in contrast to impact analysis, an audit typically implies an investigation of program compliance with the laws and regulations that govern programs and policies.

To illustrate the different uses of these tools, let's consider an example. Suppose that a government spending program involving scholarships for higher education has the goal of increasing female enrollment in science and math courses, and legislation is passed to increase the proportion of funding going to female recipients. An ex ante benefit incidence analysis of this educational spending program might consider how the existing program could benefit women and men, quantifying the number of female and male recipients of scholarships and the average size of those scholarships. An ex ante impact assessment might take this analysis further by looking at the predicted success of those scholarship winners in completing their degrees and the subsequent benefits they could obtain in terms of better jobs. An ex post incidence analysis or assessment might

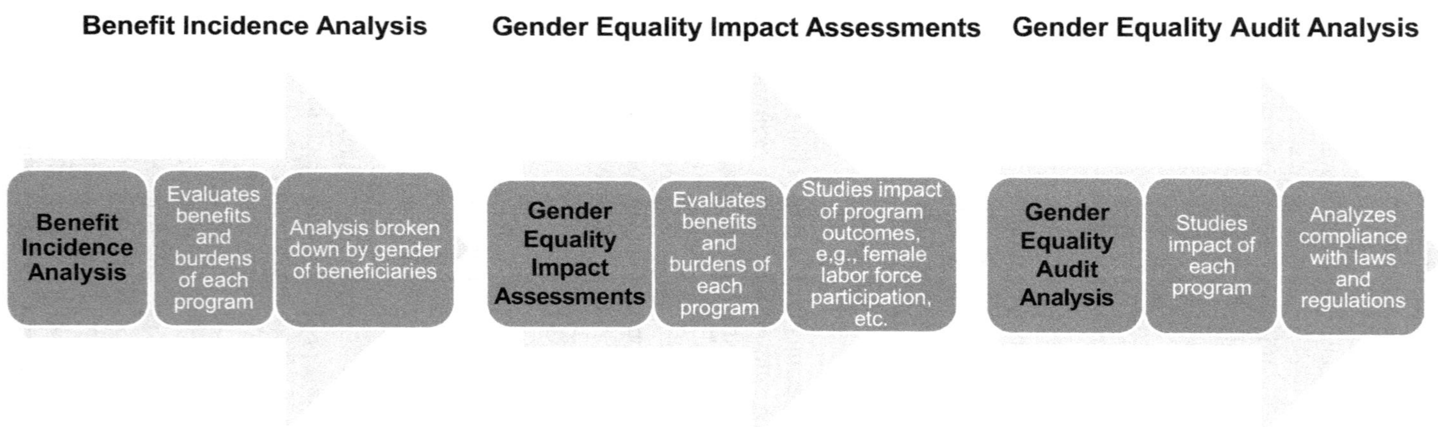

Figure 4.5 Government Evaluation Tools to Assess Quality of Gender Equality Programs and Policies

Source: Author.

be undertaken after the government's program changes were in place for some period of time to examine the effect of the change in the program structure. A gender audit might be undertaken after some period of time to assess whether the program budget was spent as intended and in accordance with revisions to the budget, and whether the gender-related objectives were met.

Few governments in developing countries have undertaken gender-specific incidence analysis themselves. However, there is a limited but growing body of research—most of it undertaken outside of government by academics and nongovernmental organizations—that provides evidence on the distribution of government programs by gender.[3] This research offers conclusions that may not apply to any particular government's own programs but do provide insight into how such analysis can be undertaken and what is typical in countries that may be similar in structure. Most of the early research did uncover gender bias against women and girls in education and health, but there was considerable variation across countries. One fairly uniform finding was that gender bias was most pronounced in lower-income countries, and for people at lower-income levels in all countries. Thus, it is important to look at both gender and income as intersecting issues, in assessing incidence analysis results.

To assess the aggregate benefit of, for example, an education or health care program comparing women and men, a unit measure of the benefit of the government service is obtained and a count of beneficiaries of each sex. For instance, in undertaking a sex-disaggregated analysis of school spending, the required data would consist of the number of students who are girls and boys, and the average cost of education, which is assumed to be the benefit. The sex-disaggregated analysis would compare the benefits to girls versus to boys, which can be assessed at different levels of education and family income. Demery and Gaddis (2009) and Mogues (2013) provide good examples of sex-disaggregated benefit incidence analysis for Kenya and Ethiopia, respectively, in a developing country context.

Although there is relatively little emphasis on auditing in gender budgeting efforts so far, there are some countries that have attempted to integrate this important step into their initiatives. In sub-Saharan Africa, a key part of Rwanda's program was the establishment of a Gender Monitoring Office with authority to ensure that gender budgetary commitments were being met. They have made available these reports to the public (Chapter 5; Stotsky, Kolovich, and Kebhaj, 2016). In Asia, the Philippines is one of the few countries where governmental departments face penalties in response to failure to live up to commitments made in their gender budgeting programs. In Korea, the government prepares gender audits and includes them in the national audit report (UN Women, 2016).

Benefit incidence analysis within households

Benefit incidence analysis can become more complex when services benefit the entire household or sex-specific data are not available. To do this analysis, it is important to have some idea of who is responsible for what activities in the household and who benefits from household resources. A body of research posits that household behavior reflects the outcome of the interactions between household members, with diverse preferences and resources that they draw upon in making their decisions (Lundberg and Pollak, 1996; Behrman, 1997; Hoddinott, Alderman, and Haddad, 1997; Vermeulen, 2002; Quisumbing, 2003; Browning, Chiappori, and Lewbel, 2013).

For policy analysis, the main implications of this line of research are that women and men may respond differently to fiscal policies and incentives, and these may have different effects on different members of the household.[4] This notion is particularly important when using models that assume the different use of time in households and how government services that substitute for domestic work (for instance, public day care for children) may have very different effects on women and men. For example, studying the differences in men and women's labor supply behavior has long been a staple of research in labor economics (Blau, Ferber, and Winkler, 1998; Blau and Kahn, 2003). For tax policy analysis, several studies (e.g., Apps and Rees, 1999; Pollak, 2011) extend models of the household to incorporate multiple individuals with different preferences.

Some government services are provided in the form of "pure public goods or services," such that their benefits can be shared by all in equal fashion. These benefits are not divisible (for example, national defense). Alternatively, there are "publicly provided goods or services," which are benefits that are not necessarily equally shared and may accrue to households or communities in a way that does not easily allow a disaggregation of the benefits by sex (for instance, water or electricity provision or fire prevention services to households).

These kinds of services pose more difficult conceptual issues in trying to undertake a sex-specific analysis of the beneficiaries of public spending. However, there are approaches in the economics literature that can be used to surmount these difficulties. For instance, one might measure the benefits of improved water supply (e.g., bore holes in villages) to households by assessing the reduction in time spent on water collection by men and boys as well as women and girls in the household and then assigning a value to the freed-up time that can be devoted to alternative activities by each household member. Such analyses could be instrumental in setting appropriate government priorities for infrastructure and other forms of spending.

Empirical studies of this type need to be better integrated into gender budgeting efforts to show how government policies affect men and women differently. Several country efforts in which formal analytical work of this type was undertaken include India, Korea, South Africa, and Tanzania, whose efforts are highlighted in Chakraborty (2016) and Stotsky, Kolovich, and Kebhaj (2016). Organization for Economic Co-operation and Development countries more commonly use these formal tools of analysis, although this analysis is rarely published (IMF, 2017).

III. Changing budget planning time horizons

Most sensible budget planning is done on a multi-year basis through "medium-term frameworks." Effective gender budgeting is no different than other budgeting in that the costs and benefits of the achievement of budget goals should be seen from a medium-term perspective. For many of the gender-related goals, especially regarding education and health, it is in fact essential to look at their outcomes over the medium term. Education and health care lead to the accumulation of human capital, which only manifests itself in improved human productivity over the medium- or long-term.

An example of a medium- to long-term impact would be a program to reduce illiteracy among women. Such a program can produce dramatic effects, but it may require the passage of an entire generation. The higher rates of literacy allow women to realize more of their productive potential in labor markets, to participate more effectively in civic governance, and most importantly to transmit socially productive values to their children. The long-term benefit will be measured more fully in the children's generation, not the mother's generation.

The length of time required to measure the most important outcomes from gender budgeting programs strengthens the argument for incorporating medium term (and even long-term) horizons into public budgeting.[5] Bangladesh is an example of a country where each ministry is required to incorporate gender-related objectives, along with those related to poverty, explicitly into the medium-term budgetary framework (UN Women, 2016).

IV. Main actors/stakeholders

The role of the ministry of finance

When looking at gender budgeting efforts, there are a wide variety of institutional arrangements that countries have adopted. In most countries, the ministry of finance is assigned primary responsibility for leading the gender budgeting initiative. It establishes requirements that must be followed by other government ministries and agencies. It is responsive to the requests of the spending ministries in the allocation of funds to programs, and it works with the revenue authorities to change tax laws or regulations. In some countries, a ministry of women's affairs or related type ministry is assigned principal responsibility and works in conjunction with the ministry of finance and other government entities. In other countries, gender budgeting efforts were initiated by legislative groups or nongovernmental organizations, and only later adopted by the ministries, in a leading role.

Where ministries of finance (and ministers of finance, specifically), lead these efforts, gender budgeting has tended to have more influence on budget policies. In some cases, the gender-related goals of the government were better integrated into the budgeting process and thus gender budgeting was applied more widely across the different areas of government activity. In sub-Saharan Africa's gender budgeting efforts, Rwanda and Uganda appeared to be most successful at ensuring that gender-related goals were established. In each case, their ministries of finance took the lead in ensuring that the rest of the ministries and agencies of the government incorporated goals relevant to their areas of responsibility into their budget plans (Chapter 5; Stotsky, Kolovich, and

Kebhaj, 2016). Sometimes, though, it is inherently difficult to establish what factors and which actors lead a government to its budgeting decisions, given the complexity of the budget process and the variety of interests that come to bear on these decisions.

The role of spending ministries

Spending ministries (e.g., education, health, justice) are responsible for developing and administering key spending programs of the government and play an important role in incorporating gender-related goals into their programs and policies. They must also report on their spending for gender-related goals to government accounting and audit offices. On the revenue side, the tax or revenue administration is responsible for ensuring that any new revenue sources or changes in spending are adapted to meet gender-related goals. There are a number of countries where government sought to achieve gender-related goals through tax policy reforms, rather than by changing existing allocations of revenue.

Effective gender budgeting requires that spending ministries take the lead in identifying gender-related goals that fall within their area of responsibility and developing programs and requesting budgets for related programs to achieve these goals. In Europe, there are several examples where ministries were asked to identify and incorporate these goals in ministerial or departmental budgets. The initiative in Austria was noteworthy in this respect. Ministries/departments were asked to include a gender-related goal, set clear performance indicators, and indicate how government programs and policies will enable them to achieve their indicated performance goal.

In Mexico, the gender budgeting efforts were led by the ministry of health (Chapter 7). In Timor-Leste, the Ministry of Education played a central role (Christie and Thakur, 2016). In Rwanda, the government initially chose four sectors as pilots—health, education, agriculture, and infrastructure—to extend gender budgeting beyond social sectors (Chapter 5). Ultimately, gender budgeting was rolled out to all sectors of the government. In Uganda, priority sectors included education, health, agriculture, roads and works, water and sanitation, and justice, law, and order (Chapter 5). Another part of their efforts focused on improving women's economic standing in the agricultural sector where most Ugandans work.

The role of parliamentary committees, women-related governmental organizations, and national women's machineries

Gender budgeting initiatives are usually advanced by coalitions of governmental and nongovernmental organizations. The governmental organization can be committees of the parliament devoted to women's issues and other women-oriented governmental organizations. The nongovernmental organizations are often called national women's machineries. Several examples of this cooperation readily come to mind. In Uganda, in the late 1990s, the Forum for Women in Democracy (FOWODE), a nongovernmental organization established by female members of parliament, led Uganda's first gender budgeting initiative and coordinated with the Parliamentary Budget Office and budget officers to advance gender budgeting (Chapter 5; Stotsky, Kolovich, and Kebhaj, 2016). In Mexico, the national women's machinery, INMUJERES, was instrumental in pushing the agenda forward, with state level machineries supplementing the federal level efforts (Chapter 7). These collaborative efforts are usually essential to provide the impetus for initiatives and to sustain them.

The catalytic role of international, bilateral, and nongovernmental organizations

Organizations outside government may also play a catalytic role in influencing the adoption of gender budgeting. The role of UN Women (formerly UNIFEM) is particularly noteworthy in this regard, as its assistance has been critical in initiating gender budgeting efforts throughout the world and helping sustain them until the present.

Gender budgeting efforts have benefited from the work of nongovernmental organizations in analyzing and reporting on gender-related issues. Several countries are particularly noteworthy in this regard. In Australia, South Africa, and Tanzania, the gender budgeting efforts were all spearheaded by nongovernmental entities.

In the United Kingdom, the government does not have a formal gender budgeting initiative and does not have any specific arrangement for coordinating discussions within government on gender-related issues related to fiscal policies. It does, however, mainstream gender equality into policy by requiring government ministries to assess the gender impact of their policies, under the 2010 Equalities Act. The Women's Budget Group (WBG), an independent, not-for-profit think tank, has a long history of commenting on the Treasury's budget proposals through a gender lens. A study has been critical of the government's fiscal policies and the lack of substantive analysis to gender-related objectives in fiscal policy (Women's Budget Group, 2016). This recent study criticized recent national budget measures because they threaten to exacerbate gender inequality and undermine essential care, education, and health services. In the view of the WBG, the political priority placed on tax cuts and a lower rate of corporate income tax benefits higher income taxpayers alone. It cites a House of Commons library analysis that found that cumulatively 86 percent of the fiscal savings of recent budget measures, in the 2010–2020 period, will be borne by women (and their households). This case is also an example of how solid research can benefit policymaking, even if the government does not have a formal gender budgeting initiative.

In the 2017 budget, Canada has formally adopted gender budgeting. This is a tribute to the determined efforts of nongovernmental organizations in the country to keep this issue on the front burner over the years, through analysis and lobbying (Smith, 2017). An initiative, known as the Alternative Federal Budget, coordinated by the Canadian Centre for Policy Alternatives, produces an annual report examining budget policies, including a chapter on gender equality. The 2016 report spoke of the need to further reduce the gender pay gap, encourage more women in the mining sector, rebalance unpaid care in the home, reduce violence against women, and increase funding for statistics and action on gender equality (Canadian Centre for Policy Alternatives, 2016).

Although the Australian government has in recent years terminated its gender budgeting efforts, a nongovernmental organization—the National Foundation of Australian Women—has tried to keep the idea alive. It has recently assessed federal budget measures from a gender lens, highlighting continued concerns about social safety nets for low-income families and the elderly, domestic violence, and housing affordability for female-headed households, among other issues (Sharp, 2016).

The United States does not have a federal gender budgeting initiative. At the subnational level, San Francisco had a gender budgeting initiative. This initiative focused on identifying priorities of women in public service provision and gaps in public infrastructure, especially for safe lighting.[6]

The role of subnational governments

Many countries have systems of government with multiple layers that are responsible for providing public services. Most large countries, and even some of the smaller ones, have at least two levels of government. Although the discussion has focused on national governments, it is equally important that gender budgeting efforts extend at least to any level of government with responsibilities for the provision of such key public services as education, health, and infrastructure, which are usually the traditional focus of gender budgeting efforts. In most countries in the developing world, even where public service provision is devolved to subnational levels, national governments remain the most significant and often, the only significant source, of public revenues, which are transferred to subnational levels through a system of intergovernmental transfers of shared revenues and grants. It may therefore be useful for national governments to create incentives for subnational governments to achieve gender-related goals relevant to their areas of public service provision by linking either the structure or amounts of intergovernmental transfers to gender budgeting efforts.

Gender budgeting has extended to subnational levels in most regions of the world. In Europe, some of the most substantive efforts were in states (including Berlin, Germany and Andalusia, Spain) (Quinn, 2016). In Latin America, local initiatives were often more substantive than national efforts (Barba and Coello, 2017). In sub-Saharan Africa, national governments more often drove the initiatives, but several extended them to local governments (Chapter 5; Stotsky, Kolovich, and Kebhaj, 2016). In Asia, state or local initiatives were also prevalent (Chapters 6 and 8; Chakraborty, 2016; UN Women, 2016). In India, gender budgeting was adopted not only at the federal level but also in more than half of the

Indian states, and some of the most substantive measures were adopted at the state level. For example, the state of Kerala introduced a statement on gender budgeting into its budget documents in 2008/09, with associated policy commitments. The state budget targeted additional spending for infrastructure to support women's greater involvement in economic and public life (Mishra and Sinha, 2017).

Notes

1 Robinson and Last (2009).
2 In program budgeting, as the name indicates, funds are allocated to a program, subprograms and activities within the subprograms. This approach provides a clear statement of the objectives of government programs and allows for monitoring through inputs, outputs, and outcomes. In line-item budgets, funds are allocated only by line items. There is no indication of outputs or outcomes. However, performance targets can still be set within line-item budgets.
3 See Stotsky (2016) and Greenspun and Lustig (2015) for surveys of these studies.
4 For example, in Rajasthan, India, the government's program to subsidize toilets for rural households, which did not have running water, led to less uptake than expected because many women felt that the additional time spent in providing the household with enough extra water to run the toilets was more costly to them than the benefits of having the toilets. The men in the household might have felt differently because they do not traditionally have the job of fetching household water in this part of India.
5 Ng (2016) examines how gender budgeting can be used to encourage more participatory budgeting.
6 San Francisco, Department of Public Works, unpublished report.

References

Apps, Patricia, and Ray Rees, 1999, "On the Taxation of Trade Within and Between Households," *Journal of Public Economics*, Vol. 73, pp. 241–263.

Barba, Lorena, and Raquel Coello, 2017, "Gender-Responsive Budgeting in Latin America: Regional Learning to Advance Financing for Gender Equality," in Zohra Khan and Nalini Burn, eds., *Financing for Gender Equality: Realising Women's Rights through Gender Responsive Budgeting* (London: Palgrave Macmillan), pp. 105–140.

Behrman, Jere, 1997, "Intrahousehold Distribution and the Family," in Mark R. Rosenzweig and Oded Stark, eds., *Handbook of Population and Family Economics*, Vol. 1A (Amsterdam: Elsevier Science), pp. 125–187.

Blau, Francine D., Marianne Ferber, and Anne Winkler, 1998, *The Economics of Men, Women, and Work*, 3rd Edition (Englewood Cliffs, NJ: Prentice-Hall).

Blau, Francine D., and Lawrence M. Kahn, 2003, "Understanding International Differences in the Gender Pay Gap," *Journal of Labor Economics*, Vol. 21, pp. 106–144.

Browning, Martin, Pierre-Andre Chiappori, and Arthur Lewbel, 2013, "Estimating Consumption Economies of Scale, Adult Equivalence Scales, and Household Bargaining Power," *Review of Economic Studies*, Vol. 80, pp. 1267–1303.

Budlender, Debbie, 2015, *Budget Call Circulars and Gender Budget Statements in the Asia Pacific: A Review*, UN Women (New York: UN Women).

Canadian Centre for Policy Alternatives, 2016, *Alternative Federal Budget* (Ottawa: Canadian Centre for Policy Alternatives).

Chakraborty, Lekha, 2016, "Asia: A Survey of Gender Budgeting Efforts," IMF Working Paper 16/150 (Washington, DC: IMF).

Christie, Tamoya A. L., and Dhanaraj Thakur, 2016, "Caribbean and Pacific Islands: A Survey of Gender Budgeting Efforts," IMF Working Paper 16/154 (Washington, DC: IMF).

Demery, Lionel, and Isis Gaddis, 2009, "Social Spending, Poverty, and Gender Equality in Kenya: A Benefit Incidence Analysis," Deutsche Gesellschaft for Technische Zusammenarbeit (Nairobi: Kenya).

Greenspun, Samantha, and Nora Lustig, 2015, "Gendered Fiscal Incidence Analysis: A Review of the Literature," unpublished manuscript.

Hoddinott, John, Harold Alderman, and Lawrence Haddad, 1997, "Testing Competing Models of Intrahousehold Allocation," in Lawrence Haddad, John Hoddinott, and Harold Alderman, eds., *Intrahousehold Resource Allocation in Developing Countries* (Baltimore: Johns Hopkins University Press), pp. 129–141.

International Monetary Fund (IMF), 2017, Gender Budgeting in G7 Countries, IMF Policy Paper (Washington, DC: IMF).

Kolovich, Lisa, and Sakina Shibuya, 2016, "Middle East and Central Asia: A Survey of Gender Budgeting Efforts," IMF Working Paper 16/151 (Washington, DC: IMF).

Lundberg, Shelly, and Robert A. Pollak, 1996, "Bargaining and Distribution in Marriage," *Journal of Economic Perspectives*, Vol. 10, pp. 139–58.

Mishra, Yamini, and Navanita Sinha, 2017, "Gender Incursions in the Domain of Budgets: The Practice of GRB in Asia Pacific," in Zohra Khan and Nalini Burn, eds., *Financing for Gender Equity: Realising Women's Rights through Gender Responsive Budgeting* (London: Palgrave Macmillan), pp. 141–175.

Mogues, Tewodaj, 2013, "The Reach of Rural Services in Ethiopia: An Asset and Gender-Based Public Expenditure Benefit Incidence Analysis," *European Journal of Development Research*, Vol. 25, pp. 230–251.

Ng, Cecilia, editor, 2016, *Gender Responsive Budgeting and Participatory Budgeting* (New York: Springer).

Quinn, Sheila, 2016, "Europe: A Survey of Gender Budgeting Efforts," IMF Working Paper 16/155 (Washington, DC: IMF).

Quisumbing, Agnes R., ed., 2003, *Household Decisions, Gender, and Development: A Synthesis of Recent Research* (Washington: International Food Policy Research Institute).

Organization for Economic Co-operation and Development (OECD), 2016, *Gender Budgeting in OECD Countries* (Paris: OECD).

Pérez Fragoso, Lucia, and Corina Rodríguez Enríquez, 2016, "Western Hemisphere: A Survey of Gender Budgeting Efforts," IMF Working Paper 16/153 (Washington, DC: IMF).

Pollak, Robert A., 2011, "Family Bargaining and Taxes: A Prolegomenon to the Analysis of Joint Taxation," *CESifo Economic Studies*, Vol. 57, pp. 216–244.

Robinson, Marc, and Duncan Last, 2009, "A Basic Model of Performance-Based Budgeting," Technical Notes and Manuals, Fiscal Affairs Department (Washington, DC: IMF).

Sharp, Rhonda, 2003, *Budgeting for Equity: Gender Budget Initiatives Within a Framework of Performance Oriented Budgeting* (New York: UNIFEM).

Sharp, Rhonda, 2016, "Following the Money in Pursuit of Gender Equality," *Australian Outlook Digest*, March 8, Australian Institute of International Affairs.

Smith, Joanna, 2017, "Liberals' Vow to Put Gender-based Analysis to Federal Budget Draws Excitement, Criticism," *National Post*, February 13.

Stotsky, Janet G., 2016, "Gender Budgeting: Fiscal Context and Current Outcomes," IMF Working Paper 16/149 (Washington, DC: IMF).

Stotsky, Janet G., Lisa Kolovich, and Suhaib Kebhaj, 2016, "Sub-Saharan Africa: A Survey of Gender Budgeting Efforts," IMF Working Paper 16/152 (Washington, DC: IMF).

UN Women, 2016, *Gender Responsive Budgeting in the Asia-Pacific Region: A Status Report* (New York: UN Women).

Vermeulen, Frederic, 2002, "Collective Household Models: Principles and Main Results," *Journal of Economic Surveys*, Vol. 16, pp. 533–564.

Women's Budget Group, 2016, *The Impact on Women of the 2016 Budget: Women Paying for the Chancellor's Tax Cuts*, unpublished manuscript.

5 Sub-Saharan Africa

A survey of gender budgeting efforts[1]

I. Introduction

This chapter examines the experience of a variety of gender budgeting initiatives in several sub-Saharan African countries. We focus on Rwanda and Uganda because of the sustained and to some degree, successful executions of their initiatives. We also look at salient aspects of the initiatives in South Africa and Tanzania, which were the original efforts in the region, and Ethiopia, which had an interesting subnational focus, and Nigeria, which had a focus on a critical healthcare need for women. We undertook both qualitative and quantitative assessments in this chapter to measure the progress of these countries relative to their peers in terms of improving key indicators of gender equality.

In qualitative terms, we find that in the countries where gender budgeting seems to be most effective, ministries of finance are taking the lead. For example, ministries of finance in Rwanda and Uganda mandate that other ministries or levels of government responsible for social welfare or women's development try to address gender gaps and women's needs in their budgets. Parliamentarians also play a catalytic role in these countries.[2] In the countries that have enjoyed the most success in gender budgeting, there is a clear consensus by officials in government that gender budgeting should contribute not only to the well-being of women and girls, but to the welfare of society as a whole. Nongovernmental organizations and donors are helpful in generating research and advocating changes in fiscal policies in these countries. Donors also may provide critical financial support to gender budgeting efforts.

Gender inequality in sub-Saharan Africa remains a significant problem

In sub-Saharan Africa, gender inequality in access to education and adequate health care and in paid employment remain pervasive, though the region has seen improvement in recent years (Chapter 2). Gender equality, as measured by our version of the United Nations' Gender Development Index (GDI), has improved in more than 90 percent of African countries for which data were available (Figure 5.1).[3]

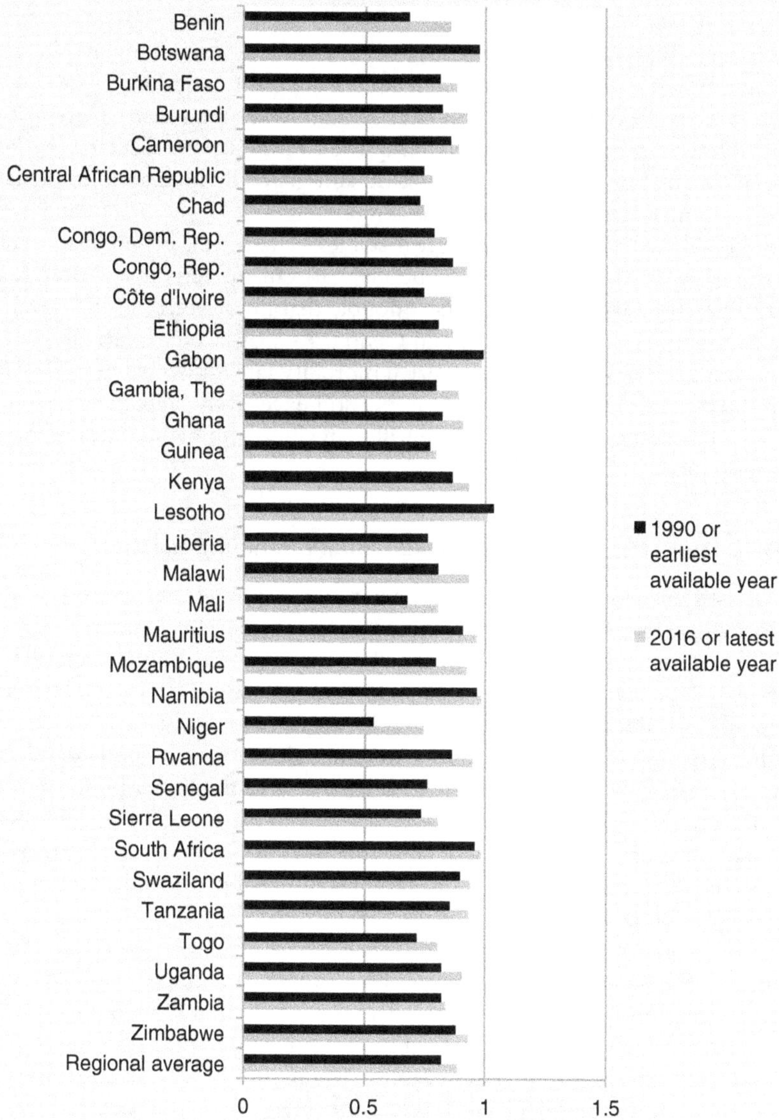

Figure 5.1 GDI, Time-Consistent Version

Source: Authors' calculations.

Notes: The time-consistent GDI was not calculated for Angola, Cape Verde, Comoros, Equatorial Guinea, Eritrea, Guinea-Bissau, Madagascar, Nigeria, Sao Tome and Principe, Seychelles, and South Sudan due to lack of relevant data. Swaziland is now called Eswatini.

The GDI generally ranges from 0 to 1, where a higher number implies more equality.

In education, female enrollment is increasing and gender gaps in primary and secondary education are being closed.[4] However, there are stark differences in the ratios of female to male enrollment rates at the secondary level across sub-Saharan Africa.

Conversely, compared with other regions in the developing world, sub-Saharan Africa has a high ratio of female to male labor force participation rates, even while women's participation rates remain lower than men's participation rates. However, women tend to be employed in the informal sector (without cash payments) or subsistence agriculture and generally hold an inferior status in the job market compared to men.

Sub-Saharan Africa has made great strides in reducing maternal mortality. In the early 1990s, the maternal mortality ratio in the region was over 1,000 deaths per 100,000 live births, almost double that in low-income and developing countries in the Middle East and Central Asia, Asia and the Pacific, or the Americas and Caribbean. The maternal mortality rate is now below 500 deaths per 100,000 live births for the region, but still excessively high. Countries that have had prolonged civil conflict are still struggling with higher rates of maternal mortality.

Sub-Saharan African countries operate within constrained budgets

Most sub-Saharan African budgets operate with limited revenue, on average below 25 percent of GDP (and some well below that level).[5] Many sub-Saharan African countries have limited ability to borrow on international financial markets and their budgets are stressed by global events (Berg et al., 2009). Public spending on education and health for all citizens is generally insufficient, even with substantial donor support in some countries.[6] Weak or underdeveloped revenue bases constrain the ability of governments to fund their public services adequately (Keen and Mansour, 2009; Ebeke and Ehrhart, 2013). Many sub-Saharan governments have undertaken reforms in public financial management in recent years (Andrews, 2010). This offers a natural opportunity to integrate gender-related goals into program-based budgeting.

Most gender budgeting initiatives in the region focus on spending allocations and the design of public programs. Although this emphasis on spending is largely appropriate, significant progress cannot be achieved without strengthening the revenue bases and ensuring that revenue policies contribute to gender equality goals. Discrimination against women in the personal income tax, once common in the region, is largely gone, but there is still scope to reform implicit biases in indirect taxation in the design of tax systems (Stotsky, 1997; Grown and Valodia, 2010).

II. International and regional initiatives supporting gender budgeting

Several key international and regional agreements have played an important role in motivating and influencing gender budgeting efforts in sub-Saharan

Africa. The United Nations General Assembly adopted the Convention on the Elimination of All Forms of Discrimination Against Women (CEDAW) in 1979 (Elson, 2006). As of 2014, all sub-Saharan African countries[7] have ratified CEDAW and put in place mechanisms to monitor progress. The "Protocol to the African Charter on Human and People's Rights on the Rights of Women in Africa," adopted in 2003, by the Assembly of the African Union emphasizes the same theme (African Union, 2003).

The "Beijing Platform for Action," adopted in 1995 at the Fourth International Conference for Women, presented an agenda for women's empowerment (UN, 1995). Countries were asked to report every five years on progress. It explicitly called for gender budgeting:

- Paragraph 345: ". . . the integration of a gender perspective in budgetary decisions on policies and programmes, as well as the adequate financing of specific programmes for securing equality between women and men."
- Paragraph 346: "Governments should make efforts to systematically review how women benefit from public sector expenditures; adjust budgets to ensure equality of access to public sector expenditures, both for enhancing productive capacity and meeting social needs. . . ."

III. Introduction of the United Nations Millennium Development Goals

In 2000, the introduction of the United Nations Millennium Development Goals (MDGs) was another milestone for international support for women's development (United Nations, 2015). Goal 3 committed countries to the promotion of gender equality and empowerment of women, and specifically set as a target that countries equal enrollment for girls and boys (and women and men) at all levels of education.[8] These goals were superseded by the Sustainable Development Goals, approved by the United Nations in 2015. Goal 5 is to "adopt and strengthen sound policies and enforceable legislation for the promotion of gender equality and the empowerment of all women and girls at all levels" (Ibid.).

The 2014 Addis Ababa Declaration of African ministers responsible for gender and women's affairs called upon member countries "to adopt gender-sensitive planning and budgeting schemes," and to strengthen domestic resource mobilization and allocation for women's and girls' rights (United Nations Economic Commission for Africa, 2015, p. 2). Only a minority of sub-Saharan African countries has a system in place for tracking spending on gender equality and women's needs, and a public record of allocations (OECD/UNDP, 2014).[9]

IV. Countries with prominent gender budgeting efforts

Rwanda

Rwanda is a low-income, agricultural-based developing country in Africa that has made impressive progress in rebuilding after civil conflict in the 1990s

(International Monetary Fund, 2014a). Budgeting to address gender equality and women's needs is embedded in the framework for developing a national budget. An organic budget law makes it mandatory for the government to include gender budget statements as part of the documentation submitted in the budget process. Monitoring takes place to ensure that all agencies of the government adhere to key features of the budget. Although Rwanda has made significant progress in closing gender gaps, women still remain at a disadvantage in key areas, including economic empowerment.

The Constitution of 2003 includes equal rights for women and men and mandates at least 30 percent women in all decision-making positions. Women constitute a majority of the lower house of parliament, and are well represented in judiciary and cabinet positions, and as provincial governors and other government positions. The Constitution also provides the basis for gender-responsive laws across a variety of areas including in the areas of inheritance, land, property rights, and protection against gender-based violence. To address gender inequality and protect women's rights, Rwanda established a Ministry of Gender and Family Promotion, a Gender Monitoring Office, and a national women's council.

Rwanda's first efforts at gender budgeting date back to 2002, with its initiative led by the Ministry of Gender and Family Promotion in collaboration with the Ministry of Finance and with support of the United Kingdom's Department for International Development (Rwanda, Ministry of Finance and Economic Planning, 2011). During this initiative, the government developed gender budget statements to be incorporated into program budgets. However, this early attempt foundered. In the government's view, the first initiative suffered because the Ministry of Finance was not the lead on this effort, and there was an over-reliance on outside experts and insufficient building of local capacity.

A second initiative was undertaken in 2008–2010, this time led by the Ministry of Finance, with support from UNIFEM, the United Nations entity responsible for women's issues (now UN Women). This initiative was premised on the view that every ministry was responsible for ensuring that women's needs were integrated into its areas of responsibility (Ibid., p. 2). The Ministry of Gender and Family Promotion and the Gender Monitoring Office were responsible for oversight and support. The initiative also aimed to avoid over-reliance on external consultants, instead trying to develop local capacity of staff.

The authorities saw this initiative as part of a process of public financial management reform taking place at that time to move Rwanda's budget from an "accounting exercise" to program budgeting. It was also intended to be rolled out within local governments as well, in view of the importance of local governments in delivering basic public services. Although local governments in Rwanda lack a strong tax base for raising their own revenues, they do have the authority to adjust budgetary programs to address gender gaps and women's needs (Ibid., p. 5).

Underlying this initiative was a National Gender Policy that placed an emphasis on gender budgeting. "Budgeting is the condition sine qua non of success of implementation of the National Gender Policy. The Policy will not succeed unless adequate resources are allocated to programmes and activities related to it" (National Gender Policy, paragraph 3.3.6, quoted in Ibid., p. 6).

The key objectives in the first phase were to sensitize planning and budgeting officers, train a core technical team, and establish sex-disaggregated data collection and monitoring at the national level. Initially, the government chose four sectors as pilots—health, education, agriculture, and infrastructure—because together they account for a substantial share of the budget. The government also intended to demonstrate that gender-related goals were relevant beyond the social sector (Ibid., p. 14). The focus was on both recurrent and capital spending, in line with the program budgeting being put in place. Because of the government's Economic Development and Poverty Reduction Strategy, the greatest priority was accorded to addressing the needs of the poor, taking account of the intersection of gender and poverty.

The key instrument for accountability was a Gender Budget Statement, a mechanism through which the government agencies could report to parliament. Ministries and agencies were required to submit the statements to the Ministry of Finance. Budget allocations were not dependent on these statements, but their submission allowed some scope for influencing budget allocations. Agencies were also required to include an analysis of gender-related goals in their Strategic Issues Papers for program discussions. Budget agencies were also asked to report on the differences in civil service employment with respect to gender.

A second phase, beginning in 2009, was intended to ensure implementation of the initiative in the four pilot areas and in local governments. It sought to build a system of monitoring and evaluation of targets, collect sex-disaggregated data, and develop indicators on gender-related goals for each sector. In 2011, the Gender Monitoring Office published a study of key gender indicators in four sectors: governance, agriculture, infrastructure, and the private sector (Rwanda, Gender Monitoring Office, 2011). Table 5.1 highlights some of the data collected.

One important accomplishment in this phase was that the Ministry of Finance submitted the national budget in 2010/2011 with gender budget statements of the four pilot sectors, following the issuance of the first budget call circular (Rwanda, Ministry of Finance and Economic Planning, 2011). The budget call circular made the submission of gender budget statements mandatory in the pilot sectors, but also required other sectors to demonstrate that gender had been integrated into budget submissions. It asked sectors to follow the multistep approach used elsewhere (i.e., an analysis of the problems and their policy implications; an assessment of how these policies could be incorporated into the budget; monitoring of execution and achievement of outputs; and evaluation of outcomes).

The addendum to the 2010/2011 national budget contained the gender budget statements of the ministries in the four pilot areas. Agencies were asked to:

- Select output by subprogram, and describe the problem, focusing on gender-related aspects, if they were present;

Table 5.1 Key Gender Indicators Collected by the Gender Monitoring Office

Indicator	*Percent Male*	*Percent Female*
Government Sector		
Percentage of men and women on boards of directors in public institutions	73.2	26.8
Percentage of men and women in the high commissariat of the police	81.0	19.0
Percentage of men and women ministers	72.7	27.2
Percentage of men and women mayors of districts	90.0	10.0
Percentage of men and women senators	65.4	34.6
Percentage of men and women judges at the Supreme Court	57.0	43.0
Percentage of men and women members on boards of directors of civil society organizations	86.7	13.3
Agriculture Sector		
Staff in agriculture institutions	66.0	34.0
Agricultural credit beneficiaries	64.0	36.0
Infrastructure Sector		
People employed within ICT companies	71.1	28.9
Number of people employed in the transport sector	71.6	28.4
Number of people accessing jobs in public infrastructure	74.6	25.4
People studying sciences and technology	67.0	33.0
Private Sector		
Percentage of employees	45.6	54.4
Percentage of private companies by gender of owners:		
a. Agriculture	85.7	14.3
b. Mining	93.2	6.8
c. Tourism	71.4	28.6
d. Manufacturing	64.0	35.5

Source: Rwanda, Gender Monitoring Office (2011).

- Identify which outputs need to be achieved to address gender- or women-related needs, taken from the medium-term expenditure framework structure;
- Identify which activities the ministry and agencies would need to conduct to achieve the identified output;
- Specify indicators to measure each output, and where available, in terms of sex-disaggregated data; and
- Indicate the allocated budget for the subprogram and where applicable the budget for gender-related activities.

The requirement of consistency between activities and program budgeting is a strength of the initiative. An extract from a local government gender budget statement on land planning and management is given in Box 5.1 (Rwanda, Ministry of Finance and Economic Planning, 2011, p. 23).

Box 5.1 Example of Gender Budgeting Statement on Land Planning and Management

Programme: Planning, Administration and Management of Land
Sub-Programme: Planning and Management of Land

Gender Analysis	*Output*	*Activities*	*Indicators*	*Budget (RFW)*
The law regulating land tenure in Rwanda gives women the right to administer and manage land as a precious family heritage. Nevertheless, many women are unaware of this right and are denied the right to manage land, and many of them do not benefit from the revenues from sale of the property of their husbands. These revenues instead benefit the husbands who use the money as they wish.	From now on, so as to promote the rights of women in respect of property in Karongi District, property will be registered in the name of both spouses-husband and wife.	Register all landholdings	All landholdings in the district are registered in the name of husbands and their wives.	10,549,095

Source: Rwanda, Ministry of Finance and Economic Planning (2011).

From fiscal year 2011/2012, the central government made gender budget statements mandatory for all ministries. For fiscal year 2013/14, the Gender Monitoring Office determined that all districts and almost all ministries complied with the gender budget statement requirement (Rwanda, Gender Monitoring Office, 2014).

In 2013, the Organic Budget Law, spearheaded by the Rwanda Ministry of Finance and Economic Planning, formally institutionalized gender budgeting (Government of Rwanda, 2014, p. 10).[10] Article 4 includes achieving gender-related goals in the budget as one of six key principles. Article 32 of the law requires that the budget framework paper contain gender budgeting statements, and Article 68 mandates activity reports of public entities to specify plans for achieving gender-related objectives (Organic Budget Law No. 12/2013/OL).

In its 2013/2014 report, the Gender Monitoring Office indicates that implementation of gender budgeting had scope for significant improvements. It assessed the degree of adherence of gender budget statements to their goals. Most ministries and districts respected the criteria on subprogram selection for inclusion, but relatively few provided an appropriate analysis, backed by sex-disaggregated data. In addition, relatively few of the gender budget statements properly linked their analysis to activities, outputs, and indicators.

Rwanda also implemented gender budgeting at the local government level. The Gender Monitoring Office found that there is scope for improving the process of identifying gender-specific indicators and tracking and monitoring outcomes. It also noted that most districts do not address violence against women (Ibid., p. 3).

Two recent studies shed light on Rwanda's progress in implementing gender budgeting. One study concluded that Rwanda is making progress in integrating gender budgeting into the budget process, though there is scope for the government to improve the initiative at the sectoral level (Mukunda, 2011). The Ministry of Youth and Ministry of Health are specifically commended for the quality of their gender budget statements.

Another study drew conclusions based on a randomized sample of stakeholders and relevant documentation (Mirwoba, 2013). Looking at the budgets and programs of the four pilot ministries in fiscal year 2010/2011, this study found that the Ministry of Agriculture spent almost one-third of its budget on gender-targeted outputs that year, the largest share of the four sectors, while the remaining ministries spent less than 15 percent each. The Ministry of Agriculture's large share reflected the priority attached to raising agricultural productivity and schooling of women, who account for the bulk of agricultural workers (Mirwoba, 2013). This focus is noteworthy in its wider applicability to other low-income agricultural-based sub-Saharan African countries, where women predominate in subsistence agriculture.

Regarding education, this study pointed to a number of programs to improve the supply of books and sanitation in schools, critical factors in encouraging girls' attendance in schools. In addition, there were programs to train teachers and parents to promote participation of girls in science and technology subjects, where girls remain significantly underrepresented. In health, there were programs to increase trained health personnel, especially related to maternity services, and a program directed to female-headed households who confront challenges in accessing subsidized health care in Rwanda. Other programs focused on mitigation of malnutrition and malaria, especially among expectant women and their children.

Trends in Rwanda compared to a synthetic control country

Figure 5.2 presents some comparisons of Rwanda's progress in key indicators of gender equality and women's development, including education, health, the labor force, and the GDI to a synthetic control country. The methodology of constructing the synthetic control country is described more fully in Appendix B but essentially uses statistical methods to create a country that has the same initial starting conditions for the variable of interest, but does not implement meaningful gender budgeting, and thereby creates a control country.

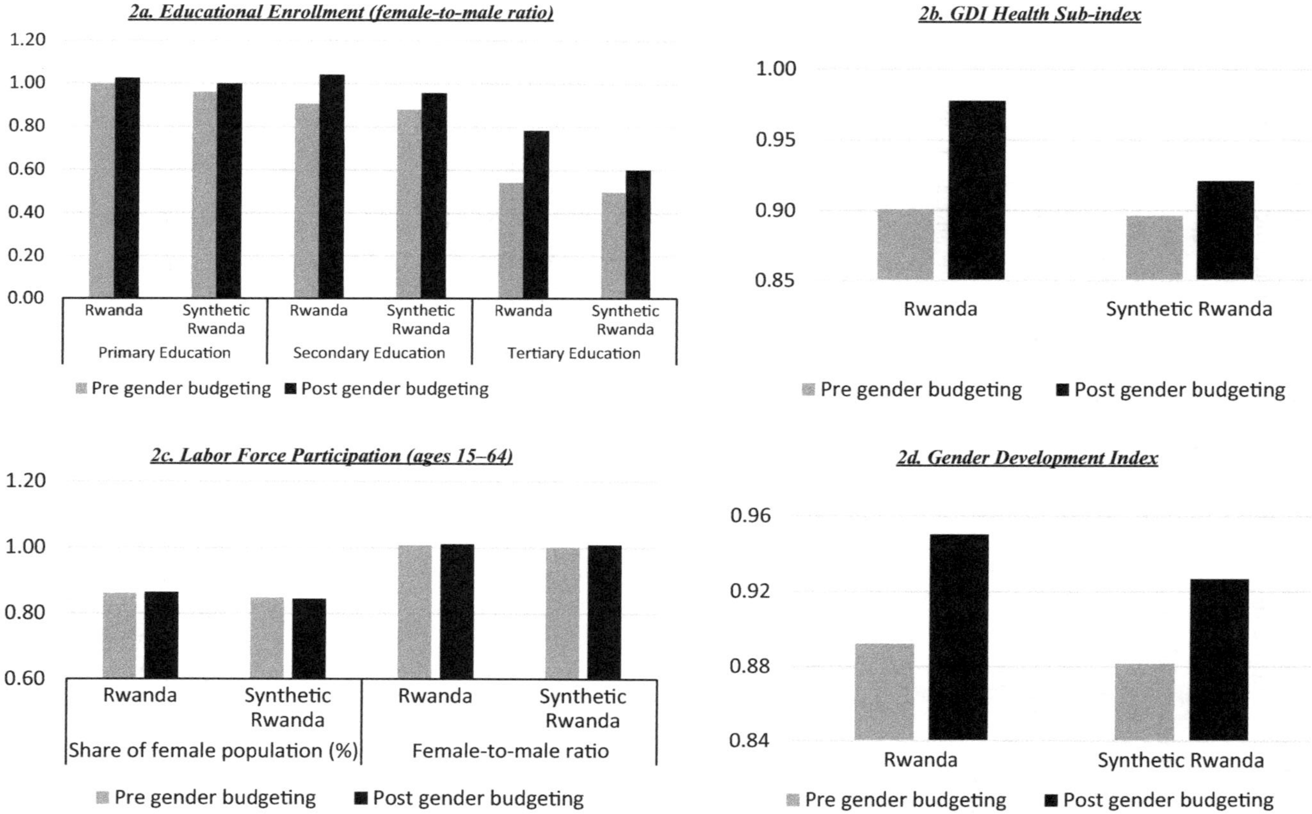

Figure 5.2 Trends in Gender Equality in Rwanda and a Synthetic Control Country

Sources: World Bank, World Development Indicators; and authors' estimates.

Notes: Synthetic Rwanda consists of a weighted average of comparable countries based on the matching feature of the SCM described in Appendix B. A higher Gender Development Index indicates greater gender equality.

The figure suggests that Rwanda made improvements in educational enrollment equality at all levels over the period 1990 to 2012. Compared to the synthetic country, it did better at the secondary and tertiary levels, but it was already starting from a very high level in primary education. The relative gains may reflect the influence of many factors, but in principle, the nature of the synthetic matching technique should control for the most important factors, thus we can attribute the relative gains, at least in part, to gender budgeting. Regarding increased life expectancy (which drives the GDI health sub-index, discussed in Chapter 2), Rwanda made substantially more progress than the synthetic country. In terms of the labor market, Rwanda was roughly on par with the control, while in terms of the overall GDI, Rwanda did somewhat better, starting from a somewhat more favorable score, but increasing by a notably wider margin.

Figures 5.3 and 5.4 capture progress that could be attributable to gender budgeting by showing the situation in the period before and after gender budgeting's introduction (we use the second initiative as the introduction date because it led to a sustained effort). We see that women closed the gap with men in primary and secondary enrollment, with some evidence of a faster rate of closure in secondary enrollment, in the period following the introduction of gender budgeting. By period end, female enrollment was, in fact, higher than male enrollment. In reducing the maternal mortality ratio, Rwanda made progress in both the period before and after the introduction of gender budgeting.

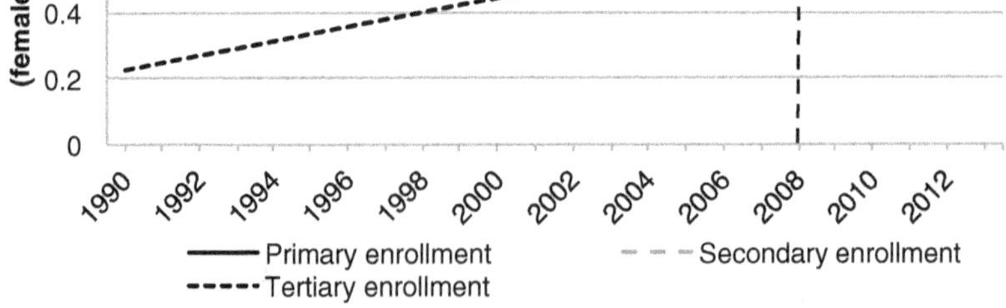

Figure 5.3 Rwanda: Trends in School Enrollment

Sources: World Bank, World Development Indicators; and authors' estimates.

Note: The vertical line indicates the start of the second gender budgeting initiative, this time led by the Ministry of Finance in 2008.

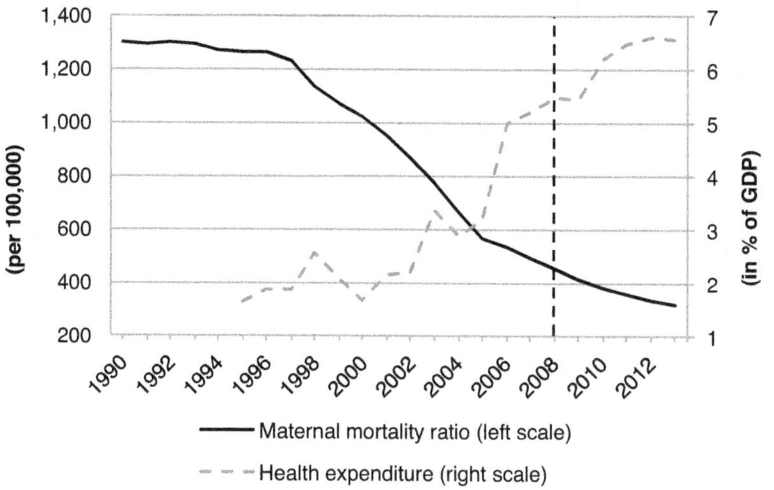

Figure 5.4 Rwanda: Trends in Maternal Mortality and Health Expenditure

Sources: World Bank, World Development Indicators; and authors' estimates.

Note: The vertical line indicates the start of the second gender budgeting initiative.

Lessons from Rwanda

Rwanda shows that it is possible to embed gender budgeting into the normal budgetary processes of national and subnational governments to address identified gender gaps, and girls' and women's needs. In Rwanda, the government and the Ministry of Finance tried to find a constructive approach to address gender-related goals through the government budget. The selection of pilots across sectors encompassing social, economic, and infrastructure issues was also notable, emphasizing the importance of addressing gender-related issues comprehensively. The authorities' objective of matching the format of gender budgeting to a program-budgeting approach likely contributed to success. Moreover, the discretion left to ministries and other government entities to identify critical issues is also a strength of gender budgeting in Rwanda in that it allowed civil servants to consider the most effective approach to addressing agreed-on goals. The Gender Monitoring Office was established to ensure that gender budgeting was put in place as intended and was serving its assigned purposes. Such an accountability mechanism is often lacking in gender budgeting initiatives found in other countries.

Uganda

Uganda is a low-income, agricultural-based developing country. Uganda's gender budgeting efforts have a primary objective to ensure that government ministries address gender issues through normal planning and budgeting processes. The country has achieved some success in addressing gender-related goals in education and health, and in strengthening justice, law, and order, to attend to women's needs through budgeting initiatives at the national and local levels.[11] These efforts reflect collaboration among central ministries of government, nongovernmental organizations, and donors. However, the data reviewed below suggest that Uganda still has a long way to go in achieving equality of women and men (Uganda Bureau of Statistics, 2014, xiv). Gender inequality is seen by the government as a significant constraint to higher growth (Uganda, Ministry of Gender, Labour and Social Development, 2014, p. 14).

In the late 1990s, the Forum for Women in Democracy (FOWODE), a nongovernmental organization established by female members of parliament, led Uganda's first gender budgeting initiative (Budlender, 2002). FOWODE coordinated with the Parliamentary Budget Office and budget officers to advance gender budgeting; in addition, the group organized workshops for legislators and technocrats (Tanzarn, 2008, p. 16). FOWODE commissioned research at the national and district levels focusing on women's needs, and its three, key sector-wide approaches centered on education, health, and agriculture. One of the goals of FOWODE's gender budgeting work was to improve maternal health, and under its sector-wide approach with the Ministry of Health, FOWODE worked to introduce "mama kits," which included items necessary for ensuring safe deliveries of babies in health facilities or at home (Ibid., p. 17).

In 1997, Uganda began implementing its Poverty Eradication Action Plan. The second revision, which came in 2000, and the third revision, in 2004, included a gender focus in the implementation strategies. The revisions highlighted infrastructure, security, health, education, agriculture, and water and sanitation as areas with the potential to reduce poverty among women (Uganda, Ministry of Gender, Labour and Social Development, 2014, p. 14). Kakande (2007) questions, though, whether the effort to incorporate gender into the plans was a priority.

During the development of the Education Sector Investment Plan, in 1998–2003, Uganda expanded access to education, seeking to equalize enrollment of boys and girls in primary and secondary school by 2015. It also sought to substantially increase female enrollment in tertiary education and in science and technology programs. The 2008/09 Ministry of Education and Sports' Policy Statement outlined specific measures to address gender inequities in education and argued for separate latrines for boys and girls in all newly constructed schools; revision of school curricula to identify and eliminate gender stereotypes; appointment of senior women to support adolescent girls and girls in post-conflict areas in the north; and affirmative action for hiring and promoting women (Tanzarn, 2008, p. 27).

Gender budgeting was formally adopted in 2004/05 when the Ministry of Finance, Planning, and Economic Development included gender budgeting in the budget call circular. Guidelines on how to address gender-related goals in the budget were attached as an annex for sector ministries and local governments. The initial focus was on the Ministries of Education; Health; Agriculture; Justice, Law, and Order; Energy; and Water and Sanitation.[12] The government also produced sex-disaggregated data to inform discussions on the budget.

The National Development Plan, covering 2010–2015, replaced the third Poverty Eradication Action Plan and focused squarely on growth, employment, and human development. Building on the formal adoption of gender budgeting, one of the objectives was to promote gender equality and women's empowerment, and the plan outlined three strategies along with more specific interventions, to meet this goal. Promoting and conducting gender budgeting and gender-responsive monitoring and evaluation is included among the interventions (Uganda, National Planning Authority, 2010). Throughout the plan, the goal of improving gender equality typically was focused on programs and interventions aimed at women and girls. But we note that the plan also acknowledges the important role that men play in achieving gender equality; one example relates to reproductive health and the availability of affordable, quality health services, which calls for promoting awareness among men, women, and communities about their roles and responsibilities for reproductive health issues.

A government review of the 2013 plan concluded that progress had been made in addressing women's poverty through improvements in their access to water, health, and education services, noting that improved access to water and sanitation reduced the time spent by women and children in fetching water (Uganda, Ministry of Gender, Labour and Social Development, 2014, p. 14). The ministry laid out achievements in other areas including increased equality in primary schooling for girls and boys; gradual improvements in the number of births attended by skilled medical personnel and in health facilities; and a reduction in unmet needs for contraception and family planning, even while progress on reducing maternal mortality has stalled in recent years.

The budget call circular has been refined over the last few fiscal years to encourage sectors to adopt gender budgeting. The Ministry of Finance, Planning, and Economic Development observed that many sectors were providing blanket or general statements about how they planned to address gender inequality in the budget framework papers (Dietl et al., 2014). Thus, the 2014/15 budget call circular required that sectors submit specific actions to address gender inequality through the budget. The 2016/17 budget call circular[13] reiterated this point and provides separate annexes with instructions on how sectors are to report on their plans. Ministries, departments, local governments, and agencies were asked to demonstrate how they are promoting gender equality and related objectives in the Sustainable Development Goals. In addition, the budget call circular directed ministries, departments, agencies, and local government to identify targets related to gender equality and measure progress toward these goals by collecting data disaggregated by sex, age, disability, and geographic location.

The Joint Programme on Gender Equality-Uganda, led by UN Women and funded by the United Kingdom's Department for International Development, was intended to bring together key international and local stakeholders advocating for gender equality to support the Government of Uganda in attaining its development goals (United Nations Joint Programme on Gender Equality, 2014). It points to some achievements on gender-related fiscal policies in recent years. These measures included Parliament's decision to eliminate the kerosene tax in fiscal year 2014/2015, even though this measure was ultimately revoked by the president. Similarly, Parliament removed the 18 percent value added tax (VAT) on agricultural inputs and equipment for fiscal year 2014/2015 benefiting farmers, the majority of whom are women (Ibid., p. 20). In addition, the Uganda Bureau of Statistics compiled documentation on the types of sex-disaggregated data collected by various ministries.[14] The United Kingdom's Department for International Development's final report on the project assigned Uganda an "A" grade for its achievements under the program, specifically citing Uganda's progress on increasing girls' education and addressing violence against women (United Kingdom, Department for International Development, 2015).

The 2015/2016 budget speech outlined specific measures designed to improve women's health and noted some of its achievements.[15]

- "Government will directly seek to address the health of mothers and children. Providing comprehensive antenatal care and malaria prevention for pregnant women, in addition to HIV voluntary counseling and testing services and nutritional supplements, will go a long way in this quest."
- The government "[i]ncreased the proportion of pregnant women living with HIV accessing Anti-Retro Viral treatment (ARVs) from 33 percent in 2007 to 87 percent in 2014 as a result of increased testing for HIV in pregnant women from 30 percent in 2008 to 95 percent in 2014."

The Uganda, Ministry of Gender, Labour and Social Development also outlined a number of activities, most of which intersected with efforts to strengthen public financial management:

- Initiating a Uganda Women's Entrepreneurship Program aimed at improving access to financial services for women and equipping them with skills for expanding their enterprises, improving value added, and marketing their products and services. The program will initially be implemented over a period of five years starting from fiscal year 2015/2016.
- Introducing a Gender and Equity Compliance Certificate into the Public Finance Management Act of 2015. The Act calls upon all ministries, departments, and agencies to ensure that their budget frameworks and Ministerial Policy statements address gender-related goals, and a certificate would be issued to reflect this.

- Instituting capacity building for senior government officials in gender budgeting. Institutions of higher learning are including these courses in their curricula.
- Requiring that all accounting officers deliver on gender equality and women's empowerment as one of their own indicators of performance on the job.
- Issuing gender mainstreaming guidelines and establishing a national coordination mechanism aimed at ensuring systematic integration of gender equality and women's empowerment issues in development plans, policies, programs, and the budget.
- Establishing a National Gender Multi-Sectoral Framework for monitoring implementation and reporting on international and regional gender equality and women's empowerment goals.
- Developing, in institutions of government, sector-specific gender policies and strategies, and establishing gender working technical committees to spearhead the gender agenda.
- Conducting, through the Ministry of Local Government, an annual assessment of local government plans, programs, and budgets for gender responsiveness. One of the key indicators under the national assessment is the allocation of resources for the gender equality and women's empowerment goals. The well-performing local governments are given incentives in terms of increased resource allocation under unconditional grants from the central government.
- Initiating a value for money audit from a gender perspective by the Auditor General's Office. The office conducts audits for sectors and local governments on an annual basis for gender responsiveness.

In addition to the policies initiated at the national level, Uganda adopted local level gender budgeting initiatives. The Ministry of Local Government established guidelines that encouraged local governments to use gender-aware budget statements and sex-disaggregated beneficiary assessments (Uganda, Ministry of Gender, Labour and Social Development/Ministry of Local Government, 2005, p. 11). Local governments were instructed to check whether their investment plans reflected gender-related goals and if the budget had allocated sufficient funds to implement the plans (Lakwo, 2009, p. 109).

Under the United Nations Joint Programme, the government developed gender-related performance indicators for local governments and assigned them to all 133 local governments in Uganda. As of fiscal year, 2014/2015, these indicators provided a measure of local government performance in planning and using resources for gender equality, and ties central government grants to good performance. Local governments have made progress in keeping girls in school, responding to violence against women, and improving water supply (United Nations Joint Programme, 2014, p. 10).

Local governments included gender-related concerns in their development plans as well. One example is the Lyantonde District Local Government

Five-Year District Development Plan for FY 2011/2012–2015/2016,[16] which offers a sex-disaggregated analysis. For example, a table on resource ownership shows that men own and control household resources. The plan also offers insight into the sex imbalance in time spent on unpaid work using a daily representative schedule for both sexes in rural areas.

Local level gender budgeting was introduced in Northern Uganda in 2012 under a one-year pilot program through a collaboration of the United Nations Development Programme the government of Japan, the Uganda, Ministry of Gender, Labour and Social Development, the Parliamentary Budget Office, and others. Northern Uganda suffered through more than 20 years of conflict. The United Nations Development Programme observed that not only was gender inequality higher in Northern Uganda than in other parts of the country, but the gaps were widening (United Nations Development Programme, 2011). An evaluation conducted at the end of the pilot found that the project had resulted in some additional allocations of money for education and health programs related to women and raised awareness about the importance of addressing gender-related concerns through the budget (Mugisha Baine, 2013).

Uganda has also instituted something called village budget clubs. FOWODE has been actively involved in these clubs, which offer a forum for local citizens to monitor the use of public resources and hold government accountable (Dietl et al., 2014).

Trends in Uganda compared to a synthetic control country

Figure 5.5 presents some comparisons of Uganda's progress in key indicators of gender equality and women's development. We note marginally greater progress in all levels of education compared to a synthetic control country, but significant regression compared to the synthetic country in health, little change in employment, and progress, though weaker than the synthetic country, in the GDI.

Figures 5.6 and 5.7 examine specific indicators of education and health before and after the introduction of gender budgeting (marked by a vertical line in the figures). Uganda continued to make progress on equalizing the number of boys and girls enrolled in education, measured in percent of the relevant population, following the introduction of gender budgeting. However, we cannot necessarily infer causality. There was some evidence of an increased rate of change, following the introduction of gender budgeting. However, women and girls still have lower enrollment in secondary and tertiary education, in the latest data. The decline in maternal mortality that began before gender budgeting continued in the years following.

Overall, then, Uganda presents a mixed picture in contrast to Rwanda. The Ugandan government has established many policies and mechanisms for improving gender equality, at both the national and local levels, and in many areas of health, education, and welfare. Nonetheless, the trends for outcomes pre- and post-gender budgeting do not demonstrate achievements

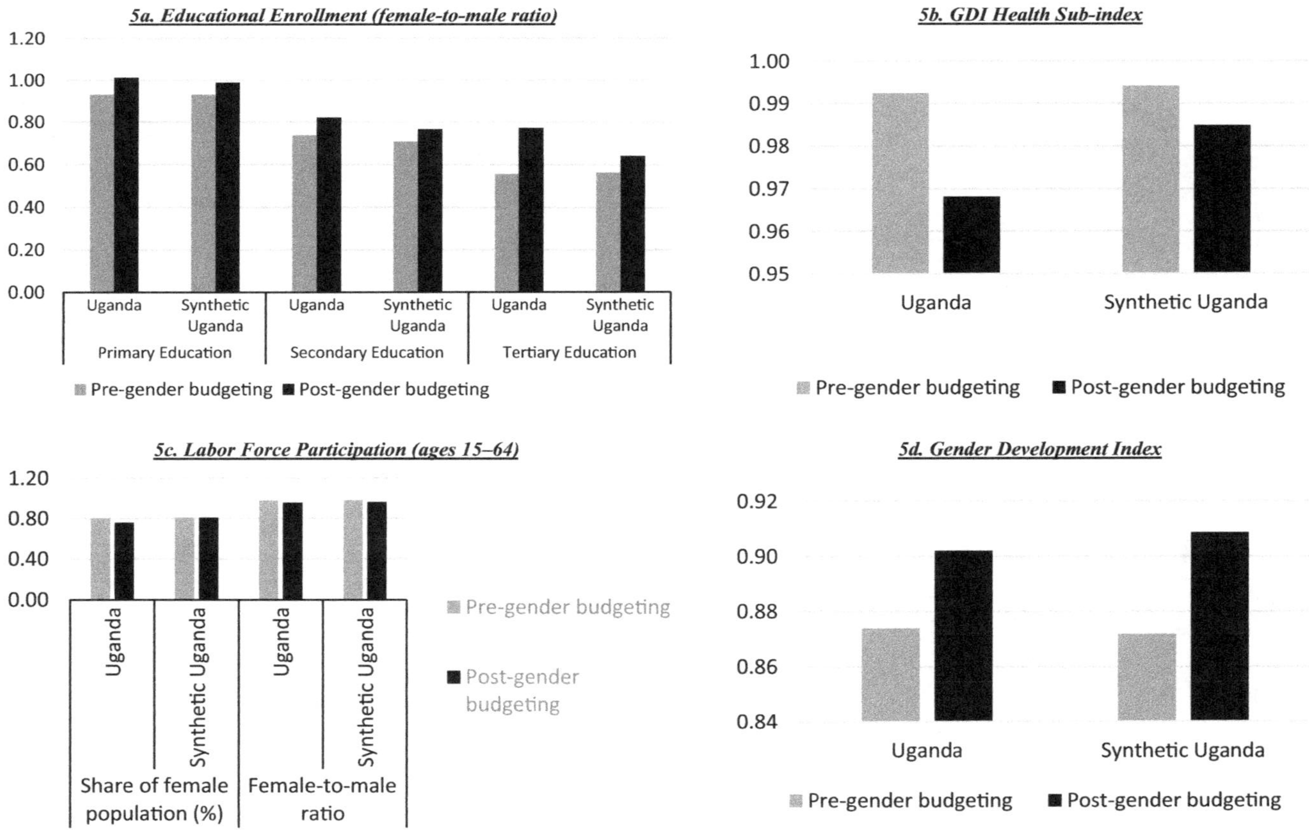

Figure 5.5 Trends in Gender Equality in Uganda and a Synthetic Control Country

Sources: World Bank, World Development Indicators; and authors' estimates.

Notes: Synthetic Uganda consists of a weighted average of comparable countries based on the matching feature of the SCM described in Appendix B. A higher Gender Development Index indicates greater gender equality.

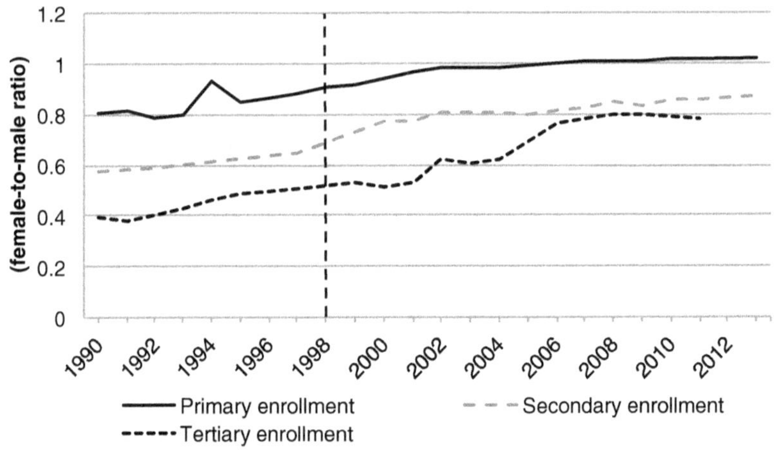

Figure 5.6 Uganda: Trends in School Enrollment

Sources: World Bank, World Development Indicators; and authors' estimates.

Note: The vertical line indicates the start of gender budgeting in the education sector marked by the start of the Education Sector Investment plan in 1998.

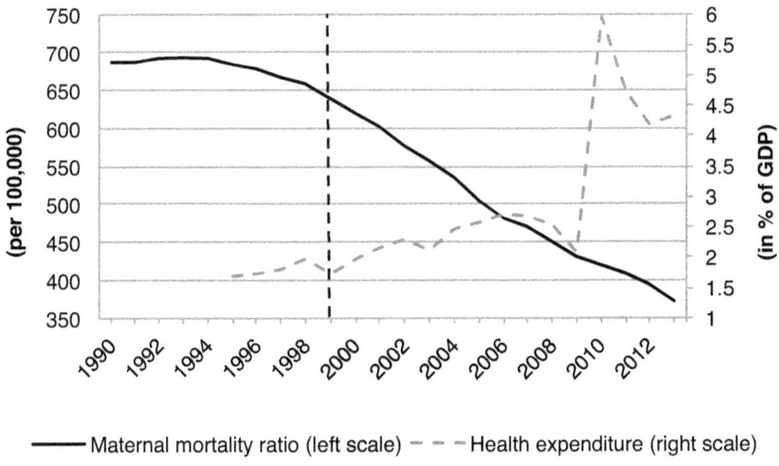

Figure 5.7 Uganda: Trends in Maternal Mortality and Health Expenditure

Sources: World Bank, World Development Indicators; and authors' estimates.

Note: The vertical line indicates the start of gender budgeting in the health sector marked by the start of FOWODE's initiative to improve maternal health in 1999.

comparable to those obtained by the Rwandan government. For example, while in 1990 Rwanda had a maternal mortality rate around 1,200 per 100,000 population, by 2013, it had been reduced to about 300 per 100,000. In contrast, Uganda started with a much lower maternal mortality rate of around 700 per 100,000 but ended the period with a rate of approximately 370 per 100,000. Whether these poorer results (and others in education and the proportion of female participation in the labor force, for example) are due to incomplete or faulty implementation, inadequate funding, or indifferent monitoring and follow-up, is not clear, but would be an appropriate topic for investigation.

Lessons from Uganda

The Ugandan experience suggests that governments can address gender-related goals through the budget by setting clear and well thought out priorities. The use of Uganda's national and subnational budgets to address gender-related gaps and women's needs in education and health demonstrates the positive role that government plays, even though progress remains slow. Many of the positive trends in women's education and health shown in Figures 5.6 and 5.7 began before gender budgeting reforms were introduced. Hence, it is not clear how much of the subsequent progress was connected to these initiatives. In fact, one might speculate that the rise in female educational levels might increase gender-equality consciousness leading to gender budgeting initiatives, not the other way around. Nonetheless, the introduction of the Certificate on Gender and Equity Compliance to monitor sectoral compliance with gender-related goals, and the linking of intergovernmental transfers to local governments to programs on gender equity are innovative policies. They suggest a genuine commitment on the part of the government to achieving gender equity and addressing women's needs through the budget.

V. Other examples of gender budgeting in sub-Saharan Africa

South Africa[17]

South Africa has had two distinct gender budgeting efforts, both of which led to some fiscal policy and administrative changes. However, both initiatives waned, even though the government maintains that it remains firmly committed to gender equality and addressing women's needs.

South Africa is a middle-income country and the most industrialized country in sub-Saharan Africa (IMF, 2014b). The government's report to the Beijing + 20 meeting lays out many of its commitments in the areas of gender equity and women's advancement (South Africa, Department of Women, Children, and People with Disabilities, 2014). It acknowledges that despite some progress in addressing poverty and gender inequality, poverty and unemployment rates remain significantly higher for women than men.

Inspired by the Australian Women's Budget (the first gender budgeting initiative), a coalition of parliamentarians and nongovernmental organizations started the Women's Budget Initiative in South African in 1995.[18] The initiative arose in the period following the end of apartheid with the adoption of a new Constitution (Budlender, 2002).

The Women's Budget was an annual publication that analyzed and provided policy prescriptions on issues of importance to women to inform budgetary discussions. The document covered a range of issues over the years including education, health care, welfare, housing, jobs, public employment, and violence against women. Over time it was expanded to cover revenue, donor, and intergovernmental finance issues. However, support for the Women's Budget Initiative gradually waned, reflecting in part the departure of a number of high-level appointees in Parliament and the Ministry of Finance over time (Ibid.).

A second initiative was piloted in 1998–1999 in the National Department of Finance (now National Treasury), with the technical support of some of the same people who had introduced the Women's Budget.[19] The South African effort was part of a broader Commonwealth Secretariat initiative that involved several Commonwealth countries. In the two years of the second South African initiative, the government discussed gender-related issues in its standard budget documents and included statistics on the role of gender in various sectors of the economy, and the actions needed to achieve a greater female presence.

Even though the initiative waned, several departments of government undertook gender budgeting-related activities subsequently. The Department of Trade and Industry was one of the first departments to observe that only a small fraction of its budget was allocated to small, medium and micro-enterprises, even though women are more likely to be owners of these types of enterprises. This observation resulted in increased allocations to the budget to promote more women's management and ownership. The Department of Social Development chose five budget programs and subprograms to assess how staff understood gender-related issues and addressed them by budgeted activities.

Over time, several fiscal policy or program changes at the national level were attributed to gender budgeting or related initiatives:[20]

- The zero rating of paraffin (i.e., kerosene) in the VAT in 2001 to reduce the tax burden on poor women who rely on this source of fuel.
- The Child Support Grant to primary caregivers (Figure 5.8).
- The increase in the allocation by the Department of Trade and Industry for small, medium, and micro enterprises, which is seen to benefit women-run businesses.
- The equalization of the amount spent on prison rations for male and female prisoners.

More recently, the Ministry of Women, Children, and People with Disabilities partnered with the Motsepe Foundation, to restart gender budgeting at the national level. After conducting a review, it offered a set of recommendations for health; agriculture, forestry, fisheries; energy; and trade and industry (Motsepe Foundation, 2013). For health, it recommended sustaining adequate

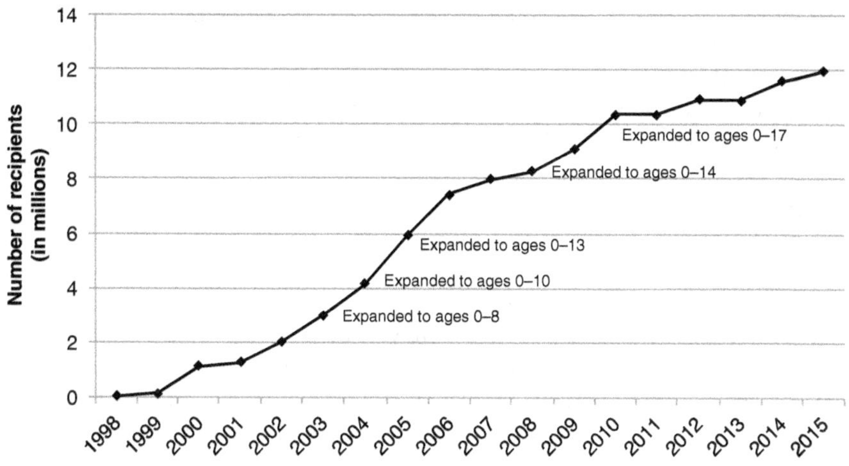

Figure 5.8 South Africa: Child Support Grant Coverage

Sources: DSD, SASSA, and UNICEF (2012); and SASSA (2013, 2014, 2015).

spending on health, particularly for programs to reduce maternal mortality and improve infrastructure for delivery of health services.

For agriculture, it pointed out the need for a policy that takes account of the importance of women both in subsistence agriculture and in paid agricultural work, in addition to a program to reduce hunger. For energy, it recommended taking full account of women's role in the household for lighting, heating, and cooking. For trade and industry, the report proposed the design of programs to support women's participation in the business sector and equitable representation of women in business activities. There were also a number of provincial initiatives. In 2003, the Premier's Office of Gauteng Province developed a policy on women's needs and incorporated relevant statements into the main budget statement. Budget officials were asked to identify outputs and outcomes—those targeting women and girls specifically and those that were not targeted but benefited women and girls and promoted gender equality in Gauteng Provincial Government. The review emphasized the importance of building institutions and making use of sex-disaggregated data. Furthermore, it proposed that government provide gender units with adequate resources, technical skills, and knowledge to translate concepts into practice; train economists in applying gender analysis; and improve monitoring mechanisms for tracking budget outcomes in terms of reducing gender gaps.

It is worth emphasizing that these recommendations, though set within a South African context, could equally well apply to the range of sub-Saharan African countries in which women have a similar role in the household and economy.

Although separate from the gender budgeting initiatives, South Africa has also reformed its tax system to be more equitable to women. In the apartheid period, the tax system contained several elements of explicit discrimination against women (Budlender, Casale, and Valodia, 2010). One important difference was that the tax schedules defined a "married person" as male with a separate category provided for "married women." Married men were taxed at a lower rate than unmarried people, and unmarried people were taxed at lower rate than married women. The distinction between married men and women was justified on the grounds that married women were secondary earners in the household. In addition, allowances for dependents accrued only to married men, among several other discriminatory measures. In 1995, in the context of income tax reform, South Africa moved to unify the rate schedule and eliminate other forms of explicit discrimination against women in the tax code. Nonetheless, concern remains that the income tax code contains elements of implicit bias against single-adult headed households, which is very common among women in South Africa.[21]

Budlender et al. (2010) also assess differential tax burdens in South Africa for indirect taxes (principally value-added taxes, excises, and the fuel levy) by household type (defined in the study). They find that there is no implicit bias overall against "female-type" households because high taxes on alcohol, tobacco, and fuel raise the relative burden on households headed by men, who consume more of these goods, and the zero-rating of basic food and paraffin has a disproportionate benefit in reducing the tax burden of households headed by women.

South Africa has many of the prerequisites for putting in place effective gender budgeting. It has well-functioning budget institutions and a legal framework for addressing gender equality and women's needs. The zero rating of paraffin and the child support grant are important achievements attributable to gender budgeting. South Africa's gender budgeting initiatives did play an important role in inspiring other initiatives in the region and elsewhere.

Tanzania

Tanzania is a low-income, agricultural-based developing country, which, like Uganda and Rwanda, has made significant progress in improving macroeconomic control and strengthening growth (International Monetary Fund, 2014c). As in these other countries, women need more education, better health care, and better work opportunities. Tanzania's gender budgeting efforts were stimulated by a coalition of nongovernmental organizations that produced considerable research for integrating women's needs in fiscal policies and employing time use data to assess the effect of unpaid labor on women's lives. Their efforts suffered because the government did not fully incorporate an approach to gender equality in the budget. Moreover, the government relied on donor funding rather than its own revenue sources to sustain funding for gender-related goals.

Tanzania was a pioneer in gender budgeting in Africa in 1997 (Rusimbi, 2002; Mhina, 2007). Its first efforts began as a civil society initiative involving a network of nongovernmental organizations such as the Tanzania Gender Networking Program and Feminist Activism. The aim of this coalition was to address gender equality and women's needs through the budget, especially in the social sectors (Rusimbi, 2002). Research to inform policymaking was a central part of their efforts. One of the coalition's first products was a book, *Budgeting with a Gender Focus*, outlining the concepts of gender budgeting. A tangible outcome was that, in 2000, the government undertook a pilot project with several ministries, including those addressing health, education, agriculture and food security, water, regional administration and local governments, community development, gender, and children's development, to integrate gender equality concerns into the budget process.

Its later efforts began in 2001, with the coalition of nongovernmental organizations continuing its focus on incorporating gender-related issues into the budget process but elevating them to macroeconomic programming (Rusimbi, 2002).

There were some achievements in girls' education: the establishment of a program for girls' secondary education to increase low-income girls' access to secondary education; scholarships for female students at the university level; a program to encourage more girls in science and math-based disciplines; and other measures to increase female enrollment and retention rates in higher levels of education (Mhina, 2007, p. 12).

Despite these efforts, the impact of gender budgeting was limited, as suggested by two reviews. A World Bank Strategic County Gender Assessment in 2004 advocated incorporating more gender-related objectives into government poverty-reduction programs (Blackden and Rwebangira, 2004). The Bank saw the efforts to mainstream gender issues in the budget as consistent with the government's move to an output and outcome-oriented budget and recommended providing more guidance to budget officers in addressing gender-related issues (Blackden and Rwebangira, 2004, p. 25). Similarly, a review by UNIFEM, in 2008, largely concurred (Kytola, 2008). It noted that awareness of budgeting was widespread, but its implementation was inconsistent (Kytola, 2008, p. 10).

A Gender Mainstreaming Working Group—Macro Policy was established to provide a forum for dialogue between the government and other stakeholders on gender-related economic policy matters and was housed in the Tanzania Ministry of Community Development, Gender and Children. It commissioned the Tanzania Gender Networking Program to study issues relevant to guiding fiscal policies, such as how to address the problems of a large number of female-headed households and the burden of home-based care in HIV/AIDS (Kytola, 2008, p. 34). The Tanzania Gender Networking Program also encouraged the government to conduct the first Tanzania study on individuals' use of time and suggested disaggregating labor into men and women in macroeconomic models, to capture the different roles of women (Rusimbi and Kikwa, 2008). It has also conducted courses though its Gender Training Institute.

The Ministry of Finance[22] and the government's Beijing + 20 report (Tanzania, MCDGC and MESWYWCD, 2014) provided an update on the status of gender budgeting in the Tanzanian government. First, the government has established a core gender budgeting team within the Ministry of Finance to oversee the implementation of gender budgeting in all sectors of the government and in local governments, working in collaboration with other groups. Second, the national government supports the integration of gender equality commitments in government programs and policies and tracking gender-related spending at the national and local levels.

Since 2010, the Ministry of Finance has given gender-specific instructions to national and local government agencies in developing their budgets. It has earmarked two ministries, the Ministry of Agriculture and the Ministry of Labor, and two local government authorities, Temeke Municipality and Morogoro District Council, to pilot a new phase of the implementation of gender budgeting.

Some of the projects influenced by the current gender budgeting efforts include:

- Education: building hostels for girls' secondary schools and encouraging girls to pursue science as a field of study in college.
- Agriculture: providing subsidies for poor families, many of which are female-headed. These subsidies cover farm inputs, such as fertilizer, seeds, and pesticides.
- Water: building water wells for 10 villages under each local government's authority to reduce the distance to fetch water.
- Tax exemptions: implementing a tax exemption on import duties for material used for production of women's sanitary towels.

In 2013, the women's caucus in Parliament, the parliamentary budget committee, and other groups planned for the implementation of gender budget statements. Permanent ministerial secretaries attended orientation sessions and staff, from 10 regions and the district councils, were trained in gender planning and budgeting. The semi-autonomous region of Zanzibar has made less progress in adopting any kind of gender budgeting (Ibid.).

Tanzania's experience with gender budgeting is mixed. The longstanding pressure of nongovernmental organizations has been instrumental in keeping efforts to address gender inequality and women's needs alive. Their push for time-use data and the elevation of gender-oriented concerns to macroeconomic modeling are notable. However, gender budgeting has not been fully embedded in the government budget. Tanzania's renewed interest in gender budgeting holds promise for it to better incorporate gender-related goals into budget policies and programs.

Ethiopia[23]

In 1993, the Ethiopian government introduced a National Policy on Women to address gender inequality and women's needs. In 1995, constitutional mandates for gender equality and women's rights followed.[24] The first efforts at gender budgeting came in 2008 when the Gender Department at the Ministry of Finance and Economic Development (MOFED) and the Ministry of Education (MOE), in partnership with UNICEF Ethiopia and the British Council, developed a manual on implementing gender budgeting to increase female school enrollment. The Prime Minister's Office and Ministries of Education and Women's Affairs, Parliament, local governments, and schools were all given guidelines and checklists to use for planning and budgeting for girls' education. For example, the Prime Minister's Office was assigned the responsibilities of checking that the budget call circular mentioned gender budgeting, ensuring an allocation of funds for gender-related purposes, and promoting the project to Parliament (Ethiopia, MOFED and MOE, 2009). Local and school authorities were instructed to focus on barriers to female enrollment and retention and determine budgetary needs for female and male pupils. This program has succeeded in significantly reducing the female dropout rate, according to the authorities. The Ministry of Finance and Economic Development has also led gender budgeting training for all federal ministries, and the ministries included gender-related goals and activities as part of their annual budget requests.

Beginning in the 2011/2012 fiscal year, Ethiopia began allocating a share of its federal budget to achieving the Millennium Development Goal targets, many of which address women's needs. The 2014/2015 fiscal year budget dedicated approximately eight percent of the total budget to these activities and programs (Ethiopia, MOFED website).[25]

Courses at the Ethiopian Civil Service University are another important highlight of the gender budgeting effort.[26] The university, which is funded primarily by the federal government, offers a two-day training course on gender budgeting, as well as other courses on analysis, audit, mainstreaming, project planning, and monitoring and evaluation.

The gender budgeting effort in Ethiopia has also benefited from the involvement of nongovernmental organizations. One such example is the program between the Poverty Action Network of Ethiopia (with help from UN Women) and an administrative unit in the north of the country.[27] The nongovernmental organization trained 30 members of the community on gender budgeting so that they could read and analyze local government budget documents and advocate for improved water facilities and access.

In October 2018, Ethiopia's new prime minister, Abiy Ahmed, drew attention to his significant step forward supporting gender equality by appointing the first women to key cabinet posts such as the minister of peace and minister of defense.[28] The prime minister expressed his hope that these appointments will lead to a greater likelihood of internal and external peace for Ethiopia and will demonstrate the capacity of women to fill roles that in Africa (and the developing world generally) have historically been filled by men.

Nigeria

The Nigerian federal government, in partnership with the United Kingdom's Department for International Development, introduced a gender budgeting initiative called "Growing Girls and Women in Nigeria" (G-WIN) in 2012. Five ministries—agriculture, public works, health, water resources, and communication and technology, were selected for this initiative. During the inaugural meeting of the Gender-Equality Community of Practice for Finance Ministers[29] in 2014, the Nigerian Minister of Finance reported on the project's early successes.

The Ministry of Health pinpointed the issue of treating women with fistulas, a debilitating post-birth condition that can lead to shame, divorce, and family rejection. According to the United States Agency for International Development, Nigeria has the highest number of women who suffer from fistulas, with about half of all cases worldwide. Under the G-WIN project, the Ministry of Health allocated resources to recruit and/or train additional doctors to perform the surgery necessary for correcting fistulas.

Nigerian female farmers account for 70 percent of all agricultural work, but have less access to agricultural inputs, contributing to female agriculture output being 40 percent lower than their male counterparts' output. The Ministry of Agriculture is trying to train more than 30,000 women on different or better farming methods. One crucial roadblock for female farmers has been access to finance because this hampered women's ability to procure seeds and fertilizers. Under the G-WIN initiative, two million female farmers received cell phones to improve access to and the exchange of information. The cell phones enabled women to use an e-wallet system to facilitate mobile money purchases of agricultural inputs. Additional highlights of the G-WIN program can be found in reports of the Ministry of Public Works and the Ministry of Water.

VI. Conclusions and lessons for improving gender budgeting in the region

Many countries in sub-Saharan Africa have adopted some form of gender budgeting over the course of almost two decades. The two most successful initiatives were in Rwanda and Uganda, where gender budgeting became integral to the budgetary process and influenced fiscal policies. Nonetheless, there remains in practice considerable scope for improving the substance of gender budgeting in both countries. The South African, Ethiopian, and Tanzanian gender budgeting initiatives, along with specific aspects of the efforts in other countries in the region, provide lessons from which future initiatives can learn.

We note several identifiable achievements. South Africa adopted a number of fiscal policies designed to assist poor women, specifically, and their families. Similarly, in Rwanda, the government's broad-based efforts to incorporate gender equality into sectoral policies and programs appear to have sped up progress on education and health-related goals. The coherent manner in which Rwanda implemented gender budgeting into its program-budgeting framework is also notable. Uganda, too, has demonstrated a sustained commitment to addressing gender equality and the advancement of women through the budget, with evident success in adapting education and health programs to address women's needs.

The use of fiscal policies and administration to address gender-related goals clearly required strong leadership from Ministries of Finance, as is seen in Ethiopia, Rwanda, and Uganda.

Successful integration of gender budgeting into ministerial, sectoral, and local government policies and programs seems to be more likely to happen when government institutions are given directives from the leadership. In fact, the presence of strong leadership from the top of the government promoting gender equality and enhanced roles for women appears to be to is critical.

Parliaments are also instrumental in playing a role in gender budgeting and can be essential as catalysts, as in Uganda. Nongovernmental organizations played an essential part as well, in keeping gender equality and women's needs in the forefront of budget discussions. In several countries, nongovernmental organizations were instrumental in launching the initiatives, in the first place.

The two countries in which one can see the most dramatic and publicly visible gains for women in high public positions (in government and/or other institutions) are Rwanda and Ethiopia. The governments of Rwanda and Ethiopia have been led at various times recently by leaders who have branded themselves as feminists.

It is perhaps not accidental that many of the African countries that have enjoyed the highest sustained rates of economic growth during the last decade or more are among those that have institutionalized, at one level or another, gender budgeting and gender-related programming. For example, during the 2015–2020 period, the average economic growth of Africa as a whole is likely to be in the 2–3 percent range, but in the four low-income countries whose gender budgeting programs we discussed in this chapter (Ethiopia, Rwanda, Tanzania, and Uganda), the economic growth rates are projected to be in the 4–10 percent range (African Development Bank Group, 2019). It should be noted that none of these countries have resource-based economies, thus the economic growth is coming from sectors of the economy that involve value added by human labor and effort.

Adequate funding for public services remains a challenge throughout sub-Saharan Africa. However, gender budgeting is a vehicle for ensuring that gender-related goals receive adequate consideration in competing for scarce funds and motivating better program design. Senior government figures typically request compliance with government priorities regarding gender equality by issuing directives. However, we see in the case of African programs, and many Asian programs discussed in the following chapter, that even where gender equality programs and policies have been included in government budgets, it appears that programmatic success has been achieved only in limited circumstances. These circumstances usually occur where there was sustained effort on the part of governments to ensure implementation. Monitoring and evaluation of outcomes that are supposed to emerge from the budgeted programs is essential. It is not enough for ministries and agencies of the government to just insert gender equality programs into the budget in order to achieve some formal level of compliance. They must also set realistic and meaningful programmatic goals, allocate an appropriate level of funding to achieve these goals, and implement the programs in the most effective manner and with the most competent personnel.

There is still a great unmet need to understand how gains in gender equality and a fuller role for women in economic life can influence the development of African societies. Research undertaken over the years, some evaluative, such as in Rwanda, and some analytical or prescriptive, as in South Africa and Tanzania, have clearly created a more fruitful environment for good policymaking. Nongovernmental organizations and others have also contributed to a greater awareness of why gender budgeting, and its full implementation through programs with measurable outputs, will produce gains for women. There is an increased consciousness in Africa today that movement toward greater gender equality will be beneficial and, in fact, necessary for the development of Africa. This is especially true regarding the needs of the poorest part of the African population that lives in villages and whose development is often neglected because it is not part of the paid, cash-based economy.

Notes

1 Suhaib Kebhaj co-authored this chapter. This chapter has benefited from the authors' earlier International Monetary Fund Working Paper (Stotsky, Kolovich, and Kebhaj, 2016), with some selective updating, chiefly of comparative economic performance and some new reference materials. More-recent information on fiscal measures that the governments have undertaken may be available from public sources.
2 Byanyima (2003) also notes the importance of parliamentary participation.
3 The GDI is a composite index that measures gender inequality on the basis of sex-disaggregated differences in schooling attainment, life expectancy, and income. The figures presented here correspond to our variant of the index, measured on a time-consistent basis (see Chapter 2 and Stotsky et al., 2016 for details).
4 Appendix A, Table 5.1, provides details.
5 Appendix A, Table 5.2, provides details.
6 African governments also have the potential to improve the efficiency of public spending (Youhou, 2015).
7 We exclude Somalia and Sudan from this summary because they are not covered in this survey.
8 The Organization for Economic Co-operation and Development (2014) reports that aid focused on the United Nations' Millennium Development Goals increased substantially over time, tripling from US$8 billion in 2002 to US$24 billion in 2012. Most of this aid went to the education and health sectors, critical areas of need in sub-Saharan Africa.
9 Holvoet and Inberg (2013) examine the effectiveness of donors in helping countries achieve gender-related education goals.
10 It drew on Austria's reform (Chapter 8).
11 Uganda government response to the IMF questionnaire, unpublished, 2015.
12 Uganda government response to the IMF questionnaire, unpublished, 2015.
13 Uganda 2016/2017 budget call circular.
14 The Bureau of Statistics developed the Compendium of Concepts and Definitions on Gender Statistics. The compendium shows that sex-disaggregated data are available for more than 20 key topics, such as education, water use, poverty, crime, and labor force participation.

15 The Ministry of Finance, Planning, and Economic Development 2015/2016 Budget Speech: "Maintaining Infrastructure Investment and Promoting Excellence in Public Services Delivery."
16 Lyantonde District Local Government Five Year District Development Plan.
17 See Stotsky, Kolovich, and Kebhaj (2016).
18 The two nongovernmental organizations were the Budget Information Office of the Institute for Democracy in Africa (IDASA) and Community Agency for Social Enquiry (CASE), with lead researcher Debbie Budlender.
19 These were Debbie Budlender, Diane Elson, and Rhonda Sharp, who developed the analytical tools for gender budgeting. The Commonwealth Secretariat also developed a number of tools to promote the adoption of gender budgeting, such as the incorporation of gender-oriented considerations into medium-term budgetary planning, gender-aware policy appraisal, and budget statements; gender-disaggregated beneficiary assessments and public expenditure and tax incidence analysis; and a gender-disaggregated analysis of the impact of the budget on time use. See Budlender and Hewitt (2002, 2003) and Budlender et al. (2002).
20 As reported in South African delegation (2012).
21 Budlender, Casale, and Valodia (2010, p. 212).
22 Tanzania government response to IMF questionnaire, unpublished, 2015.
23 This section draws extensively from the Ethiopia government response to the IMF questionnaire, unpublished, 2015.
24 In addition to establishing equal rights for men and women, the Ethiopian constitution states that

> [c]onsidering that women have traditionally been viewed with inferiority and are discriminated against, they have the right to the benefit of affirmative actions undertaken for the purpose of introducing corrective changes to such heritage. The aim of such measures is to ensure that special attention is given to enabling women to participate and compete equally with men in the political, economic and social fields both within public and private organisations.

Furthermore, oppressive "stereotyped ideas and customs" that negatively impact women were prohibited. Other notable features include provisions for maternity leave and equal marriage and property rights. Proclamations in 2003 and 2007 prohibited gender-based discrimination in employment and wages, while the Civil Servants Proclamation 515/2007 provided for affirmative action for female civil service candidates (Authorities' questionnaire response, 2015).
25 MOFED website, accessed on 12 April 2016.
26 The Ethiopian Civil Service University website, accessed on 12 April 2016: www.ecsu.edu.et/content/cross-cutting-issues.
27 UN Women website, accessed on 12 April 2016: www.unwomen.org/en/news/stories/2013/8/in-ethiopia-rural-women-improve-their-lives-befriending-budgets.
28 Afrika News, "Ethiopia's Political Journey toward Gender Equality." Downloaded from https://afrika-news.com/ethiopia-political-journey-gender-equality/.
29 Then Nigerian Finance Minister Ngozi Okonjo-Iweala pitched the idea of creating a Gender Equality Community of Practice during the World Bank/IMF Annual Meetings in the fall of 2013. Shortly thereafter, in April 2014, the inaugural meeting of the group took place with eight finance ministers, the president of the World Bank, and the executive director of UN Women in attendance.

References

Abadie, Alberto, and Javier Gardeazabal, 2003, "The Economic Costs of Conflict: A Case Study of the Basque Country," *American Economic Review*, Vol. 93, pp. 112–132.

Abadie, Alberto, Alexis Diamond, and Jens Hainmueller, 2010, "Synthetic Control Methods for Comparative Case Studies: Estimating the Effect of California's Tobacco Control Program," *Journal of the American Statistical Association*, Vol. 105, pp. 493–505.

Adhikari, Bibek, Romain Duval, Bingjie Hu, and Prakash Loungani, 2016, "Can Reform Waves Turn the Tide? Some Case Studies Using the Synthetic Control Method," IMF Working Paper 16/171 (Washington, DC: IMF).

African Development Bank Group, 2019, *East Africa Economic Outlook 2019* (Abidjan: Africa Development Bank Group).

African Union, 2003, *Protocol to the African Charter on Human and People's Rights on the Rights of Women in Africa* (the Maputo Protocol), (Addis Ababa: African Union).

Andrews, Matthew, 2010, "How Far Have Public Financial Management Reforms Come in Africa?" HKS Faculty Research Working Paper Series, RWP10–018, John F. Kennedy School of Government, Harvard University (Cambridge).

Berg, Andrew, Norbert Funke, Alejandro Hajdenberg, Victor Lledo, Rolando Ossowski, Martin Schindler, Antonio Spilimbergo, Shamsuddin Tareq, and Irene Yackovlev, 2009, "Fiscal Policy in Sub-Saharan Africa in Response to the Impact of the Global Crisis," International Monetary Fund Staff Position Note 09/10 (Washington, DC: IMF).

Blackden, C. Mark, and Magdalena Rwebangira, and with support from Zahia Lolila Ramin, 2004, *Tanzania Strategic Country Gender Assessment* (Washington, DC: World Bank).

Budlender, Debbie, 2002, "A Profile of Country Activities," in Debbie Budlender, Diane Elson, Guy Hewitt, and Tanni Mukhopadhyay (contributing eds.), *Gender Budgets Make Cents* (London: Commonwealth Secretariat), pp. 131–164.

Budlender, Debbie, and Guy Hewitt, eds., 2002, *Gender Budgets Make More Cents: Country Studies and Good Practice* (London: Commonwealth Secretariat).

Budlender, Debbie, Diane Elson, Guy Hewitt, and Tanni Mukhopadhyay, contributing editors, 2002, *Gender Budgets Make Cents* (London: Commonwealth Secretariat).

Budlender, Debbie and Guy Hewitt, 2003, *Engendering Budgets: A Practitioner's Guide to Understanding and Implementing Gender-Responsive Budgets* (London: Commonwealth Secretariat).

Budlender, Debbie, Daniela Casale, and Imraan Valodia, 2010, "Gender Equality and Taxation in South Africa," in Caren Grown and Imraan Valodia, (eds.), *Taxation and Gender Equity* (New York: Routledge), pp. 206–232.

Byanyima, Winnie, 2003, "Politics, Good Governance and Gender: The Experience of Three African Countries," paper presented at the Fifth Global Forum on Re-Inventing Government, Mexico, November.

Dietl, Susanne, Luise Gubitzer, Consolata Kabonesa, and Elisabeth Klatzer, 2014, "The Budget Process in Uganda: Entry Points for Gender and Gender Responsive Budgeting in the Budget Process in Uganda," Working Paper, Austrian Development Cooperation (Vienna).

DSD, SASSA, and UNICEF, 2012, *The South African Child Support Grant Impact Assessment: Evidence from a survey of children, adolescents and their households* (Pretoria: UNICEF).

Ebeke, Christian, and Helene Ehrhart, 2013, *Tax Revenue Instability in Sub-Saharan Africa: Consequences and Remedies* (Paris: Banque De France).

Elson, Diane, 2006, *Budgeting for Women's Rights: Monitoring Government Budgets for Compliance with CEDAW* (New York: UNIFEM).

Ethiopia, Ministry of Finance and Economic Development (MOFED) and Ministry of Education (MOE), 2009, *Guidelines for Gender Sensitive Budgeting in Girls' Education* (Addis Ababa: Ethiopia).

Grown, Caren, and Imraan Valodia, eds., 2010, *Taxation and Gender Equity: A Comparative Analysis of Direct and Indirect Taxes in Developing and Developed Countries* (New York: Routledge).

Holvoet, Nathalie, and Liesbeth Inberg, 2013, "Multiple Pathways to Gender-Sensitive Budget Support in the Education Sector Analyzing the Effectiveness of Sex-Disaggregated Indicators in Performance Assessment Frameworks and Gender Working Groups in (education) Budget Support to Sub-Saharan Africa Countries," *UNU-World Institute for Development Economics Research*, Working Paper-No. 2013/105 (Helsinki).

International Monetary Fund (IMF), 2014a, *Rwanda*, IMF Country Report No. 14/343 (Washington, DC: IMF).

International Monetary Fund (IMF), 2014b, *South Africa*, IMF Country Report No. 14/338 (Washington, DC: IMF).

International Monetary Fund (IMF), 2014c, *United Republic of Tanzania*, IMF Country Report No. 14/120 (Washington, DC: IMF).

Kakande, Margaret, 2007, "Financing for Gender Equality and Empowerment of Women: Uganda's Experience," EGM/FFGE/2007/E.8 (New York: United Nations).

Keen, Michael, and Mario Mansour, 2009, "Revenue Mobilization in Sub-Saharan Africa: Challenges from Globalization," International Monetary Fund Working Paper 09/157 (Washington, DC: IMF).

Kytola, Liisa, 2008, *Integrating Gender Responsive Budgeting into the Aid Effectiveness Agenda: Tanzania Country Report* (New York: UNIFEM).

Lakwo, Alfred, 2009, "Making Decentralization Work for Women in Uganda," *African Studies Collection*, Vol.16 (Leiden: African Studies Centre).

Mhina, Edward Hiza, 2007, *Financing for Gender Equality and the Empowerment of Women: Experiences from Tanzania* (Dar Es Salaam).

Mirwoba, Siringi Elijah, 2013, "Macro, Mezzo and Micro-Level Analysis of Gender-Responsive Budgeting in Rwanda," *Journal of Development and Agricultural Economics*, Vol. 5, pp. 71–83.

Motsepe Foundation, 2013, *Doing More with Less: A South African Gender Budget Analysis for Health, Agriculture, Forestry and Fisheries, Energy and Trade and Industry (2012/2012)* (Pretoria).

Mugisha Baine, Euzobia M., 2013, *A Terminal Evaluation Report for the Project 'Gender Budgeting for Northern Uganda, Recovery, Reconstruction and Development.'* (New York: UNDP).

Mukunda, Julius, 2011, *Progress Towards Achieving Gender Responsive Budget in Rwanda: A CSO Response to Sectoral GB Statements for the FY 2011/12* (Kigali).

Organization for Economic Co-operation and Development (OECD), 2014, *Financing the Unfinished Business of Gender and Women's Rights: Priorities for the Post-2015 Framework: Technical Brief* (Paris: OECD).

Organization for Economic Co-operation and Development/United Nations Development Programme (OECD/UNDP), 2014, *Making Development Co-operation More Effective: 2014 Progress Report* (Paris: OECD).

Rusimbi, Mary, 2002, "Mainstreaming Gender into Policy, Planning and Budgeting in Tanzania," in Karen Judd (ed.), *Gender Budget Initiatives: Strategies, Concepts and Experiences* (New York: UNIFEM), pp. 119–125.

Rusimbi, Mary, and Anna Kikwa, 2008, *Research Paper on Just Budgets: Increasing Accountability and Effectiveness Through Gender Budget Analysis in Tanzania* (London: One World Action).

Rwanda, Gender Monitoring Office, 2011, *Key Gender Indicators and Baseline in Four Sectors: Governance, Agriculture, Infrastructure, and Private Sector* (Kigali, Government of Rwanda).

Rwanda, Gender Monitoring Office, 2014, *Gender Monitoring Office Annual Report 2013–2014* (Kigali, Government of Rwanda).

Rwanda, Ministry of Finance and Economic Planning (MINECOFIN), 2011, *Gender Responsive Budgeting Programme in Rwanda, 2008–2010* (Kigali: Government of Rwanda).

Rwanda, 2014, *Report on the Implementation of the Beijing Declaration and Platform for Action (1995) and the Outcomes of the Twenty-Third Special Session of the General Assembly (2000)* (Kigali: Government of Rwanda).

South Africa, Department of Women, Children, and People with Disabilities, 2014, *South Africa's Beijing +20 Report* (Pretoria: Republic of South Africa).

South African delegation, 2012, "GRBI Profile Brief and Template," International Conference of Gender Budgeting in Marrakech in November 2012, organized by the Ministry of Economy and Finance of Morocco.

Stotsky, Janet G., 1997, "Gender Bias in Tax Systems," *Tax Notes International* (June 9), pp. 1913–23.

Stotsky, Janet G., Lisa Kolovich, and Suhaib Kebhaj, 2016, "Sub-Saharan Africa: A Survey of Gender Budgeting Efforts," IMF Working Paper 16/152 (Washington, DC: IMF).

Tanzania, Ministry of Community Development, Gender, and Children (MCDGC), and Ministry of Empowerment, Social Welfare, Youth, Women, and Children Development (MESWYWCD), 2014, *Country Report on the Review and Progress Made and Challenges Encountered in Implementation of the Beijing Declaration and Platform for Action and Outcomes of the Twenty Third Special Session of the General Assembly—Beijing +20* (Dar es Salaam and Zanzibar: Governments of Tanzania and Zanzibar).

Tanzarn, Nite, 2008, *Integrating Gender Responsive Budgeting into the Aid Effectiveness Agenda: Uganda Country Report* (New York: UNIFEM).

Uganda, Bureau of Statistics (UBOS), 2014, *Uganda National Household Survey 2012/2013* (Kampala: Government of Uganda).

Uganda, Ministry of Gender, Labour and Social Development/Ministry of Local Government, 2005, *Gender Budgeting Guidelines and Analytical Tools for Lower Local Governments* (Kampala: Government of Uganda).

Uganda, Ministry of Gender, Labour and Social Development, 2014, *National Report on Implementation of the Beijing Platform for Action (1995) and the Outcome of the Twenty Third Special Session of the United Nations General Assembly (2000)* (Kampala: Government of Uganda).

Uganda, National Planning Authority (NPA), 2010, *First National Development Plan (NDP I) 2010/11–2014/15* (Kampala: Government of Uganda).

United Kingdom, Department for International Development, 2015, "Project Completion Review," report on the UN Joint Programme on Gender Equality—Uganda, unpublished.

United Nations Development Programme (UNDP), 2011, *Gender Budget Project for Northern Uganda Recovery, Reconstruction and Development* (New York: UNDP).

United Nations (UN), 1995, "Platform for Action," Fourth World Congress on Women. www.un.org/womenwatch/daw/beijing/platform/plat2.htm.

United Nations (UN), 2015, *Transforming our World: The 2030 Agenda for Sustainable Development*, A/RES/70/1 (New York: United Nations).

United Nations Economic Commission for Africa (UNECA), 2015, *Addis Ababa Declaration on Accelerating the Implementation of the Beijing Platform for Action: Towards a Transformational Change for Women and Girls in Africa* (Addis Ababa: United Nations).

United Nations Joint Programme on Gender Equality (UNJPGE)—Uganda, 2014, *Annual Narrative Report* (New York: UN).

Youhou, Djedje Hermann, 2015, "In Search of Fiscal Space in Africa: The Role of the Quality of Government Spending," *Etudes et Documents*, No. 27, CERDI.

Appendix A

Table 5.1A Selected Indicators of Gender and Income Equality

Country	*GDI, time-consistent (2016)*	*Gini coefficient*[1] *(scale 0–100)*	*Gross secondary enrollment*		*Labor force participation rate (ages 15–64)*		*Maternal mortality ratio (per 100,000)*	*Legislation exists on domestic violence*	*Married men and women have equal ownership rights to property*
			female-to-male ratio	*Female (percent)*	*female-to-male ratio*	*Female (percent)*			
Angola	0.83	40.7	0.63	39%	0.84	65%	477	Yes	Yes
Benin	0.85	47.8	0.76	51%	0.89	69%	405	Yes	Yes
Botswana	0.97	51.2	1.09	82%	0.89	73%	129	Yes	Yes
Burkina Faso	0.88	35.3	0.95	35%	0.86	76%	371	No	Yes
Burundi	0.92	38.6	0.97	48%	1.01	84%	712	Yes	Yes
Cabo Verde	0.94	43.3	1.10	88%	0.66	55%	42	Yes	Yes
Cameroon	0.89	46.6	0.86	57%	0.84	66%	596	No	No
Central African Rep.	0.78	56.2	n.a.	n.a.	0.86	72%	882	Yes	Yes
Chad	0.74	43.3	0.46	14%	0.81	65%	856	No	No
Comoros	n.a.[2]	45.3	n.a.	n.a.	0.48	37%	335	Yes	Yes
Congo, Dem. Rep.	0.84	42.1	0.64	36%	0.96	70%	693	No	No
Congo, Rep.	0.92	48.9	n.a.	n.a.	0.94	68%	442	No	No
Cote d'Ivoire	0.85	41.5	n.a.	n.a.	0.67	53%	645	No	No
Equatorial Guinea	n.a.	50.2	n.a.	n.a.	0.90	78%	342	No	No
Eritrea	n.a.	n.a.	0.87	30%	0.89	80%	501	No	Yes
Ethiopia	0.86	39.1	0.96	34%	0.89	79%	353	Yes	Yes
Gabon	0.98	38.0	n.a.	n.a.	0.86	57%	291	No	No
Gambia, The	0.89	35.9	n.a.	n.a.	0.87	71%	706	Yes	Yes
Ghana	0.90	42.4	0.97	69%	0.92	67%	319	Yes	Yes
Guinea	0.79	33.7	0.66	32%	0.86	66%	679	No	Yes
Guinea-Bissau	n.a.	50.7	n.a.	n.a.	0.88	69%	549	Yes	No
Kenya	0.93	40.8	0.90	55%	0.88	63%	510	Yes	Yes

(Continued)

Table 5.1A (Continued)

Country	*GDI, time-consistent (2016)*	*Gini coefficient*[1] *(scale 0–100)*	*Gross secondary enrollment*		*Labor force participation rate (ages 15–64)*		*Maternal mortality ratio(per 100,000)*	*Legislation exists on domestic violence*	*Married men and women have equal ownership rights to property*
			female-to-male ratio	*Female (percent)*	*female-to-male ratio*	*Female (percent)*			
Lesotho	1.01	54.2	1.35	60%	0.81	60%	487	No	Yes
Liberia	0.78	33.2	n.a.	n.a.	0.91	58%	725	No	Yes
Madagascar	n.a.	42.7	0.99	38%	0.93	82%	353	No	Yes
Malawi	0.93	44.3	0.89	35%	1.03	83%	634	Yes	Yes
Mali	0.80	33.0	0.74	37%	0.57	40%	587	No	Yes
Mauritius	0.96	35.8	1.05	100%	0.62	45%	53	Yes	Yes
Mozambique	0.92	50.5	0.91	32%	1.02	83%	489	Yes	Yes
Namibia	0.98	58.1	1.15	69%	0.81	58%	265	Yes	Yes
Niger	0.74	34.3	0.73	20%	0.48	43%	553	No	Yes
Nigeria	n.a.	43.9	0.90	40%	0.76	48%	814	Yes	Yes
Rwanda	0.95	45.1	1.10	38%	1.02	86%	290	Yes	Yes
Sao Tome and Principe	0.90	30.8	1.13	88%	0.62	47%	156	Yes	Yes
Senegal	0.89	40.3	1.06	48%	0.76	64%	315	Yes	Yes
Seychelles	n.a.	41.3	1.07	96%	n.a.	n.a.	n.a.	Yes	Yes
Sierra Leone	0.80	34.0	n.a.	n.a.	0.96	66%	1360	Yes	Yes
South Africa	0.98	63.0	1.09	105%	0.74	47%	138	Yes	Yes
South Sudan	n.a.	46.3	n.a.	n.a.	n.a.	n.a.	789	No	Yes
Swaziland	0.94	51.5	0.98	72%	0.63	45%	389	No	Yes
Tanzania	0.93	37.8	n.a.	n.a.	0.97	87%	398	No	Yes
Togo	0.80	43.1	0.71	50%	0.99	80%	368	No	Yes
Uganda	0.90	42.8	0.83	25%	0.96	75%	343	Yes	Yes
Zambia	n.a.	57.1	n.a.	n.a.	0.87	73%	224	Yes	Yes
Zimbabwe	0.93	40.4	0.98	47%	0.93	84%	443	Yes	Yes
Regional average	**0.89**	**43.5**	**0.92**	**52%**	**0.84**	**66%**	**477**		

Sources: World Bank, World Development Indicators database; World Bank, Women, Business and the Law (2015); Stotsky et al. (2016); and authors' calculations.

Note: Values are for 2016 or the latest year available. Swaziland is now Eswatini.

[1] A higher Gini coefficient implies more inequality.
[2] Data are not available.

Table 5.2A Sub-Saharan African Fiscal Indicators

Country	*Fiscal Aggregates*[1] *(average 2015–2018; unless otherwise indicated)*[2] *(percent of GDP)*						*Public Financial Management*
	Total revenue	*Total expenditure*	*Overall*[3] *balance*	*Gross*[4] *debt*	*Education*[5] *expenditure*	*Health*[6] *expenditure*	*Public Expenditure and Financial Accountability (PEFA), overall score*[7]
Angola	22.1	19.7	2.4	88.1	3.5	2.9	n.a.[8]
Benin	18.6	23.3	−4.7	54.6	4.0	3.9	2.0
Botswana	28.8	31.9	−3.1	12.9	n.a.	5.5	2.6
Burkina Faso	22.8	27.5	−4.7	43.0	4.2	6.8	2.9
Burundi	13.7	22.3	−8.6	58.4	4.3	6.2	2.3
Cabo Verde	28.2	30.9	−2.7	127.7	5.2	5.2	2.8
Cameroon	15.8	18.5	−2.7	37.7	3.1	4.7	n.a.
Central African Republic	17.5	16.8	0.7	48.5	1.2	4.3	1.7
Chad	16.0	14.6	1.4	46.6	2.9	4.5	n.a.
Comoros	28.3	30.1	−1.8	31.2	4.3	7.6	1.4
Democratic Republic of the Congo	12.2	12.7	−0.5	15.7	1.5	3.9	n.a.
Republic of Congo	30.4	25.0	5.4	98.5	4.6	4.6	1.6
Côte d'Ivoire	19.7	23.7	−4.0	52.2	4.4	4.4	1.6
Equatorial Guinea	19.0	16.2	2.8	35.9	n.a.	3.4	n.a.
Eritrea	15.1	28.3	−13.2	129.4	n.a.	3.0	n.a.
Ethiopia	13.1	16.1	−3.0	61.1	4.7	4.0	2.7
Gabon	18.2	16.7	1.5	58.2	2.7	3.1	1.6
The Gambia	14.8	21.4	−6.6	83.2	3.1	4.4	n.a.
Ghana	14.6	21.6	−7.0	59.6	4.5	4.4	1.9
Guinea	15.4	17.5	−2.0	38.7	2.2	5.5	n.a.
Guinea-Bissau	16.7	21.8	−5.1	56.1	2.1	6.1	1.1
Kenya	18.3	25.6	−7.3	57.2	5.2	4.5	2.4
Lesotho	41.4	46.3	−4.9	39.0	6.4	8.1	1.9
Liberia	27.3	32.8	−5.6	40.5	3.8	9.6	1.9
Madagascar	14.9	17.1	−2.2	39.7	2.8	6.0	1.9
Malawi	23.5	28.6	−5.1	61.3	4.0	9.8	2.1
Mali	15.4	20.2	−4.7	36.6	3.1	3.8	2.8
Mauritius	22.5	24.9	−2.4	65.2	5.0	5.7	3.2
Mozambique	26.0	31.3	−5.3	100.4	6.5	5.1	2.9
Namibia	30.5	36.3	−5.9	47.1	3.1	9.1	n.a.
Niger	21.4	26.3	−4.9	55.1	3.5	6.2	2.1

(Continued)

Table 5.2A (Continued)

Country	*Fiscal Aggregates*[1] *(average 2015–2018; unless otherwise indicated)*[2] *(percent of GDP)*						*Public Financial Management*
	Total revenue	*Total expenditure*	*Overall*[3] *balance*	*Gross*[4] *debt*	*Education*[5] *expenditure*	*Health*[6] *expenditure*	*Public Expenditure and Financial Accountability (PEFA), overall score*[7]
Nigeria	8.0	12.5	–4.5	28.4	n.a.	3.6	n.a.
Rwanda	24.1	26.7	–2.6	40.7	3.2	6.8	3.0
São Tomé and Príncipe	22.6	24.7	–2.1	81.3	4.9	6.0	1.8
Senegal	18.7	22.1	–3.4	64.4	6.2	5.5	2.3
Seychelles	37.7	37.3	0.5	58.2	4.4	3.9	2.6
Sierra Leone	16.9	23.6	–6.8	71.3	4.6	16.5	2.4
South Africa	29.1	33.6	–4.4	56.7	6.1	8.1	3.6
South Sudan	43.9	44.9	–1.0	43.8	1.0	n.a.	1.7
Swaziland	25.1	35.1	–10.1	34.9	7.1	7.7	2.1
Tanzania	15.1	16.9	–1.8	36.0	3.5	4.1	2.4
Togo	24.3	27.4	–3.1	74.6	5.1	6.6	1.4
Uganda	15.6	20.4	–4.8	42.2	2.6	6.2	2.5
Zambia	18.4	24.9	–6.5	72.4	n.a.	4.5	2.2
Zimbabwe	10.3	14.1	–3.8	29.8	7.5	9.4	n.a.
Regional average	**21.2**	**24.7**	**–3.5**	**55.9**	**4.1**	**5.8**	**2.2**

Sources: World Economic Outlook (WEO), World Bank Development Indicators (WDI), and authors' calculations.

[1] All figures except for health and education expenditure are drawn from the latest WEO publication, and the concept of government corresponds to that in the WEO. Please see the WEO for further details. Health and education expenditure are drawn from World Bank Development Indicators (WDI) and correspond to the general government concept. Swaziland is now Eswatini.
[2] The figures are based on the average over the number of years in this period for which data were available.
[3] Corresponds to the concept of total revenue minus total expenditure.
[4] Gross debt does not net out holdings of debt by other entities of the government.
[5] The figures for education expenditure are based on 2014–2017 averages or the number of years for which data are available in this period. The 2017 data are the latest available.
[6] The figures for health expenditure are based on 2013–2016 averages or the number of years for which data are available in this period. The 2016 data are the latest available.
[7] PEFA is a performance monitoring framework used to assess the public financial management systems in developing countries. It is an initiative jointly supported by the World Bank, IMF, European Commission, and other development and government institutions. The framework consists of 28 indicators with each indicator scored on a scale from A (highest) to D (lowest). PEFA scores reported above are an average of the 28 indicators and convert the four ordinal PEFA scores (A,B,C,D) to numerical scores (4,3,2,1) with "+" score given 0.5 point. A higher PEFA score implies stronger administration of public finance. On a global basis, the lowest score is 1.1 and highest score is 3.6. Please see www.pefa.org/ for further details.
[8] Data are not available.

Appendix B

Synthetic control methodology

The synthetic control method (SCM) allows us to create a counterfactual country outcome for any variable in our country of interest, after the adoption of any given policy, for example, gender budgeting. If we wish to consider the effect of gender budgeting on a variable such as educational enrollment, we compare educational enrollment before and after gender budgeting was instituted in the country of focus to educational enrollment in the same time periods in a synthetic control country. Abadie and Gardeazabal (2003) and Abadie, Diamond, and Hainmueller (2010) discuss the approach to the SCM and Adhikari et al. (2016) apply the SCM to the analysis of the effect of structural reforms on growth.

For each country and variable of interest, we create the synthetic control by selecting a comparator group of countries based on set criteria. For our analysis, we use per capita income, the natural logarithm of GDP, the population of the country, and the initial starting position of our variable of interest. For example, when our variable of interest is educational enrollment, one criterion required for the comparator country would be that educational enrollment for women and girls relative to men and boys be similar to that of our country of interest, in the period before intervention. We further limit the comparator country sample in our Africa analysis to low-income developing countries in Africa; for our Asian country analysis we limit the comparator country sample to other emerging markets and developing countries (Chapter 6). We exclude countries that had important gender budgeting initiatives ongoing, to avoid biasing the results.

For each country highlighted in our analysis, the pre-period refers to an average value from the beginning of our data sample until the year when gender budgeting was put in place. The post-period refers to an average value for the subsequent years to the end of the sampling period. The weights, treatment values, and synthetic values for each country and variable—for Rwanda and Uganda in this chapter and India, the Philippines, and Bangladesh in Chapter 6—are available from the authors along with the statistical programming that was used to compute the synthetic control country results.

6 Asia

A survey of gender budgeting efforts[1]

I. Introduction

Gender inequality remains pervasive in Asia, though progress is evident in all the countries of the region. Two of the largest countries, India and China, have marked gender imbalances in the number of children born, giving rise to the so-called "missing women" problem (Klasen and Wink, 2003). The nature of gender-related concerns varies across the Asian region, ranging from redressing female disadvantages or unmet needs in education and health, to addressing the lack of equal opportunities in paid employment, to grappling with the burden of the unpaid care economy on women's efforts to advance in all spheres of life.

Twenty-nine countries in the Asian region have some type of gender budgeting initiative, and most of these programs were instituted in the early to mid-2000s (Mishra and Sinha, 2017). A few have achieved some notable successes in instituting a legal basis or implementing important fiscal policy or managerial practices (Chakraborty, 2016; Mishra and Sinha, 2017).

This chapter reviews gender budgeting in Asia and is organized as follows. Section II provides a summary of trends in key gender inequality indicators in the region. Section III presents the fiscal context for understanding gender budgeting in Asia. Section IV surveys several countries that have already instituted gender budgeting efforts. Our analysis focuses on country-specific case studies. This should allow us to identify countries that seem to have made progress in their efforts versus those where the results are less promising. Section V offers some thoughts on the path forward.

II. Indicators of gender inequality

Asian countries are at various stages of development, with most falling into the middle- or lower-income groups. The developmental trends in Asia are of great importance, not only because over half of the world's population resides on this continent, but also because most of the economic growth in the world during the 21st century will likely occur in Asia. Asian countries have generally made progress in addressing gender inequality in the areas of health, education, and political participation. This progress is clearly visible from the data in the figures below (with details in the Appendix Table 6.1). Nonetheless, difficult challenges to gender equality include still low female economic participation, a high incidence of violence against women and girls, and a need for more female political leadership in local and national life.

Figure 6.1 shows the female-to-male ratio in secondary school enrollment, where improvements in the relative enrollment of girls are visible in a large majority of the Asian less developed countries. Figure 6.2 shows maternal mortality, a key indicator of women's advancement. Even while it remains relatively high in some countries, there is almost a universal trend of declining maternal mortality (van den Broek and Falconer, 2011).

Figure 6.3 shows the female-to-male ratio in labor force participation rates, where the general trend is toward equality, though notably a number of countries show a declining ratio.

Finally, Figure 6.4 shows female participation in parliaments across the region, where the trends point to an increased role for women in virtually every country. It is interesting that the levels of female participation in parliaments are not necessarily a function of the level of income or development of a country. In the latest year of the sample, the countries with the highest

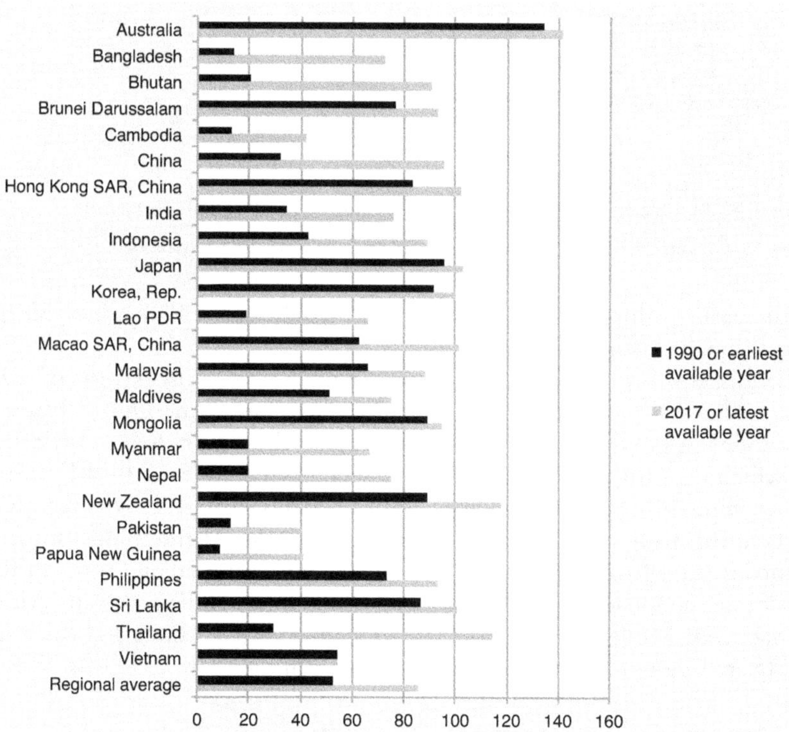

Figure 6.1 Gross Secondary Enrollment (female-to-male ratio)

Sources: World Bank, World Development Indicators database; and authors' estimates.

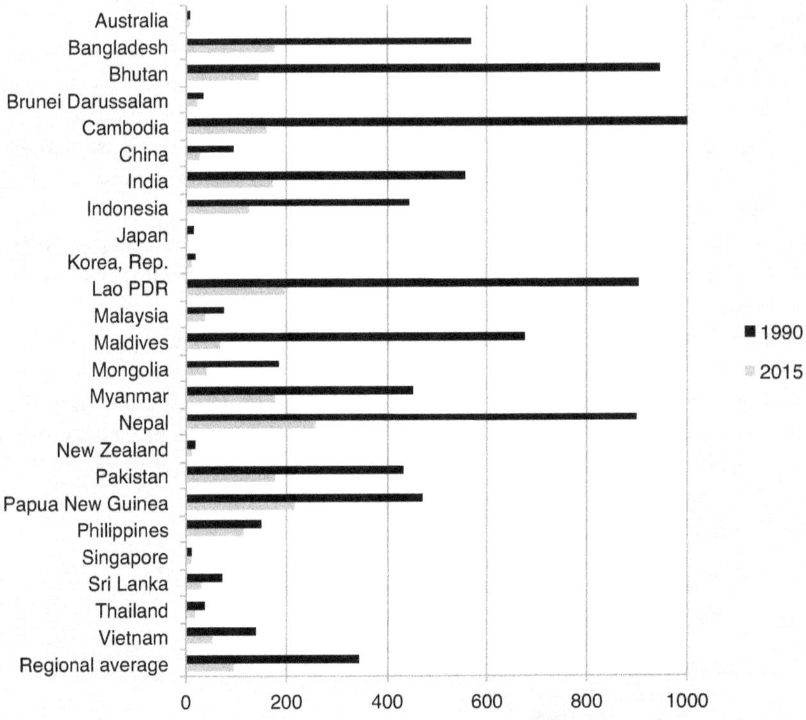

Figure 6.2 Maternal Mortality Ratio (modeled estimate, per 100,000 live births)

Sources: World Bank, World Development Indicators database; and authors' estimates.

female participation were Australia, New Zealand, Nepal, Philippines, Singapore, China, Vietnam, and Laos.

Gender equality indices provide a useful summary of an aggregation of indicators. Figure 6.5 presents a summary of our version of the United Nations Development Program's GDI for countries across the region, for the latest year for which data are available.[2] This index generally ranges from 0 to 1, where higher numbers represent more equality. The results suggest that the region as a whole has made progress in recent decades. Developed and middle-income countries (e.g., Japan, Hong Kong, Australia, and Malaysia) and some of the developing countries (e.g., Thailand and Philippines) are approaching parity in their GDI, while the large South Asian countries (e.g., India and Pakistan) clearly are lagging, although much improved from their low 1990 base.

III. Overview of gender budgeting in Asia and the fiscal context

Despite being signatory to various gender conventions, many countries in the Asian region have not yet initiated or implemented a sustainable process

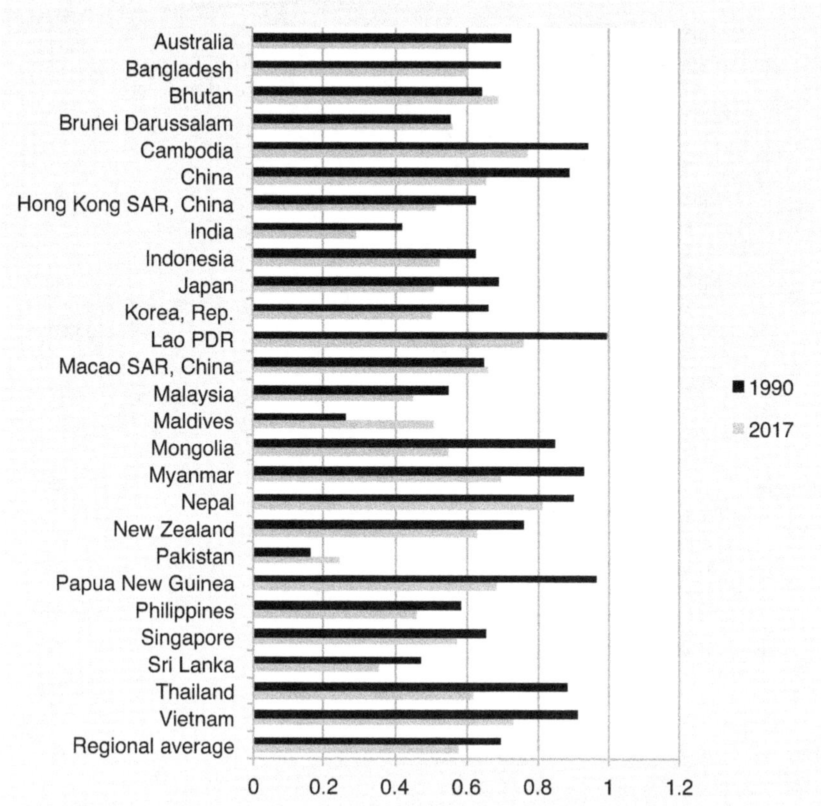

Figure 6.3 Labor Force Participation Rate, Ages 15–64 (female-to-male ratio)

Sources: World Bank World Development Indicators database; and authors' estimates.

of using fiscal tools (or gender budgeting) for addressing developmental needs of women and gender inequality. Elson (2006) provided an early landmark effort to compare public budgeted expenditures in Asia promoting gender equality for specifically targeted programs for women in several Asian countries.[3]

Various Asian nations have undertaken sustained gender budgeting efforts. External donors often provide the stimulus for these efforts, but domestic government support, especially in the ministry of finance, is required to sustain efforts over the long run (UN Women, 2016). An analysis of successful gender budgeting initiatives in the Asian region shows that the most successful efforts involve collaboration between governments and external partners. For example, in the Philippines and Nepal, initiatives were the result of effective collaborations between the Ministry of Finance, the Ministry of Planning, and the national women's ministry (UN Women, 2016). On the other hand, in India, the Ministry of Finance spearheaded the gender budgeting process, and

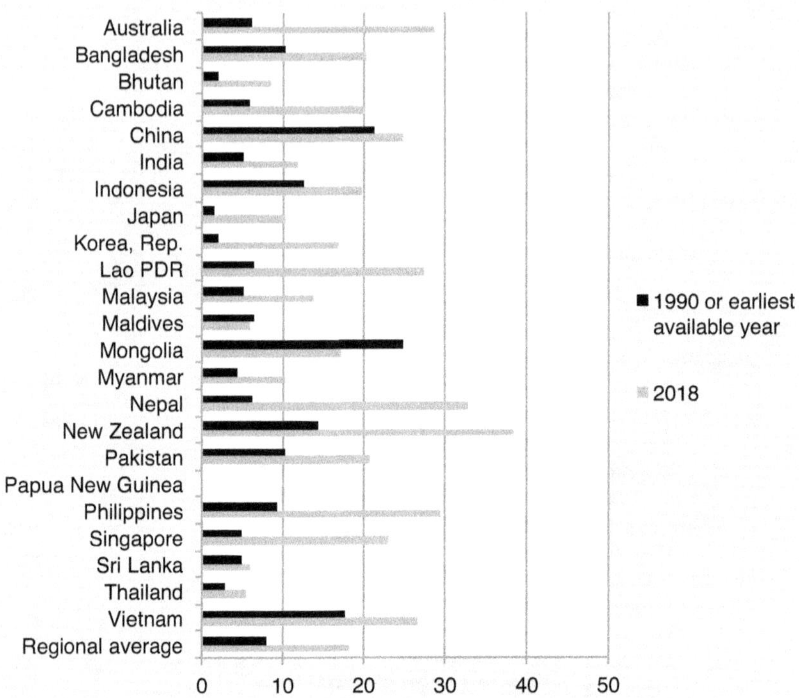

Figure 6.4 Seats Held by Women in National Parliaments (percent of total)

Sources: World Bank, World Development Indicators database; and authors' estimates.

then left the management to the Ministry of Women and Child Development, civil society organizations, and external donors, as discussed below (Ibid.).

Figure 6.6 shows the key actors in promoting gender budgeting initiatives in the Asian countries studied in this chapter. In these countries, national and local governments were the most important actors responsible for spearheading efforts and sustaining them through implementation (Mishra and Sinha, 2017). Civil society organizations have played a much less important role, although they were influential in the Philippines and Indonesia. Nonetheless, the authors conclude that the original impetus for gender budgeting reforms in most Asian countries came from external donor-led initiatives. The most important of these donors have typically been United Nations and Asian development organizations and bilateral partners from the developed world (Ibid.).

Fiscal attributes that favor effective gender budgeting implementation

As discussed in Chapter 4, performance-based budgeting is more likely to lead to effective gender budgeting implementation and monitoring compared to

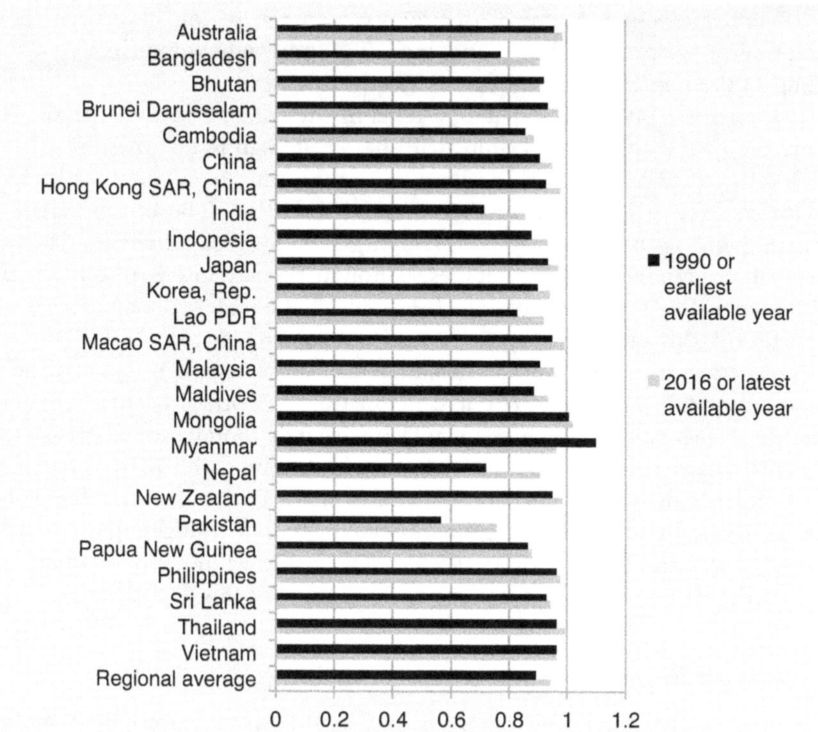

Figure 6.5 GDI, Time-Consistent Version

Sources: Authors' estimates.

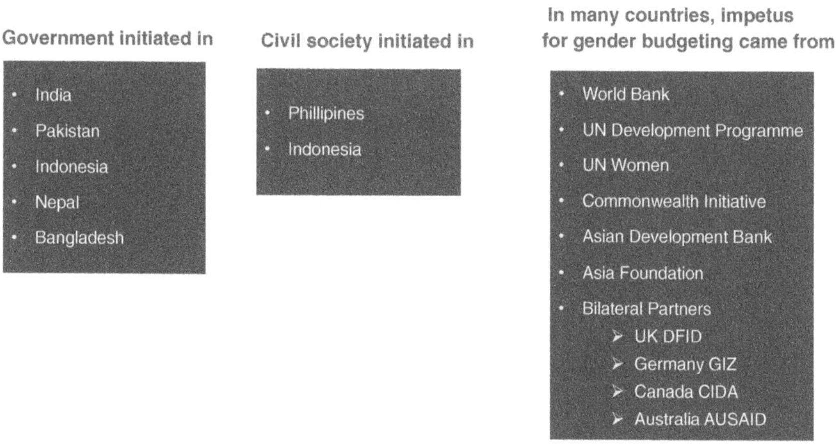

Figure 6.6 Key Actors in Promoting Gender Budgeting Initiatives in Asian Countries

Source: Adapted from Mishra and Sinha (2017).

Note: UK DFID stands for United Kingdom Department for International Development. Germany GIZ stands for German Gesellschaft fur Internationale Zusammenarbeit. Canada CIDA stands for Canadian International Development Agency. Australia AUSAID stands for the Australian Agency for International Development.

line-item budgeting. Some of the countries in the region have been moving toward performance budgeting, including India, which in principle would support the implementation of gender budgeting.

Monitoring budget transparency remains a challenge in the region. The International Budget Partnership (IBP) has created an index, the Open Budget Index (OBI), denoting the level of transparency of a country's budget, with data for 2017 shown in Figure 6.7 (IBP, 2019). The best performing Asian countries of the group of developing and emerging countries that year were Indonesia and the Philippines, although their scores were only in the 60s—considered sufficient by the IBP—out of a possible score of 100.

One of the great challenges in institutionalizing gender budgeting as a permanent feature of government budgeting in the region is to give it legal standing within each Asian country. Legislation supporting gender budgeting would, in principle, make it irreversible, but is rarely found. Nonetheless, a few countries have mandated gender budgeting in the law (Table 6.1).

Gender budgeting is generally sustained more by commitments at the policy or managerial level, not as a legal requirement. India's "Budgeting for Gender Equity" was adapted as a mission statement by the Ministry of Women and Child Development in 2004–05 and is an example of this approach.

Scope of gender budgeting: in part or all of the budget?

Gender equality advocates often claim that the entire government budget should employ a gender budgeting perspective because no budget section is gender-neutral, including the ministries that address economic issues, such as

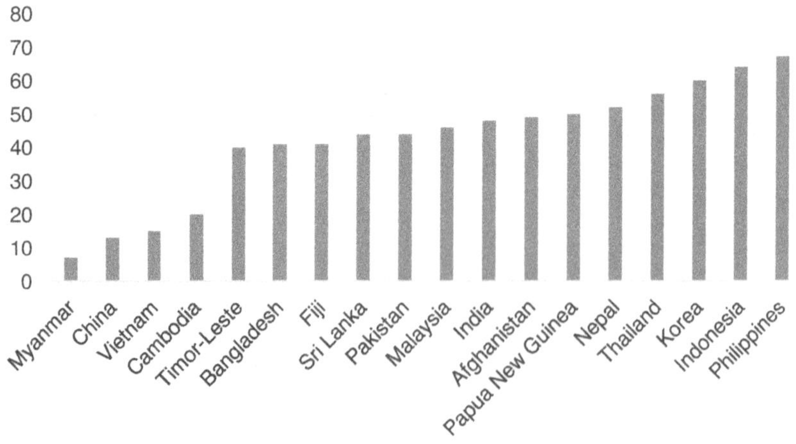

Figure 6.7 Measuring the Level of Budget Transparency with the OBI

Source: IBP (2019).

Table 6.1 Legal Fiat of Gender Budgeting

Country	*Law*	*Year of Commencement*
The Philippines	Gender and Development Budget, earmarking 5 percent of all sectoral budgets for women.	1995
The Republic of Korea	National Finance Law (Articles 16, 26, 57, 68-2, 73-2) to introduce gender budgeting principles and statements, and to do gender analysis.	2006

Source: Adapted from Chakraborty (2016).

trade, infrastructure, and industry. Others feel that gender budgeting should only be applied as an initial strategy (at least) to sectors such as health, nutrition, and education addressing human capital needs.

Mishra and Sinha state that the experience of Asian countries leads to the conclusion that from an advocacy perspective, focusing on a few ministries where the gender connection is prominent is a better initial strategy than applying gender budgeting to the whole budget (Mishra and Sinha, 2017). In their view, success in the initial limited sectors of the budget can provide a proof of principle to support extending gender budgeting to other sectors later. An example of this sort of gender budgeting strategy comes from Indonesia, which initiated gender budgeting in 2012 with 10 ministries, with the intention of extending it to all 34 ministries by 2014 (Ibid.). In Rwanda, gender budgeting started in four pilot sectors and then became mandatory in the entire budget.

Gender budgeting at the subnational level

Gender budgeting at the national level, as important as it is in setting priorities, does not fully address the fiscal challenges to countries with heterogeneous regions and populations. Fiscal decentralization is pursued in many countries in the region, and subnational governments have important spending responsibilities for basic public services. Subnational gender budgeting exercises are also important and are beginning to expand, even though they are still confined to a few countries. We discuss subnational gender budgeting in a number of the case studies.

Gender budgeting and the care economy

Gender budgeting has provided an opportunity to incorporate unpaid work and the care economy into planning frameworks in the region. The valuation of work done by women employing time-use data and incorporating it to gender budgeting policies came about as an offshoot of this process (Chakraborty, 2014a). Exercises to incorporate time-use in planning has led governments to realize that policies which were considered gender neutral were in fact not so.

Table 6.2 Examples of Revenue-Side Gender Budgeting

Content	*Revenue Policy*	*Countries*
Direct income taxes	Tax exemption policy.	India, different tax exemption for women in the personal income tax, subsequently revoked. Vietnam, tax exemption for women entrepreneurs in small and medium enterprises.
Filing of direct taxes	Personal filing of taxes instead of joint filing of direct taxes.	India, Thailand (recently debated), Australia.
Property taxes	Differential rates for women property owners.	India (in certain states, including New Delhi).
Mining taxes and royalties (Nontax revenue)	Linking of mining revenue for human development.	India (discussed).
Indirect taxes	Tax incidence analysis across income quintiles, region-wise.	India (examining the incidence of different households, headed by women and men).

Source: Chakraborty (2016).

The revenue side of gender budgeting

The revenue side of gender budgeting is still in its nascent stages (Stotsky, 1997; Grown and Valodia, 2010). Revenue policies that provide favorable treatment to women may help to improve their paid work efforts, access to land and property, and their ability to accumulate financial savings and investments. These policies enhance their children's access to education and health and increase their role in intra-household decisions. Typically, the examination of revenues in gender budgeting has centered on the design of personal income taxes (Table 6.2). However, there is a more recent focus on indirect taxes as well, such as property and mineral taxes.

IV. Country-specific gender budgeting efforts in Asia

We next turn to a survey and assessment of gender budgeting experiences in the region and feature those countries whose experience with gender budgeting is notable or interesting. We provide case studies of the following Asian countries, which are all developing countries: India, the Philippines, Bangladesh, Nepal, Indonesia, and Pakistan. The Republic of Korea (Korea), which has a notable gender budgeting effort, is covered in Chapter 8, which features developed economies.

India

India's gender budgeting efforts stand out globally because they have not only encompassed expenditure and revenue policies, but also have extended to national and subnational governments. The goal of gender budgeting in India is to ensure greater efficiency and gender equity in overall fiscal policy. Gender budgeting has been integrated into many aspects of public finance, which include altering fiscal policies, revising budget classification procedures, influencing fiscal decentralization efforts and local budgeting, and leading to the development of tools to analyze public expenditure, including through benefit incidence analysis.

Development of gender budgeting in India

Historically, the Indian government has expressed a commitment to gender equality in its constitution, in its five-year development plans, and in its national policy for women's empowerment (UN Women, 2016). India's budgetary transparency is considered limited and insufficient (IBP, 2019), but the budget is available to the public.

The Ministry of Finance initially played a leading role in incorporating gender budgeting via budget circulars, expenditure budgets, and performance or outcome budgets. In 2002, the government of India commissioned the National Institute of Public Finance and Policy (NIPFP) to undertake a comprehensive study on gender budgeting. This pioneering study, reported in Lahiri, Chakraborty, and Bhattacharyya (2002), analyzed the fiscal data submitted by all the ministries and departments of the central government to identify the programs and schemes which existed, if any, for women. The NIPFP study assessed the benefit incidence of budget allocations and traced the link between fiscal policy and gender development.[4]

The Minister of Finance announced in the Union Budget speech 2005–06 that India would institutionalize gender budgeting in the country from the 2006 Union Budget onwards. A gender budgeting secretariat was placed in the Ministry of Finance, and gender budgeting cells were created in sectoral ministries.

Starting from 2005–06 onwards, gender budget statements have been included in Indian government budgets. Until 2006, the Ministry of Finance played the leading role in promoting gender budgeting. Since then, the Ministry of Women and Child Development has been the main driver of gender equity-related programming (Chakraborty, 2014b). Out of a total of 95 ministries and departments in the Indian government budget, the number reflecting allocations from the gender budgeting statement has increased from nine in 2005–06 to 35 in 2015–16 (India, Ministry of Women and Child Development, 2015a).

Initiatives on gender budgeting have been undertaken in gender-neutral ministries like Finance, Science and Technology, Road Transport and Highways, Communications and IT, Corporate Affairs, Ocean Development, and Petroleum and Natural Gas, and have led to the development of policies to improve gender equity and achieve women's development goals (India, Ministry of Women and Child Development, 2015b; Jhamb and Mishra, 2015).

Revenue side gender budgeting and tax incidence analysis

Analysis of the revenue side of gender budgeting is still in its elementary stages because of a lack of sex-disaggregated tax data. In India, the legislation defining different types of income does not make any specific provision for gender except in the personal income tax (Chakraborty, P., Chakraborty, Karmakar, and Kapila, 2010). In India, the personal income tax system recognizes both individual taxation and the Hindu undivided family as a separate legal entity, reflecting an economic arrangement that is inherently biased against women as it assigns tax liability to the oldest male member of an extended family. Given this structure, tax exemptions in India offer a limited benefit to women as only 4 percent of economically active women are in the formal paid employment sector. On the other hand, gender-differentiated duties imposed on property transfers may offer a better means to provide favorable treatment for women. For instance, in New Delhi, the duties are set at 4 percent if the property is registered in the name of a woman and 6 percent if registered in the name of a man.

Shortcomings of the Indian attempt to incorporate gender budgeting

The Indian experience demonstrates that not all programming that is designated for gender budgeting or gender equality purposes is targeted exclusively at women. Furthermore, there is a paucity of reporting on the actual number of beneficiaries in addition to a shortage of sex-disaggregated data. Also, there appears to be a poor commitment by the Indian government to monitoring and auditing existing programs (UN Women, 2016).

Not surprisingly, Indian government data shows that while in 2006–07, 5.1 percent of the total government budget was devoted to gender equality issues, by 2015–16 only 4.5 percent was allocated (UN Women, 2016). During the entire intervening period, the gender budgeting allocation never exceeded 6 percent of the budget.[5] Thus, regardless of the degree of inequality, and the formal budget statements and policy declarations in favor of gender budgeting, there was no increase in relative funding for gender equity programs during this period. In recent years, the Ministry of Women and Child Development has tried to institute auditing of gender budgeting programs in order to increase their relevance and enhance the likelihood that they will be executed. In these efforts, the ministry is aided by civil society and external donor organizations. Among the latter, more prominent are organizations such as UN Women, Ford Foundation, United Nations Development Programme, and Oxfam India.

Gender budgeting at the subnational level and the case of Kerala

State level gender budgeting in India has also been adopted using the national level approach.[6] For instance, a successful example of subnational level gender budgeting was adopted by the state of Karnataka and the state of Kerala (India, Ministry of Women and Child Development, 2015b; Chakraborty, 2016).

The "Kerala model" of development is widely referred to in the economic development literature because it refers to the unusual situation where human development indicators are high, even while the per capita income level remains low (Chakraborty, 2016; George, 2016). Kerala has also been a leader in institutionalizing gender budgeting, starting in 2008.

Against the backdrop of the budget announcement in 2006, the state government entrusted the Centre for Development Studies Unit on Local Self Government to study state-level gender budgeting. A report entitled "Analysis of Kerala State Budget 2007–08 Through a Gender Lens" was prepared.[7] This Centre for Development Studies report provided a roadmap for institutionalizing gender budgeting within the Kerala Department of Finance. Subsequently, a significant move in this direction began in Kerala with the announcement by the finance minister in his Budget Speech 2008 that from next year onwards, a special Statement on Gender would be submitted to the legislature along with the budget, as is done in the central government.

In Kerala, democratic decentralization occurred in the mid-90s, and a Women Component Plan was earmarked for gender budgeting. The details of this process are provided in Isaac and Franke (2000) and Isaac (2004). Kerala has local citizens' forums that make governing decisions, and most participants are female (George, 2016). In fact, 50 percent of the seats in these governing bodies are reserved for women. Women leaders and activists in Kerala have been at the forefront of designing programs in nutrition and education specifically directed at women and children.

In subsequent years, innovative infrastructure projects related to gender have been consistently undertaken by the state government. For instance, in 2013, Kerala introduced *She-Taxi* to ensure safe mobility of women, driven by women, which has a database of all emergency response systems in the city. Safe night shelters and hospitals are available for women, and vehicles are proactively monitored from a 24x7 security control room. This is one of the flagship programs of "Gender Park," introduced by the Department of Social Justice, in the government of Kerala. Gender Park was conceptualized by the former finance minister of Kerala, Thomas Isaac, and announced in his Budget Speech 2011–12.[8]

Gender Park was the first such large scale initiative in India to reduce gender inequalities through innovative projects. Though delayed in its full execution, it was officially inaugurated by the president of India in February 2016.[9] Two additional innovative schemes in areas not traditionally seen as "women-related" have also been instituted in Kerala—an income support scheme and a food security scheme, both targeted specifically at women (Mishra, 2011).

In 2019, Kerala became the first state in India to implement the "She Pad" scheme, designed to distribute clean sanitary pads to all school students across the state with the support of local self-government institutions.[10]

Integrating gender in intergovernmental transfers to subnational governments in India

In India and in other federal countries, resources for supporting public expenditures at the state and local levels are insufficient, and the lower levels of the government depend heavily on intergovernmental transfers from the national government.[11] There is an ongoing debate in India whether to integrate gender in formula-based fiscal transfers (Chakraborty, 2010a). The Fourteenth Finance Commission of India, which reported in January 2015, integrated "climate change" variables in the formula-based transfers, setting a precedent for gender development variables (Government of India, 2015).

The Fourteenth Finance Commission undertook to devolve 42 percent of the tax pool of the central government to states (Chakraborty, P., 2015). This may allow states to raise spending on gender-sensitive human development relating to health and education, which are state responsibilities in the Indian federal system. The flow of unconditional funds to the subnational governments can also provide space for state priorities on gender development. Earlier studies noted that lack of flexibility of intergovernmental transfers and unfunded mandates were two deterrents to implementing gender budgeting effectively. Anand and Chakraborty (2016) analyzed progressivity of fiscal transfers following the incorporation of gender as a criterion. They found that the transfers, in fact, are progressive in terms of gender equality purposes.

Strengthening accountability mechanisms, capacity building, and gender mainstreaming

The Gender Budget Statement has helped women activists and civil society organizations lobby for better funding and provisioning for women's rights on much stronger grounds (UN Women, 2012; Mishra and Sinha, 2012). Though the Lahiri Committee has provided a comprehensive framework for accounting in gender budgeting, it has not yet been completely implemented in India, at the national and subnational levels (India, Ministry of Women and Child Development, 2015b; Jhamb and Mishra, 2015). Further effort is clearly required to strengthen the implementation of gender budgeting and build strong accountability mechanisms.

Trends of India compared to a synthetic control country

Figure 6.8 presents some comparisons of India's progress in key indicators of gender equality and women's development, including education, health, the labor force, and the GDI compared to a synthetic control country. The figure suggests that India made improvements in educational enrollment at all levels over the period, with greater progress than the synthetic country at the primary and secondary but not at the tertiary levels, which may reflect the influence of state level gender budgeting efforts. In increasing life expectancy, India made

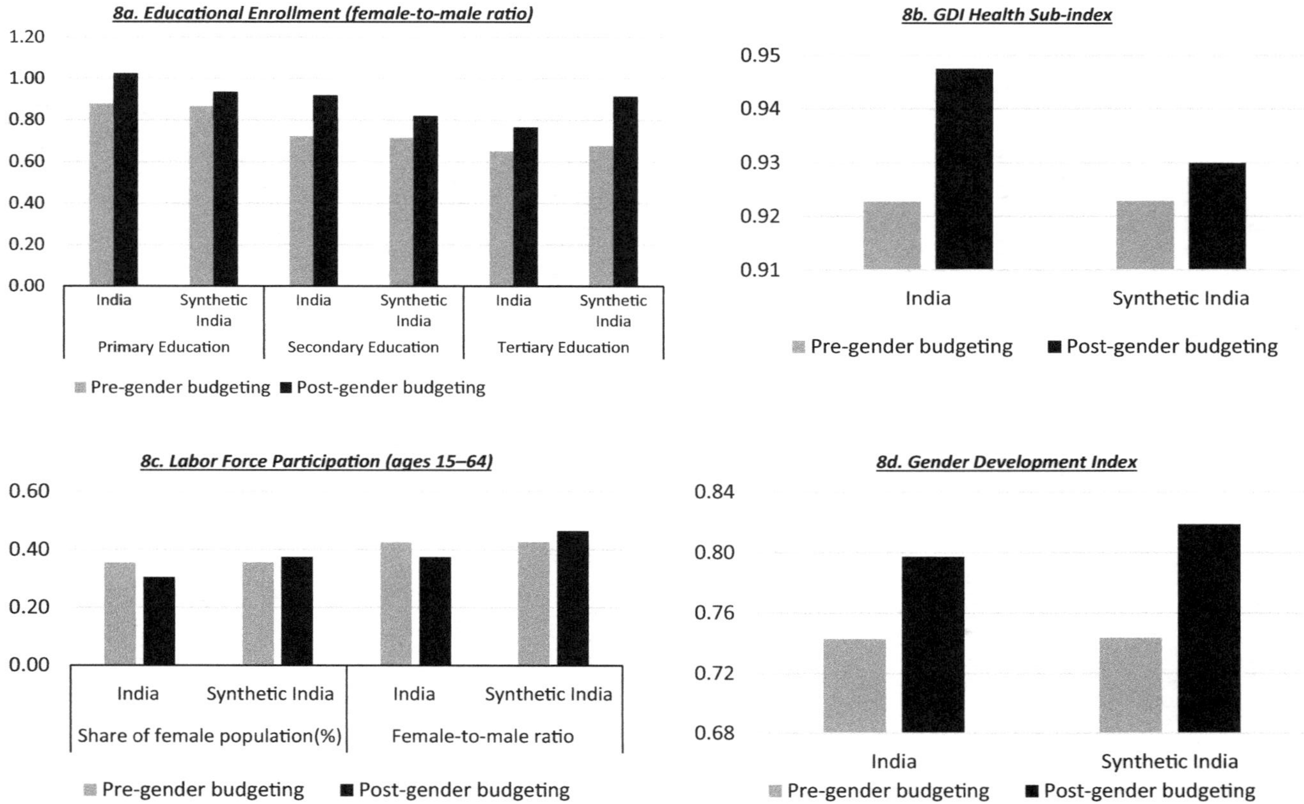

Figure 6.8 Trends in Gender Equality in India and a Synthetic Control Country

Sources: World Bank, World Development Indicators; and authors' estimates.

Notes: Synthetic India consists of a weighted average of comparable countries based on the matching feature of the SCM described in Chapter 5 Appendix B. A higher Gender Development Index indicates greater gender equality.

more progress than the synthetic country, but performed worse on the labor market and GDI indicators. Its employment indicators worsened, compared to the synthetic country, and while the GDI improved, it improved less than the synthetic country, and for both indicators, India started out in a somewhat weaker position. Overall, the analysis is consistent with our assessment of India's mixed record on gender budgeting, with primary and secondary education appearing to be a bright spot in relative performance.

The Philippines

The Philippines provides an interesting example of how gender budgeting can be legislated into law and then applied at both national and subnational levels. Republic Act "Women in Development and Nation-Building Act" was signed into law by Philippine President Corazon C. Aquino in 1992. Under the law, the Philippine state is responsible for providing women rights and opportunities equal to that of men. Three strategies were designed to achieve this goal (Illo et al., 2010):

1. Setting aside and using a portion of development assistance to fund programs and activities for women;
2. Ensuring that women participate and benefit equally to men in all programs of government departments;
3. Gender mainstreaming or removing gender bias in regulations and procedures of all government departments and agencies.

Gender-responsive budget policy initiatives started at the national level in the Philippines with the gender and development budget in 1995 (Chakraborty, 2016). The gender and development budget made a provision for earmarking at least 5 percent of all departmental expenditures on programs for women in national and subnational budgets, and hence, it has led to a sectoral analysis across spending ministries. The gender and development budget policy led to the formulation of annual gender plans and budgets in all government departments, including their attached agencies, bureaus, state universities and colleges, government-owned and -controlled corporations, and local government units. The authorities reported in 2015 that gender and development planning is integrated into the regular activities of agencies and that the cost of implementing this is at least five percent of their total annual appropriation, based on the General Appropriations Act.[12]

Chakraborty (2016) notes that setting a floor for spending on gender-related aims resulted in a misallocation of resources in various departments. It also resulted in the marginalization of gender issues from mainstream budgeting, as floor limits were taken as ceilings in various departments. Earmarking a specific proportion of a budget allocation for women is not likely to lead to efficient use of public funds, though at times it may have its uses where programs are chronically underfunded.

Under quota-based gender budgeting, money was initially earmarked for such activities as ballroom dancing in certain government departments. As there was no penalty for not using the gender and development budget fully and efficiently, many departments ended up with an unspent surplus in this budget. However, the 5 percent requirement was eventually made more flexible so that departments could spend money only on what was truly needed.

There have been no gender budgeting initiatives on the tax side or with respect to employment or procurement policies. Gender budgeting led to initiatives related to improving sex-disaggregated data and statistics in reports of programs and projects.

Since 1995, the Philippine Commission on Women, considered to be the national machinery on women, has been the primary agency responsible for monitoring compliance with gender budgeting mandates. Civil society organizations act as the watchdog of formulation and implementation of gender budgeting, while the legislative branch and parliamentary committees play a role through committees and public hearings.

Subnational gender budgeting in the Philippines

Gender budget initiatives at the local level can be found in a few local units in the Philippines, particularly in Sorsogon and Hilongos, where selective attempts were made to identify specific gender needs before drafting the budget (Chakraborty, 2016). These initiatives, which came from the Department of Interior and Local Government and the National Commission on the Role of Filipino Women, with the support of UNIFEM in 2004, identified entry points for results-oriented gender budgeting.

In Sorsogon, the initiative was taken in the health sector, where gender-related health goals were identified in the Millennium Development Goals. In Hilongos, the initiative was taken in the agricultural sector. By strengthening the agricultural sector, the goal was to reduce the forced migration of women and enhance their income-earning opportunities, because women predominate in agriculture. For instance, since women are key contributors to intra-household food and nutrition security, decentralization has implicit gender dimensions. One component of the local gender budgeting in Hilongos was revamping the irrigation system and strengthening other policies to increase agricultural productivity.

Trends of the Philippines compared to a synthetic control country

Figure 6.9 presents some comparisons of the Philippines' progress in key indicators of gender equality and women's development, including education, health, labor force participation, and the GDI to a synthetic country. In education, there is little change in either the Philippines or the synthetic country, though in all cases, there is already a high degree of educational enrollment equality, and in fact, at the secondary and tertiary levels, female enrollment

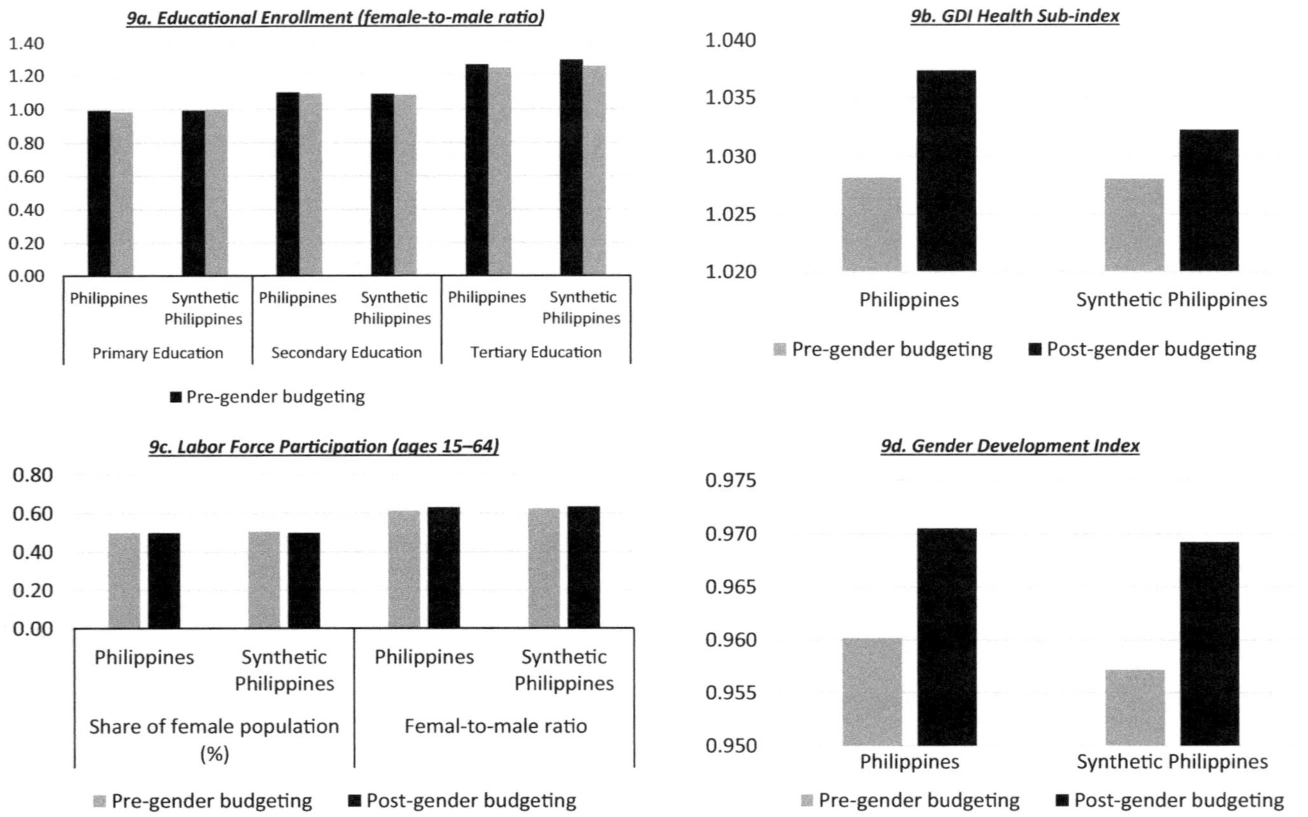

Figure 6.9 Trends in Gender Equality in the Philippines and a Synthetic Control Country

Sources: World Bank, World Development Indicators; and authors' estimates.

Notes: Synthetic Philippines consists of a weighted average of comparable countries based on the matching feature of the SCM described in Chapter 5 Appendix B.

A higher Gender Development Index indicates greater gender equality.

exceeds male enrollment in the Philippines and the synthetic country, a phenomenon increasingly found throughout the developed world. In terms of life expectancy, the Philippines made greater progress than the synthetic country. In terms of employment, there is little change in either the Philippines or the synthetic country, and in terms of the GDI, the Philippines started at a somewhat higher level but made less overall progress. These indicators thus show a mixed record of success, and the only clear area of gain is in the area of health. Without looking more precisely at health programs launched by the government in this field and determining whether they can be attributed to the gender budgeting initiative, it is hard to conclude whether the improved performance in health is a result of gender budgeting efforts.

Bangladesh

Integrating gender-related concerns into national policies became prominent in Bangladesh with the formulation of the Fifth Five-Year Plan, 1997–2002 (Chakraborty, 2010b). The adoption of a National Policy for the Advancement of Women and a National Action Plan for the Advancement of Women in 1997 has led to implementation of gender budgeting. The Ministry of Health has also piloted a gender-disaggregated beneficiary assessment of community health services. After the findings of this analysis were presented to the Ministry of Finance, the ministry agreed to incorporate gender-related and anti-poverty concerns into the budget. The Ministry of Finance and the Ministry of Women and Children's Affairs have led this initiative. Several ministries carried out gender mainstreaming separately, but the major task of gender mainstreaming was given to the Ministry of Women and Children's Affairs.

The gender budgeting effort encompassed an analysis of gender-related concerns in a number of ministries and also the assignment of Women in Development focal points in 47 specific ministries. Section 3 of the budget circular instructs the ministries to assess the impact of their strategies on gender-related and anti-poverty objectives, while Section 4 requires them to assess the impact of their activities on the outlined gender and poverty goals (Sharp et al., 2009). Gender "shares" for each expenditure are calculated using the specially developed Recurrent, Capital, Gender and Poverty database and methodology (Budlender, 2015). A Financial Management Reform Program involved gender budgeting training for all ministries engaged in the Medium-Term Budgetary Framework and the program on Policy Leadership and Advocacy for Gender Equality–Phase II. This training strengthens the capacity of partner ministries to analyze gender-related concerns and mainstream gender across their programs.

Gender budgeting in Bangladesh has focused on the analysis of ministry budgets to determine whether they are gender responsive or not. The government produces a document along with the budget, which explains how different activities of various ministries/divisions have implications for women's advancement and rights. In the first year, such analysis was done for four ministries, and in the second year, this was done for 10 ministries. Since 2009, the Bangladesh government has been producing an annual gender budget report that can be considered a form of a gender budget statement (Budlender, 2015). In 2012, a review of 20 ministries was carried out and concluded that Bangladesh had been successful in institutionalizing the gender budgeting process. The focus of the Bangladesh gender budgeting effort has been to encourage all ministries to consider the impact of their programs on the goals of poverty reduction and women's advancement. Mishra and Sinha (2017) note that the gender budget allocation in Bangladesh, like in India, has stagnated. Since 2009–2010, is has been around 26 percent of the budget.

Apart from gender budgeting, the Bangladesh Food for Education (FFE) program, introduced in 1993, constitutes an innovative approach to raising enrollment rates and reducing dropout rates of students in school while also improving nutrition. An evaluation of this program suggested that the government could improve how it targets food subsidies to benefit the education of children and other needy populations (Ahmed and Arends-Kuenning, 2006). The FFE program entailed determining the appropriate geographical targets (i.e., focusing on communities, municipalities, urban areas, etc.) and categorical targets (i.e., girls, families, HIV orphans, displaced people, and war-affected people) for government-funded food subsidies, in order to motivate families to improve school enrollment and retention rates. An International Food Policy Research Institute study found that there was an enrollment increase for all children, and it was greater for girls than for boys, but the quality of education remained a problem for all children (Ahmad and del Ninno, 2002).

Trends of Bangladesh compared to a synthetic control country

Figure 6.10 presents some comparisons of Bangladesh's progress in key indicators of gender equality and women's development compared to the synthetic country. In education, Bangladesh made progress in educational enrollment and relatively more than the synthetic country at the primary and secondary levels, but not the tertiary level. In health and the GDI, Bangladesh started from a weaker position but made substantially more progress, and in employment, it made marginally more progress. Overall, Bangladesh's record is quite good, and some part may be attributable to its various gender budgeting and gender-equality initiatives.

Nepal

In 2005, the Ministry of Finance in the Nepal government created a gender-responsive budget committee to guide the process of gender budgeting reform (Nepal, 2016). In the fiscal year 2007–2008, the Ministry of Finance introduced gender budgeting (Nepal, 2016; Chakraborty, 2016). A new classification of budgetary transactions was introduced to incorporate gender budgeting

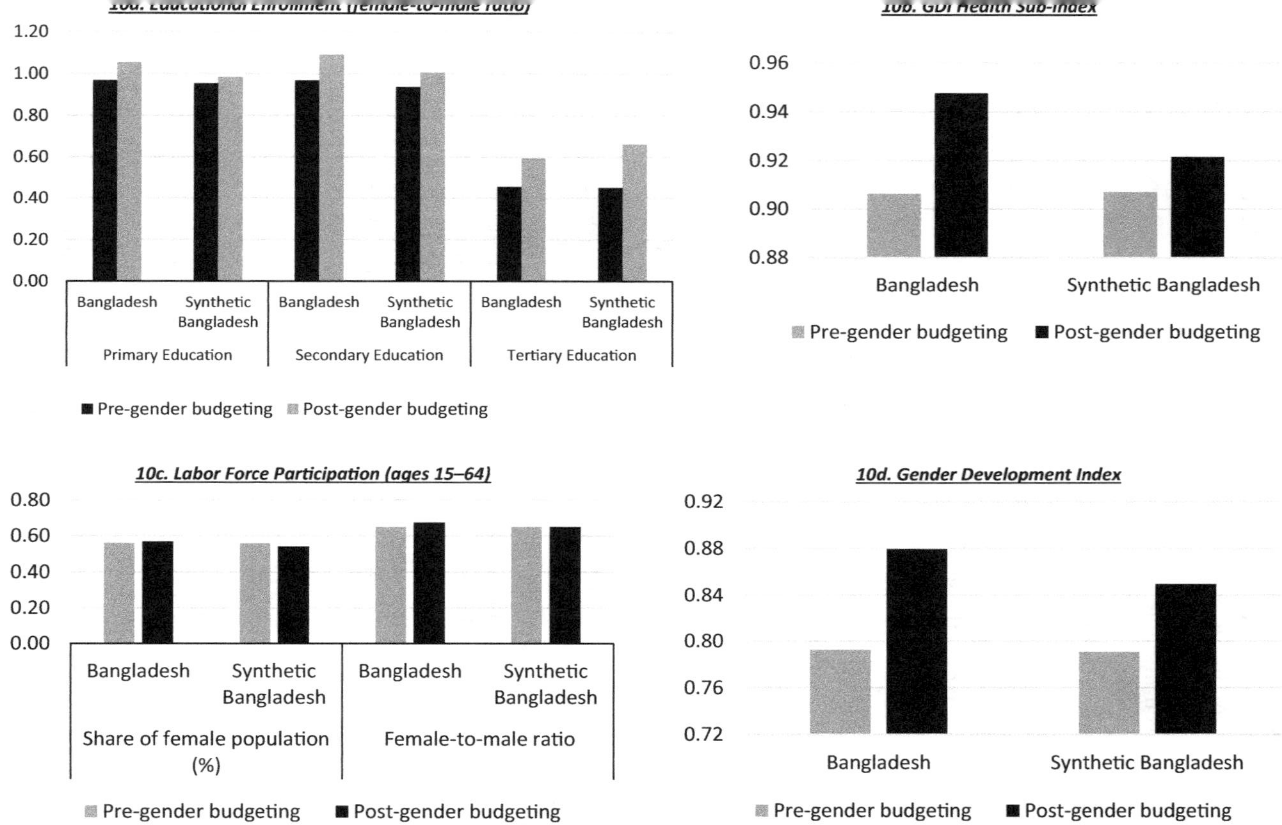

Figure 6.10 Trends in Gender Equality in Bangladesh and a Synthetic Control Country

Sources: World Bank, World Development Indicators; and authors' estimates.

Notes: Synthetic Bangladesh consists of a weighted average of comparable countries based on the matching feature of the SCM described in Chapter 5 Appendix B.

A higher Gender Development Index indicates greater gender equality.

into the budget. Similar to India and Bangladesh, the new classification mainly entailed categorizing public expenditure according to benefits to women.

According to the government's guidelines, all line ministries, departments, and project/program units at all levels must provide information classifying their demands for new programs into the three categories: directly gender responsive (G01), indirectly gender responsive (G2) and neutral, scoring as per the indicators. The gender budgeting classification criteria and corresponding scores are given in Table 6.3. Scoring is done by planning units in every ministry together with the Minister of Finance. Public budget expenditures are classified into three categories:

1 Those that are more than half related to programs directly responsive to gender (> 50 percent);
2 Those that are indirectly gender responsive (> 20 to < 50 percent); and
3 Those that are neutral (< 20 percent).

The scoring system takes account of different aspects of gender sensitivity, participation, capacity building, benefit sharing, and increased access to employment and income-earning opportunities and a reduction in women's workload. These indicators have been allocated different potential percentage points that signify their importance. Programs scoring 50 percent or more are classified as directly supportive of women, those scoring 20 to 50 percent as indirectly supportive, and those scoring less than 20 percent as neutral (Nepal, 2007). The complexity and subjectivity of the scoring method of gender budgeting may be one of the reasons for the lack of universal acceptance of Nepal's experience with gender budgeting.

Practically speaking, gender budgeting efforts in Nepal seem to be producing visible results in both the amount of funding being allocated by the government that directly benefits women and the programmatic outcomes achieved. Budget allocations increased gradually from 11.3 percent in fiscal year 2007–2008 to 21.8 percent in fiscal year 2013–2014 (Nepal, 2016). Despite this apparent increase, it seems that a major portion of the budget for women and children went to school and road construction and, in some places,

Table 6.3 Nepal: Criteria of Gender Budgeting and Scores

No.	Criteria	Score
1	Women's participation in informing and implementing the program	20
2	Women's capacity development	20
3	Women's share in the benefit	30
4	Promoting employment and income generation for women	20
5	Qualitative improvement of women's time-use or reduced workload	10

Source: Budget Speech (2015–2016), Nepal, Ministry of Finance.

electrification. These results demonstrate that groups targeted as beneficiaries in gender budgeting (women and children) often have little say over how allocated funds are spent.

In Nepal, gender audits of programming were conducted in many of the government ministries, and these audits revealed a number of significant achievements in the period 2007–2012 (Nepal, 2016), such as the following:

1 At the ward level of governance, 33 percent female representation is mandated, as is a 10 percent allocation to women's programs.
2 Maternal mortality rates were reduced from 510 to 229 per 100,000 women, via improvements in maternity care and cash grants for regular checkups before delivery.
3 School dropout rates for girls were reduced from 16 percent to 5 percent between 2001–2002 and 2011–2012, by installing girls' toilet rooms in public schools and by providing scholarships.
4 Equal wages for men and women are mandated at the local level.

Indonesia

The Indonesian government's commitment to gender-responsive budgeting was communicated starting in 1978, when it formed the Ministry of Women's Empowerment and Child Protection (Salim, 2016). It wasn't until the year 2000, though, that a gender budgeting initiative really was enacted with Presidential Instruction No. 9/2000 on Gender Mainstreaming in National Development. Gender mainstreaming is the term that the Indonesian government uses to describe its strategy of integrating gender-based perspectives into planning, budgeting, implementing, monitoring, and evaluating policy and development programs (Salim, 2016).

By 2004, 34 gender-responsive programs were implemented in different development sectors, including those normally associated with gender concerns—such as health, education, family planning, and social welfare. Other sectors not typically connected to women's issues—such as labor, law, agriculture, and environment—were also part of this gender budgeting initiative (ibid.).

Indonesia has 38 ministries, and gender budget statements were introduced incrementally starting with pilot projects in seven ministries in 2010. By 2014, more than 20 ministries submitted gender budget statements. Table 6.4 is an example of a gender budget statement submitted to the Indonesian government (Budlender, 2015).

In 2014, an instrument for monitoring gender budget statement implementation was piloted in certain provinces and districts. The instrument was designed to match the format of the gender budget statement. The purpose of this instrument was to determine whether activities planned in the statement were implemented.

As part of the 1998 democratic reform process, participation from local governments and civil society organizations at the subnational level became more

Table 6.4 Indonesia: Example of a Gender Budget Statement

Program	Land Transportation Service Delivery and Management
Activity	Education and development in an urban transportation system
Output	Purchase of a bus for urban transportation
Objective	To improve the mass transportation service that addresses communities' needs for better, safe, convenient, timely, and affordable mass transportation for all (adults, children, elderly people, and people with disabilities)
Situation Analysis	• Low availability of gender-responsive buses • Accumulation of passengers at certain times and routes, disorganized bus service frequency, and lack of responsiveness to gender needs • Existence of sexual harassment because of high population density using buses, which is caused by a shortage of bus vehicles

Source: Budlender (2015).

prominent. However, at the provincial level, gender budgeting activities were not prioritized, and the human resources necessary for implementation of programs were also considered weak (Salim, 2016).

One of the notable features of the Indonesia gender budgeting experience was the central involvement of civil society organizations such as PATTIRO in providing advocacy, technical assistance, and critiques of shortcomings in local gender budgeting efforts. In Indonesia in particular, civil society organizations have pushed for greater government commitment to women's needs by increasing budgetary allocations for programs such as maternal and child health, literacy, and other gender-equity efforts. Generally, civil society organizations in Indonesia have found that gender budgeting efforts by the government have been characterized by inadequate budgets and ineffective, inefficient, and unequal programs and activities (Salim, 2016).

Pakistan

The Ministry of Women and Development called for gender budgeting in 2001 in a paper on gender and poverty issues put forward as part of Pakistan's application for an IMF loan under the Poverty Reduction Growth Facility (Chakraborty, 2016). The introduction of budget reforms and changes in public resource management processes provided opportunities for the emergence of a gender budgeting initiative (Pakistan, Ministry of Women Development, Social Welfare and Special Education, 2002).

The Gender Resource Budgeting Initiative in Pakistan began in the federal government and in Punjab province, in coordination with the United Nations Development Programme and other bilateral agencies in 2005. The initiative was integrated into the Strengthening Poverty Reduction Strategy Monitoring (SPRSM) funded by the United Nations Development Programme (2008–2012). It was implemented in the federal government and in three provinces. However, the initiative was not confined to SPRSM. The Medium-Term Budgetary Framework Secretariat in the federal government has integrated gender in medium-term output-based budgets. The primary objective of the initiative was to analyze public expenditure in sectors that contribute to poverty reduction through a gender lens. The key focal areas/priority sectors of the initiative during 2008–2012 remained in the social sector—such as health, education, women's development, population welfare, and labor.

The first time-use survey in Pakistan was carried out in 2007 by the Federal Bureau of Statistics. It engaged close to 20,000 households from across the country to uncover the macroeconomic implications of unpaid care work and to strengthen public policies to support men and women to realize their productive potential. Drawing on these data, further research was commissioned, to measure the value of unpaid care work in Pakistan, and the results were made available to government officials and the public (Mahbub and Budlender, 2007).

The Budget Call Circular 2006–2007, issued by the Finance Department, Government of the Punjab, for the first time asked for some sex-disaggregated information. The data given in response to the budget call circular provided information on gender patterns in public sector employment and remuneration. These data helped in increasing women's employment in the government and reducing the gender wage gap. It also led to publicly-funded day care centers to promote women's participation in paid activities.

In the second phase, 2008–2012, the initiative led to establishing targets in the output-based budgeting system at the national level, across all ministries. The Ministry of Finance reported that gender budgeting initiatives relate neither to tax nor to government employment or procurement practices. However, the initiative provided support to strengthening the statistical function in reporting of the Millennium Development Goals.

Against the backdrop of an International Monetary Fund–supported economic program, the federal government reinvigorated the work on gender-disaggregated analysis and carried out a gender-responsive analysis of the 2015/2016 fiscal year budget to ensure that fiscal policies incorporate gender-equality principles and are geared to attaining inclusive economic growth. This work contributed to a baseline for the 2016/2017 fiscal year budget to foster gender equality in education and labor force participation, and it also has applications at the subnational level (International Monetary Fund, 2016).

V. Conclusion

From the research on country-specific experiences, we can broadly conclude that gender budgeting in the region is sustainable and adds substantively to fiscal policy, but it succeeds only if the ministry of finance takes a direct and strong role in leading the effort. The experience of the region suggests that initiatives on gender budgeting should begin with the ministry of finance and require adequate support from all stakeholders, including civil society, parliamentarians, and external donors. For instance, the heterogeneous stakeholders in the process who supported the Ministry of Finance in India in introducing gender budgeting include policy think tanks, the Ministry of Women and Child Development,

UN entities, and civil society organizations. Although gender budgeting has the potential to transform gender equality in the region, the results are still modest in most of the lower-income countries except India and the Philippines, where the efforts have led to the enactment of substantive fiscal policies.

Country-specific outcomes

- **India**: The pivotal role of the Ministry of Finance in gender budgeting, with the support of policy think tanks, has led to the successful institutionalization of gender budgeting at both the national and subnational levels. Gender budgeting has also led to the regular integration of gender-related considerations in budgetary programming, even in sectors that appear gender-neutral, such as industry. Gender budgeting has helped to improve accountability and transparency. In the state of Kerala, gender budgeting initiatives have resulted in many innovative programs in health, education, and transportation, producing a high level of human development given the low level of income in the state.
- **The Philippines**: The original design of the gender budgeting effort, which entailed earmarking a portion of the budget for women in every ministry or department, was poorly conceived and has been made more flexible over time. Gender-related allocations are now linked to results or performance-related programming, a sounder approach and consistent with modern budget management trends.
- **Bangladesh**: Although not introduced as part of a gender budgeting initiative, the successful Food for Education program was carried out, which improved the school enrollment and retention rates of children and improved their nutrition levels. There was some evidence suggesting that it had a more meaningful effect on girls. Bangladesh has outperformed the synthetic country control in most variables analyzed, and this may be attributable partly to gender budgeting.
- **Nepal**: The integration of time-use statistics and the statistically invisible care economy in gender budgeting is almost nonexistent in the Asian region except in Nepal, where it was integrated in analytical matrices of gender budgeting.
- **Indonesia**: Gender budgeting has led to increased civil society pressure on government to produce results.
- **Pakistan**: Gender budgeting has led to some substantive accomplishments for women and girls in terms of equalizing opportunities in education and the workplace. It has also led to an increased use of time-use and other sex-disaggregated data. Nonetheless, the efforts remain inadequate to the task.

Overall outcomes for the region

The overall outcomes for the region regarding the value and impact of gender budgeting can be summarized as follows:

- Gender budgeting has led in some countries to fiscal policies that were intended to improve gender equality and advance women and ensure that even in areas of the budget that appear gender-neutral, gender-related objectives are considered.
- Subnational gender budgeting is a key feature in the region and is critical, given the size and importance of these governments in Asia and their responsibility for critical services such as education and health. India, Indonesia, and the Philippines are most notable.
- Public financial management in the region has benefited from the introduction of gender budgeting, specifically using gender as a theme in budgeting. This fits especially well into results or performance-budgeting systems.
- Gender budgeting has led to public expenditure benefit incidence analysis and expenditure tracking disaggregated by gender, along with other assessment and auditing techniques, to evaluate how public spending differentially affects women and girls.
- Gender budgeting statements within budget documents help ensure transparency in the budgetary allocations for women. However, there is still room to improve their content.
- Gender budgeting has spurred the involvement of civil society organizations and activists for women's rights.
- Gender budgeting has led to some reconsideration of revenue-side issues, but so far, there have been only a few countries that have tried to examine income and other taxes from a gender perspective.

Notes

1 Ellen Shnidman co-authored this chapter. It has benefited from Chakraborty (2016) and other reference materials. More-recent information on fiscal measures that governments have undertaken may be available from public sources.
2 See Chapter 2 for the time-consistent version of the United Nations Development Program's GDI.
3 The Appendix Table 6.2 provides details on fiscal aggregates.
4 The NIPFP diagnosed the existing degree of gender inequality in India through the sex disaggregation of relevant macro data, the quantification of existing non-Systems of National Accounts unpaid care economy work of women, an econometric investigation into the link between public expenditures and gender development, an assessment of budgetary policies through a gender lens, and the identification of policy alternatives to build in a gender-sensitive national budgeting process (Lahiri, Chakraborty, and Bhattacharyya, 2002).
5 However, it is unclear whether all initiatives with gender-related implications were included in this measure.
6 The state-level gender budgeting initiatives are summarized in the Gender Budgeting Handbook, published by the government of India, Ministry of Women and Child Development (2015b). Broadly, all states followed the national-level gender budgeting for their own initiatives. However, comparative financial information is hard to obtain.
7 Chakraborty (2008).
8 Kerala, Budget Speech 2011–2012 (Kerala: Ministry of Finance). Found at www.finance.kerala.gov.in/index.php?option=com_content&view=article&id=448: kerala-budget-2011-12&catid=18: state-budget.

9 Government of India, Press Information Bureau, February 27, 2016 (New Delhi: Government of India). Found at: http://pib.nic.in/newsite/PrintRelease.aspx?relid=136959.
10 Abraham, Bobins, 2017, "In A First, Kerala Makes Sanitary Napkin Vending Machines Mandatory In All Schools," India Times, May 20. Found at: www.indiatimes.com/news/india/in-a-first-kerala-makes-sanitary-napkin-vending-machines-mandatory-in-all-schools-321966.html?fbclid=IwAR2Xyuqoyx5bgVw1aSSL8A3q5MsVa9pW2chnOxz9X6DWP3EjhE80Hw8EYqY.
11 The fiscal transfers and gender budgeting experiences on India can be found in Chakraborty (2007, 2010a).
12 Authorities' response to the IMF questionnaire, unpublished, 2015.

References

Ahmed, A.U., and M. Arends-Kuenning, 2006, "Do Crowded Classrooms Crowd Out Learning? Evidence from the Food for Education Program in Bangladesh," *World Development*, Vol. 34, pp. 665–684.

Ahmad, A.U., and del Ninno, Carlo, 2002, "The Food for Education Program in Bangladesh: An Evaluation of Its Impact on Educational Attainment and Food Security," Discussion Paper Brief 138 (Washington, DC: International Food Policy Research Institute).

Anand, Abhishek, and Lekha Chakraborty, 2016, "Integrating Gender Criteria in Intergovernmental Transfers in India," paper accepted for 25th IAFFE Conference on 'Transitions and Transformations in Gender Equality,' National University of Ireland, Galway, Ireland.

Abraham, Bobins, 2017, "In A First, Kerala Makes Sanitary Napkin Vending Machines Mandatory In All Schools," *India Times*, May 20.

Budlender, Debbie, 2015, *Budget Call Circular and Gender Budget Statements: A Review* (New Delhi: UNIFEM).

Chakraborty, Lekha S., 2007, "Gender Responsive Budgeting and Fiscal Decentralisation in India: A Preliminary Appraisal," Working Paper 46 (New Delhi, NIPFP).

Chakraborty, Lekha S., 2008, "Analysis of Kerala State Budget 2007–08 Through a Gender Lens," (Thiruvananthapuram: Centre for Development Studies).

Chakraborty, Lekha S., 2010a, "Determining Gender Equity in Fiscal Federalism: Analytical Issues and Empirical Evidence from India," Working Paper No. 590 (New York: Levy Economics Institute).

Chakraborty, Lekha S., 2010b, *Gender-Sensitive Fiscal Policies: Experience of Ex-Post and Ex-Ante Gender Budgets in Asia-Pacific* (Bangkok: UNDP).

Chakraborty, Lekha S., 2014a, "Integrating Time in Public Policy: Empirical Description of Gender-Specific Outcomes and Budgeting," Working Paper No. 785 (New York: Levy Economics Institute).

Chakraborty, Lekha S., 2014b, "Gender-Responsive Budgeting as Fiscal Innovation: Evidence from India on Processes," Working Paper No. 797 (New York: Levy Economics Institute).

Chakraborty, Lekha S., 2016, "Asia: A Survey of Gender Budgeting Efforts," IMF Working Paper 16/150 (Washington, DC: IMF).

Chakraborty, Pinaki, 2015, "Getting the Federal Transfers Right," *The Hindu*, May 8.

Chakraborty, Pinaki, Lekha Chakraborty, Krishanu Karmakar, and Shashi M. Kapila, 2010, "Gender Equality and Taxation in India: An Unequal Burden?," in Caren Grown and Imraan Valodia, eds., *Taxation and Gender Equity: A Comparative Analysis of Direct and Indirect Taxes in Developing and Developed Countries* (New York: Routledge), pp. 94–118.

Elson, Diane, 2006, *Budgeting for Women's Rights: Monitoring Government Budgets for Compliance with CEDAW* (New York: UNIFEM).

George, Sunny, 2016, "Community Participation and Women's Empowerment: The Kerala Experience of Participatory Planning and Budgeting," in Cecilia Ng, ed., *Gender Responsive and Participatory Budgeting: Imperatives for Equitable Public Expenditure* (Heidelberg: Springer International), pp. 81–95.

Government of India, Press Information Bureau, February 27, 2016 (New Delhi: Government of India).

Grown, Caren, and Imraan Valodia, eds., 2010, *Taxation and Gender Equity: A Comparative Analysis of Direct and Indirect Taxes in Developing and Developed Countries* (New York: Routledge).

Illo, Jeanne Frances I., Jean Encinas-Franco, Jon Michael R. Villasenor, Maria Daryl L. Leyesa, and Frances Chariza I. de los Trino, 2010, *Accounting for Gender Results: A Review of the Philippine GAD Budget Policy* (Quezon City: Women and Gender Institute, Miriam College).

India, 2015, *Fourteenth Finance Commission Report* (New Delhi: Government of India).

India, Ministry of Women and Child Development, 2015a, *Annual Report 2014–15* (New Delhi: Government of India).

India, Ministry of Women and Child Development, 2015b, *Gender Budgeting Handbook* (New Delhi: Government of India).

International Budget Partnership (IBP), 2019, *Open Budget Initiative* (Washington, DC: International Budget Partnership). Available at: www.internationalbudget.org/open-budget-survey/open-budget-index-rankings/.

International Monetary Fund (IMF), 2016, "Pakistan: Tenth Review under the Extended Arrangement and Request for Modification of Performance Criteria," (Washington, DC: International Monetary Fund).

International Monetary Fund (IMF), various years, *World Economic Outlook* (Washington, DC: International Monetary Fund).

Isaac, Thomas T.M., 2004, "Democratic Decentralization and Women Empowerment: Kerala Model," paper presented at Local Level Gender Responsive Budgeting International Expert Group Meeting, NIPFP, New Delhi.

Isaac, Thomas T.M., and Richard W. Franke, 2000, *Local Democracy and Development* (New Delhi: Left Word).

Jhamb, Bhumika, and Yamini Mishra, 2015, "Gender Budgeting," *Economic and Political Weekly*, Vol. 50, pp. 54–62.

Kerala, Budget Speech, 2011–2012 (Kerala: Ministry of Finance).

Klasen, Stephan, and Claudia Wink, 2003, "Missing Women: Revisiting the Debate," *Feminist Economics*, Vol. 9, pp. 263–299.

Lahiri, Ashok, Lekha Chakraborty, and P.N. Bhattacharyya, 2002, "Gender Budgeting in India," *Follow the Money Series* (New York: UNIFEM).

Mahbub, Nadeem, and Debbie Budlender, 2007, *Gender Responsive Budgeting in Pakistan: Experience and Lessons Learned* (New York: UNIFEM).

Mishra, Yamini, 2011, *Breaking New Frontiers for Gender Responsive Budgeting: The Kerala Model* (New Delhi: UN Women).

Mishra, Yamini, and Navanita Sinha, 2012, "Gender Responsive Budgeting in India: What Has Gone Wrong?" *Economic & Political Weekly*, Vol. 28, pp. 50–57.

Mishra, Yamini, and Navanita Sinha, 2017, "Gender Incursions in the Domain of Budgets: The Practice of GFB in Asia Pacific," in Zohra Khan and Nalini Burn, eds., *Financing for Gender Equity* (London: Palgrave Macmillan), pp. 141–175.

Nepal, 2007, "Gender Assessment and Gender Budget Audit in Seven Ministries," Compilation of Synopsis of Executive Summary and Conclusion and Recommendations of the Studies (Kathmandu: Lumbini Publications, published jointly by the Government of Nepal, Ministry of Finance, Ministry of Women, Children and Social Welfare, and UNIFEM Office).

Nepal, Purusottam, 2016, "Institutionalizing Gender Responsive Budgeting in National and Local Governments in Nepal," in Cecilia Ng, ed., *Gender Responsive and Participatory Budgeting: Imperatives for Equitable Public Expenditure* (Heidelberg: Springer International), pp. 163–178.

Pakistan, Ministry of Women Development, Social Welfare and Special Education, 2002, "Major/Important Achievements made by the Ministry of Women Development," (Islamabad: Government of Pakistan).

Salim, Agus, 2016, "Gender Responsive Budgeting: State and Civil Society Initiatives at National and Sub-National Levels in Indonesia," in Cecilia Ng, ed., *Gender Responsive and Participatory Budgeting: Imperatives for Equitable Public Expenditure* (Heidelberg: Springer International), pp. 179–193.

Sharp, Rhonda, Diane Elson, Monica Costa, Sanjugta Vas Dev, and A. Mundkur, 2009, "Republic of Bangladesh: Gender Responsive Budgeting in the Asia Pacific Region," (Bangladesh: UNISA).

Stotsky, Janet G., 1997, "Gender Bias in Tax Systems," Tax Notes International, June 9, pp. 1913–1923.

Stotsky, Janet G., Sakina Shibuya, Lisa Kolovich, and Suhaib Kebhaj, 2016, "Trends in Gender Equality and Women's Advancement," International Monetary Fund Working Paper, 16/21 (Washington, DC: IMF).

United Nations Development Programme (UNDP), various years, *Human Development Report* (New York: UNDP).

UN Women, 2012, *Gender Budgeting: Evaluation Report* (New Delhi: UN Women).

UN Women, 2016, *Gender-responsive Budgeting in the Asia-Pacific Region: A Status Report* (New York: UN Women).

van den Broek, N.R., and A.D. Falconer 2011, "Maternal Mortality and Millennium Development Goal 5," British Medical Bulletin, Vol. 99, pp. 25–38.

World Bank, various years, *World Development Indicators Database* (Washington, DC: World Bank).

Appendix

Table 6.1A Selected Indicators of Gender and Income Equality

Country	*GDI, Time-consistent (2016)*	*Gini Coefficient*[1] *(scale 0–100)*	*Gross Secondary Enrollment*		*Labor Force Participation Rate (ages 15–64)*		*Maternal Mortality Ratio (per 100,000)*	*Legislation Exists on Domestic Violence*	*Married Men and Women Have Equal Ownership Rights to Property*
			Female-to-male ratio	*Female (percent)*	*Female-to-male ratio*	*Female (percent)*			
Australia	0.980	n.a.	n.a.	n.a.	0.84	60%	6	Yes	Yes
Bangladesh	0.907	32.39	1.10	72%	0.72	60%	176	Yes	Yes
Bhutan	0.908	37.44	1.10	88%	0.87	69%	148	Yes	Yes
Brunei Darussalam	0.967	n.a.	1.01	94%	0.76	56%	23	Yes	Yes
Cambodia	0.884	30.76	0.85	42%	0.89	77%	161	Yes	Yes
China	0.947	34.7	1.02	96%	0.83	66%	27	Yes	Yes
Hong Kong SAR, China	n.a.[2]	n.a.	0.97	101%	0.76	51%	n.a.	n.a.	n.a.
India	0.855	34.60	1.02	76%	0.36	29%	174	Yes	Yes
Indonesia	0.931	37.28	1.04	88%	0.64	53%	126	Yes	Yes
Japan	0.968	n.a.	n.a.	n.a.	0.72	51%	5	Yes	Yes
Korea, Rep.	0.944	n.a.	1.00	100%	0.71	50%	n.a.	n.a.	n.a.
Lao P.D.R.	0.918	36.39	0.93	64%	0.95	76%	n.a.	n.a.	n.a.
Macao SAR, China	0.992	n.a.	1.00	99%	0.86	66%	n.a.	n.a.	n.a.
Malaysia	0.957	40.3	1.06	88%	0.59	45%	40	Yes	Yes
Maldives	n.a.	37.34	1.17	75%	0.65	51%	68	Yes	Yes
Mongolia	1.017	32.35	1.07	95%	0.82	55%	44	Yes	Yes
Myanmar	n.a.	38.07	1.10	63%	0.88	70%	178	No	Yes
Nepal	0.908	32.84	1.07	72%	0.94	81%	258	Yes	Yes
New Zealand	0.983	23.6	1.06	118%	0.84	63%	11	Yes	Yes
Pakistan	0.757	33.45	0.81	41%	0.29	24%	178	Yes	Yes

(*Continued*)

Table 6.1A (Continued)

Country	*GDI, Time-consistent (2016)*	*Gini Coefficient*[1] *(scale 0–100)*	*Gross Secondary Enrollment*		*Labor Force Participation Rate (ages 15–64)*		*Maternal Mortality Ratio (per 100,000)*	*Legislation Exists on Domestic Violence*	*Married Men and Women Have Equal Ownership Rights to Property*
			Female-to-male ratio	*Female (percent)*	*Female-to-male ratio*	*Female (percent)*			
Papua New Guinea	n.a.	41.85	n.a.	n.a.	n.a.	n.a.	n.a.	n.a.	n.a.
Philippines	0.973	40.11	1.10	93%	0.60	46%	114	Yes	Yes
Singapore	0.967	n.a.	n.a.	n.a.	0.76	57%	10	Yes	Yes
Sri Lanka	0.940	40.41	n.a.	n.a.	0.48	35%	30	Yes	Yes
Thailand	0.988	35.99	0.99	118%	0.80	62%	20	Yes	Yes
Vietnam	n.a.	35.27	n.a.	n.a.	0.90	73%	54	Yes	Yes
Regional average	**0.937**	**35.548**	**1.02**	**0.841**	**0.73**	**0.563**	**94.263**		

Sources: World Bank, World Development Indicators database; World Bank, Women, Business and the Law (2015); Stotsky et al. (2016); and authors' calculations.

Note: Values are for 2016 or the latest year available.

[1] A higher Gini coefficient implies more inequality.
[2] Data are not available.

Table 6.2A Asian Fiscal Aggregates

Fiscal Aggregates[1] (average 2016–2019; unless otherwise indicated)[2] (percent of GDP)						
Country	*Total Revenue*	*Total Expenditure*	*Overall[3] Balance*	*Gross[4] Debt*	*Education[5] Expenditure*	*Health[5] Expenditure*
Australia	35.8	37.1	-1.3	40.9	5.3	9.2
Bangladesh	10.2	14.3	-4.2	34.8	1.8	2.4
Bhutan	26.6	26.0	0.6	103.2	6.8	3.5
Brunei Darussalam	22.3	32.3	-10.1	2.6	3.9	2.2
Cambodia	22.1	24.1	-2.0	29.5	1.9	6.3
China	28.9	34.4	-5.4	52.9	n.a.	4.9
Hong Kong SAR, China	20.6	18.9	1.7	0.0	3.4	n.a.
India	20.5	27.3	-6.8	69.4	3.8	3.6
Indonesia	14.9	16.7	-1.8	29.2	3.5	3.1
Japan	33.9	37.0	-3.0	237.3	3.5	10.9
Korea, Rep.	24.4	22.0	2.4	40.6	5.3	7.1
Lao PDR	16.2	20.9	-4.7	63.5	2.9	2.4
Macao SAR, China	32.1	18.0	14.2	n.a.	2.8	n.a.
Malaysia	19.6	23.0	-3.3	56.3	4.9	3.8
Maldives	26.6	31.7	-5.0	61.5	4.1	9.1
Mongolia	26.1	30.5	-4.4	n.a.	4.5	3.8
Myanmar	17.5	20.6	-3.1	38.7	1.1	5.1
Nepal	27.3	33.1	-5.8	31.8	4.3	6.1
New Zealand	37.3	37.0	0.2	28.7	6.3	9.3
Pakistan	15.1	22.0	-6.9	74.6	2.6	2.7
Papua New Guinea	17.5	20.2	-2.7	37.3	n.a.	2.7
Philippines	20.1	21.2	-1.1	39.4	n.a.	4.3
Singapore	21.4	17.3	4.1	108.9	2.9	4.2
Sri Lanka	14.3	19.3	-4.9	83.5	2.6	3.8
Thailand	21.4	21.6	-0.2	41.8	4.1	3.7
Vietnam	23.6	28.2	-4.6	57.5	5.7	5.7
Regional average	**22.9**	**25.2**	**-2.2**	**56.8**	**3.8**	**5.0**

Sources: World Economic Outlook (WEO); World Bank Development Indicators (WDI); and authors' calculations.

Notes:

[1] All figures except for health and education expenditure are drawn from the latest WEO publication, and the concept of government corresponds to that in the WEO. Please see the WEO for further details. Health and education expenditure are drawn from World Bank Development Indicators (WDI) and correspond to the general government concept.

[2] The figures are based on the average over the number of years in this period for which data were available.

[3] Corresponds to the concept of total revenue minus total expenditure.

[4] Gross debt does not net out holdings of debt by other entities of the government.

[5] The figures for education and health expenditure are based on 2014–2017 averages or the number of years for which data are available in this period. The 2017 data are the latest available.

7 Emerging markets and developing countries

A survey of gender budgeting efforts

I. Introduction

This chapter surveys gender budgeting in selected emerging markets and developing countries. Mexico, Morocco, and Ukraine have achieved notable success in their efforts to establish gender budgeting policies and programs. In addition, Argentina, Brazil, and Chile have achieved significant fiscal policy reforms in reaching gender-equality and anti-poverty goals, albeit outside the framework of gender budgeting.

Emerging markets and developing countries are diverse, both in terms of their economic and fiscal policy and managerial structures and in terms of the degree of gender equality that they have achieved. Thus, it is difficult to generalize about how they have approached or should approach gender budgeting. Nonetheless, they are generally at a stage where they have made sufficient progress on gender equality that the most pressing gender-related objectives, such as equalizing primary education enrollment and achieving high life expectancy, are within grasp. Hence, there is an opportunity to shift focus to achieving goals such as increasing women's labor supply, equalizing women's economic opportunities, or strengthening social safety nets for low-income or elderly women. As a result of the diversity of accomplishments among the countries in this category, the range of issues dealt with varies considerably from one country to another.

The countries selected for this chapter encompass those from three distinct regions of the world: North Africa, Eastern Europe, and Latin America. This points to the reality that gender budgeting efforts can take root in places with different cultural milieus and differing paths of economic development.

The specific countries reviewed in this chapter range from those on the lower end of middle income to the upper reaches of middle income, including two countries, Mexico and Chile, that became members of the Organization for Economic Co-operation and Development (OECD) in recent decades. The countries also differ greatly in their prevailing culture and background. Morocco is a predominantly Muslim country, which was a French colony and is thus heavily influenced by both Islamic and French traditions. Ukraine is an Eastern European country, which has largely been dominated by Russian

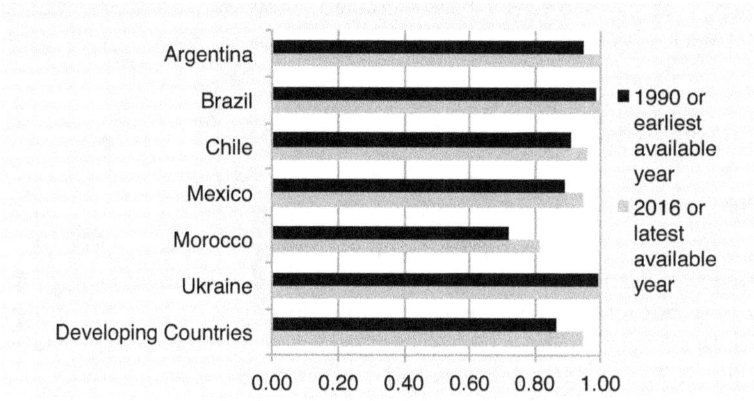

Figure 7.1 GDI, Time-Consistent Version

Sources: World Bank, World Development Indicators database; and authors' estimates.

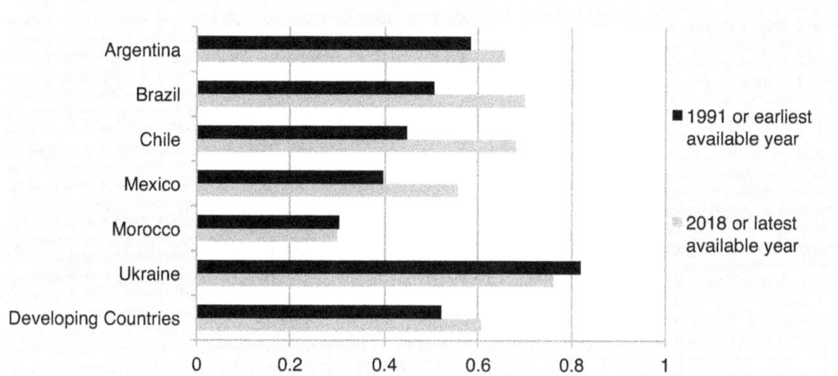

Figure 7.2 Employment (female-to-male ratio)

Sources: World Bank, World Development Indicators database; and authors' estimates.

influences and only briefly enjoyed independence throughout history. It was part of the Soviet Union's communist system until independence in 1991, when it began a transition to a market-based economy and democratic rule. The Latin American countries include Mexico and Brazil, which are diversified emerging markets but still struggle with pockets of underdevelopment, and Argentina and Chile, which face fewer problems of underdevelopment.

Figures 7.1 and 7.2 present some summary indicators of the progress of these countries relative to their peers in the same income group in both the GDI and the female-to-male employment ratio, respectively. We can see that all the countries improved their GDI score, especially Morocco. With respect to the employment ratio, performance was more mixed, and Ukraine's ratio declined, whereas Morocco's barely budged. However, the improvement in Latin America is notable.

II. Country case studies

Morocco[1]

Morocco is a middle-income developing country in North Africa that has achieved significant economic, social, and human development gains in recent years, with both women and men benefiting from this progress (World Bank, 2015a). In education, Morocco has significantly narrowed gender gaps in access for women. The female-to-male enrollment ratio for the primary level jumped from around 70 percent in the mid-90s to close to parity today. Similarly, the gender gap for secondary and tertiary education has narrowed significantly. Women have wider access to health care and have made progress in some health indicators, such as reproductive health. Meanwhile, other indicators, such as maternal mortality, remain poor.

Morocco has considerably reformed its legal frameworks, with the intent to enshrine gender equality in its laws (World Bank, 2015a; Constitute Project, 2012). The Constitution, revised in 2011, provides for equality of Moroccan citizens and obligates public bodies to promote liberty and equality for male and female citizens. The Moudawana (Family Code) was revised in 2004, expanding the rights of women in areas such as guardianship, marriage and child custody, and access to divorce. Nonetheless, polygamy and inequality in inheritance remain legal. Gender equality is enshrined in a number of key laws, including the (revised) Labor Code (2003), which mandates equal pay for equal work, and the Law on Nationality (2008), which allows children to inherit Moroccan citizenship from their mothers. In 2009, the government established a quota on women's representation in local government. Some institutions were established to implement the reforms, such as the Family Solidarity Fund and an enhanced family court system. In principle, women enjoy more freedom than ever before to travel, access employment and education, and negotiate marriage and divorce.

Nonetheless, Moroccan women continue to face significant obstacles to full equality in the economic, social, and political spheres (World Bank, 2015a). Legal equality continues to be undermined by weak implementation of laws, specifically when provisions for legal equality conflict with social norms. Women's labor force participation remains low and has hardly risen in recent years. Gender segregation in employment is pervasive, with women restricted to predominantly low-productivity sectors and low-skill occupations. The gender wage gap remains large (World Bank, 2015a). Although Morocco scores relatively high on measures of gender equality for the North Africa and Middle East region (World Bank, 2019), it compares unfavorably to the rest of the world.

Origins of gender budgeting

Gender budgeting has lagged as an initiative among countries in the Middle East and North Africa, even while gender inequality is pervasive in the region and gender gaps in employment are among the worst in the world. Morocco is notable for having a long-standing gender budgeting effort, initiated in 2002, when the government, under the leadership of the Ministry of Finance and Privatization, took steps to examine the "methodological feasibility of budgetary accounts for gender and childhood" (Chafiki and Touimi-Benjelloun, 2007).[2] The initiative was divided into two phases: the first, in 2003–2004, sought to introduce the idea to government ministries and develop tools for its implementation, and the second, in 2005–2008, attempted to institutionalize a gender report. One of Morocco's key objectives in undertaking gender budgeting was to improve its performance in meeting the United Nation's Millennium Development Goals. Early efforts focused on adapting sectoral budgets for the Ministry of Education and Training, Ministry of Health, and Ministry of Agriculture and Rural Development, to address these goals (UNIFEM, 2007). There was also an emphasis on increasing women's public employment and collecting sex-disaggregated data.

The publication of a gender budgeting handbook and the Gender Report accompanied the Finance Bill in 2005. The Prime Minister's Budget Circular letter for 2007 was the first to call upon the line ministries to include gender indicators in budget performance indicators. The Gender Report now covers most spending in the federal budget and is designed as an annex to the Economic and Financial Report to the annual Finance Bill presented to parliament (Morocco, Ministry of Economy and Finance, 2013). As a cornerstone of Morocco's gender budgeting initiative, the Gender Report highlights key priorities and targets for the various ministries, along with accomplishments.

In the 2008 Gender Report, the Ministry of Justice discussed the evolution of increased gender equality in family, penal, and nationality laws. The report highlights how the Ministry of Justice has created a gender unit and offers an analysis of gender-related goals in the budget. More recent reports include data on the share of women employed in each department as well as information on what percentage of women are in management positions. The reports serve as an accountability and monitoring tool (UN Women, 2014a).

The summary of the 2015 Gender Report assesses progress under the new Constitution and subsequent legislation and in establishing the new institutions designed to achieve gender equality. Areas of priority were combating violence against women and improving conditions of work and employment for domestic workers.

Morocco linked its gender budgeting initiative to its national development strategy. The Government Plan for Equality for 2012–2016 included 143 measures aimed at improving gender equality in education, health, and labor market opportunities and at increasing the social, political, and economic empowerment of women (Morocco, Ministry of Economy and Finances, 2013). The plan's key goals mirror several Millennium Development Goals, such as eliminating all discrimination and violence against women, providing equal access to health and education services, and appointing women to decision-making positions.

The introduction of gender budgeting was accompanied by supporting public financial management reforms to implement a performance-based budgeting system. A reformed organic finance law was adopted in 2014, with two key components designed to strengthen gender budgeting (Morocco, Ministry of Economy and Finances, 2015; UN Women, 2014b). First, the law requires that each budget program be associated with defined gender-related objectives as well as indicators to measure results. Second, the law requires that a gender report be included as part of each year's finance bill. Gender budgeting in Morocco still has a way to go to reach its objectives. Although the gender reports have evolved over time, they still lack strong accountability and a sufficiently close connection to the performance-based budgeting system.

Morocco continues to work with international organizations to strengthen its gender budgeting efforts. In 2013, UN Women established one of three Gender-responsive Budgeting Centers for Excellence in Morocco, based in the Ministry of Economy and Finance (UN Women, 2014c).

In the area of revenues, the World Bank (2015b) notes, Morocco is one of the 16 out of 173 countries that have a tax system that directly favors men through legal provisions of the tax code (El Bouazzaoui et al., 2010). This direct bias relates to Article 74, which provides a dependent deduction for men but not for women. That is, a male taxpayer may claim a deduction for his wife and dependent children, but unless a wife is able to prove legally that her husband and children are dependent on her, she may not claim a similar deduction. In addition, El Bouazzaoui et al. (2010) note that an implicit bias is that there are no deductions for child care, as is commonly found in income tax codes, which may hinder women's ability to fully participate in the workforce.

Practical outcomes

As we discussed in Chapter 3 on fiscal policies, labeled or conditional cash transfers can play an important role in gender budgeting programs. There we cited the work of Benhassine et al. (2015), who examined the impact of a labeled cash transfer for education. In this program, small sums of cash were transferred to fathers of school-age children in poor rural communities in Morocco, in order to encourage them to improve their children's participation in formal schooling. The authors found that these transfers produced significant gains in school participation and that adding conditionality (as opposed to just labeling the transfer for education) or targeting mothers as the recipient of the transfer made almost no difference in the outcomes. These results suggest that labeled or conditional cash transfers can boost enrollment, not only of boys but also of girls, in traditional societies where girls' enrollment lags. (See data summary in Figures 7.3–7.5.)

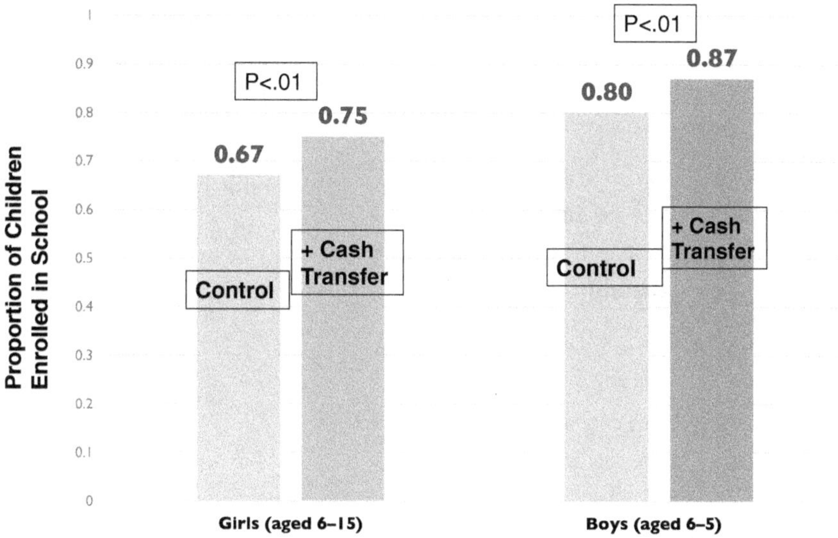

Figure 7.3 Labeled Cash Transfer Programs Boost School Enrollment of Boys and Girls
Source: Adapted from Benhassine, Devoto, Duflo, Dupas, and Pouliquen (2015).

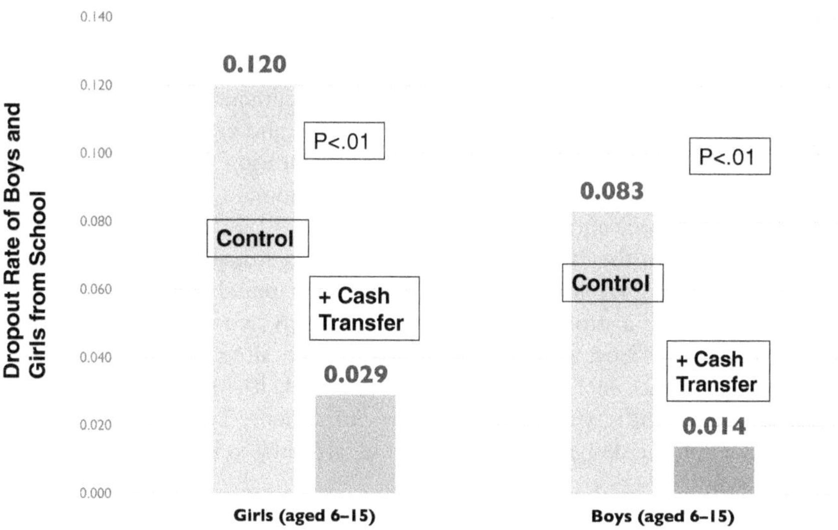

Figure 7.4 Labeled Cash Transfer Programs Reduce Dropout Rate of Boys and Girls
Source: Adapted from Benhassine, Devoto, Duflo, Dupas, and Pouliquen (2015).

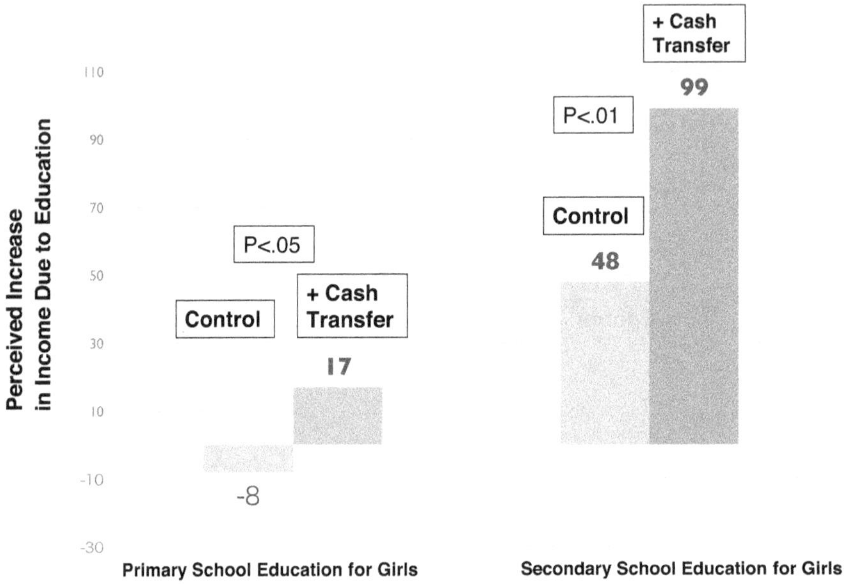

Figure 7.5 Labeled Cash Transfer Programs Influence Parental Attitude about the Value of Education, Especially for Girls

Source: Adapted from Benhassine, Devoto, Duflo, Dupas, and Pouliquen (2015).

The results of the cash transfer program described by Benhassine et al. (2015) show that the program increased end-of-year enrollment for boys and girls (Figure 7.3), reduced the dropout rate for both boys and girls (Figure 7.4), and influenced parental attitudes toward the value of education (Figure 7.5). Figure 7.5 shows that the existence of the cash transfer program encourages parents to view both primary and secondary education for girls as a vehicle for raising their income when they finish school (data for boys, not shown, also demonstrated a similar but smaller extent of influence on parental attitudes).

In societies with a strong cultural bias against girls, where girls' enrollment lags behind that of boys and is likely to do so even after applying a gender-neutral cash transfer such as the one just described, it should be possible to create further incentives to increasing girls' enrollment. These incentives can be embedded in the design of this type of a fiscal policy to help achieve gender equality goals.

Ukraine[3]

Ukraine is a middle-income country in Eastern Europe whose economy and institutions are still in transition from the Soviet era. One of Ukraine's major achievements is developing a national legislative framework on gender equality and in particular, the law On Ensuring Equal Rights and Opportunities of Women and Men, enacted in 2005 (Ukraine, 2014; Ukraine, Ministry of Finance, 2016). The passage of this law led to the further development of a national gender-equality legislative framework, including in the area of labor law and the civil code. The latest national and regional programs were developed from a collaboration between the government, nongovernmental organizations, and international organizations, on the basis of international best practices. Starting in 2001, the government began collecting sex-disaggregated data.

Women in Ukraine are more at risk of poverty as young adults because of child care responsibilities and in old age because of more limited pensions. Women also have a reduced ability to earn and borrow money, which limits their financial resources. Women constitute a disproportionate share of employees in some areas of the public sector and thus are at risk of bearing a heavy burden as these areas are retrenched. Minority women are also at risk, including Roma and those displaced from the Crimea. Other identified goals are in the area of improving women's and girls' education, where the principal concern is to reduce stereotyping, which prevents professional training for well-educated women, and infectious disease, which include the reduction of HIV/AIDS and tuberculosis. Additional goals include improving access to centralized water and reducing poverty, both of which were seen to have gender-specific dimensions (Ukraine, 2014). Health, in general, is seen as gender neutral. However, attention is focused on ensuring that lower-income women have equal access to high-quality health care and improving reproductive health care for all women and girls to bring them up to European standards.

Practical outcomes

In terms of early achievements, the most progress was made in bringing about a better balance of civil service employment between women and men, but less progress was made in closing the gender wage gap and in improving the proportion of women as elected representatives (Ukraine, 2014). In education, women's enrollment in secondary and higher education exceeds men's enrollment. In 2001, Ukraine was the first former Soviet country to develop a law on preventing violence against women in the family. Subsequent efforts are being made to bring this law and implementation up to European standards, including through social services for victims and domestic enforcement against offenders. Countering human trafficking is another element of this program.

The Ministry of Finance is currently leading a seven-year gender budgeting initiative, at the national and regional levels, which is being supported by the Swedish International Development Cooperation Agency (SIDA) (Schmitz, 2019). The principle goals of this effort are to support the development of methods and legislative documents to institutionalize gender budgeting and examine government funding for gender equality. In addition, a gender budgeting method has been issued as an Order of the Ministry of Finance: Order on Methodological Recommendations on Gender Budgeting for All Ministries and Agencies in Ukraine. Therefore, as of January 2019, all the ministries and agencies of Ukraine are expected to analyze their budget programs to assess their differential impact on women and men and to promote gender equality more broadly.

Latin America

Gender budgeting efforts in Latin America have been evolving for about 20 years and have taken varied forms. Most have focused on the expenditure side of the budget. However, a few have examined aspects of the tax system. Interestingly, given the importance of fiscal decentralization in the region, the efforts have focused on both the national and subnational levels, and some of the greatest successes have been achieved at the subnational level (Barba and Coello, 2017).

These initiatives have focused on various aspects of the budget process to institutionalize gender budgeting. Barba and Coello (2017) group initiatives into those that focus on the following:

1 Changing the regulatory and legal framework for the budget, including the organic or budget laws and budget call circulars;
2 Programming and budgeting formats, manuals, and guidelines;
3 Accounting and financial systems, including budget classification codes and budgetary reports;
4 Setting up institutional structures or mechanisms, including specific gender units within Ministries of Finance or Planning or their local and legislative equivalents.

Barba and Coello (2017)[4] reported, in their survey of 21 initiatives, chiefly those supported by UN Women, on achievements in a number of distinct areas. For example, two-thirds (14) were able to modify regulatory and legal frameworks, including in Ecuador, Bolivia, and Brazil, at times with significant support from civil society. Nine were able to change formats and manuals that are used to elaborate and implement programs and budgets; seven changed accounting and financial systems; five changed budget reports; and nine changed institutional structures. Of the nine that were able to change programming and budget formats, these initiatives most commonly led to formulating gender-related activities, results, and indicators and to defining specific budget allocations for gender-equality activities. Others led to elaborating a diagnosis of gender-related problems; disaggregating data by sex; and establishing links to a gender-related strategy.

Mexico[5]

Gender budgeting at the national level

Mexico has been a leader among countries in the region concerning gender budgeting initiatives. It has had two parallel gender budgeting initiatives at the national level. Since 2003, the national parliament, under the leadership of female parliamentarians, and El Instituto Nacional de las Mujeres (INMUJERES), the National Institute for Women, have worked to ensure that greater resources were devoted to policies and programs that address women's needs (United Nations Economic Commission for Latin America and the Caribbean, 2013; INMUJERES, 2010). Starting in 2008, the federal government earmarked and registered these resources in an annex of the Budget of the Federation.[6] The earmarked programs are dedicated mainly to women's health and economic empowerment programs. This earmarking is a considerable achievement in ensuring that resources are expended where they are assigned, even though the share of the budget earmarked for achieving equality between women and men remains small.

The second parallel gender budgeting initiative in Mexico started with a focus on health. In 2003, the Gender Equity, Citizenship, Work, and Family AC, a civil society organization, joined the Secretariat of Health to integrate gender into budget policies and programs in the health sector by using a method that entailed determining gender-related needs. They also determined whether an existing program or policy met those needs and what resources were needed to fund a government program (Pérez Fragoso and Rangel Granado, 2004). In 2004, a guide was developed to aid in the formulation of public budgets in the health sector by using a gender perspective.

This method was adapted to be applied across a wider range of the national government's spending areas and also to municipal budgets. INMUJERES promotes the aforementioned method, to integrate gender budgeting at the national level according to the following stages:

1 Government institutions prepare gender-related proposals with the help of INMUJERES.
2 These proposals are harmonized with sectoral programs, in accordance with the government's program for gender equality.
3 These programs are included in the budget proposal.
4 When the budget is adopted by Parliament, funds are allocated to each government institution based on the agreed-on programs.
5 The Secretariat of Finance and INMUJERES undertake quarterly monitoring for compliance.[7]

Legislative framework and institutional basis

In 2006, the Mexican Parliament adopted the federal Budget and Financial Responsibility Law, which stipulates that the administration of public resources be based on a number of criteria, including gender equality. This law provides guidelines for how gender-related considerations can be incorporated into all aspects of the budget. Article 17 states that it is necessary to ensure that budget planning incorporates a gender perspective and that the budget complies with programs, projects, and actions promoting gender equality.

In 2006, a law on Equality between Women and Men was enacted, which stipulates, in Article 12, that the national government budget allocate resources for compliance with the National Policy on Equality and No Discrimination against Women. In 2007, the promotion of gender equality and the authority of INMUJERES to deliver quarterly reports on the actions promoting women were also incorporated into the Budget Decree on Expenditure of the Federation. These laws helped institutionalize gender budgeting in the budget law and regulatory framework (United Nations Economic Commission for Latin America and the Caribbean, 2013). The Law on Planning entered into force in June 2011 and guarantees equality of opportunity between women and men. There is work to extend its main parameters, requiring analysis of differentiated impact on women and men and programs formulated from a gender perspective, across the country, with assistance from INMUJERES (INMUJERES-UNWOMEN, 2015).

Mexico DF (Mexico City)

In 2007, Mexico City launched a continuing gender budgeting initiative (INMUJERES DF (2013). The strength of the initiative is the cooperation among the Secretariat of Finance from the city, which is responsible for preparing the budgets, and the Mexico City Institute for Women (INMUJERES Ciudad de Mexico), and the organization Gender Equity, Citizenship, Work and Family AC.

In 2008, Mexico City's government issued Budget with Equity. Its first few pages were dedicated to explaining gender budgeting and provided programs focused on and resources allocated to gender equality. The Secretariat of Finance, whose support was critical, committed to integrating a gender perspective in the process of planning, programming, and budgeting.[8] Each of the departments in the government was asked to include in its budget some policy, program, or action leading to gender equality.

Gender budgeting in Mexico City has continued to evolve. The number of programs, participating agencies, and resources allocated has generally increased over time, even while the spending share of these programs has continued to represent only a small part of Mexico City's budget (INMUJERES DF, 2016). In this way, most government departments have at least one program directed to addressing gender inequality. In the 2015 budget, the main programs were for the following (INMUJERES DF, 2016):

- i) Women's employment, self-employment, economic empowerment, and specifically for migrant and young women's employment;
- ii) Strengthening legal and social services for women and discouraging the use of gender stereotypes in radio and television;
- iii) Social services for women in vulnerable situations, with application to indigenous women, women in prison, women with drug addictions, and female-headed households.

Practical outcomes

Among the most important results of Mexico City's gender budgeting is that public transport buses exclusively for women were set up in conjunction with the Viajemos Seguras (Let's Travel Safely) Program. This program ensures that women can travel safely around the city, which is essential for their integration into work life. Similarly, security was increased on the public metro system (subway) and on the other transport systems in the city. In addition, programs were put in place to address violence against women and to provide legal advice, shelters, and psychological counseling programs to aid victims.

Conclusions from the Mexican experience

Some lessons from the Mexican experience hold true for other middle-income countries, such as Brazil (discussed next), and for low-income countries discussed in Chapters 5 and 6.

The Mexican government, at both the national and the subnational levels, has supported the notion that gender equality can be achieved through fiscal policies. Mexico has led Latin America in embodying gender budgeting in budget legislation and processes and has spearheaded the development of tools for budget analysis and preparation. The participation of the Ministry of Finance, Parliament, and civil organizations is a notable achievement and has helped to ensure the success of the initiatives across federal and state levels.[9]

However, INMUJERES has concluded that gender budgeting has not yet lived up to its promise, because there is an insufficient institutional capacity to monitor and assess programs, not enough of the government's budget has incorporated a gender perspective, and the national and state laws lack harmonization in terms of objectives and approach.[10]

As in the case of Morocco, conditional cash transfer programs have been executed and seem to produce positive outcomes, though on a limited scale. Such programs could be expanded to play a more important role in gender budgeting programs. In Chapter 3, we cited an example of this type of initiative from the work of Attanasio, Meghir, and Santiago (2011), who examined the impact of a Mexican conditional cash transfer program called PROGRESA. This program, introduced in 1998, provided cash transfers to poor rural families conditional on specific behaviors, for the purpose of improving nutrition, health, and education. Mothers in the poorest households in a set of targeted villages were given grants to keep their children in school. They found that the program had a positive effect on child enrollment, especially after primary school. The design drew on the specific culture of Mexico, where mothers were viewed as likely to make the best decisions with regard to spending on children. This is an example of a fiscal policy taking advantage of a prevailing cultural norm to promote social progress.

Brazil

Brazil has a long history of governments, at different levels, undertaking budget analysis for the purpose of strengthening civil society. As part of this process, Brazil has launched a number of gender budgeting initiatives, with a significant innovation being the integration of gender budgeting and citizenship training through the development of participatory budgets.

The oldest gender budgeting initiatives in the Latin American region were carried out in Brazil.[11] The city of Recife has been doing participatory budgeting with a gender perspective from 2001 onward.[12] The city established the Coordinating Committee for Women in 2001 to advance gender equality and encourage higher female participation in democracy (UNIFEM, 2008). In 2010, the Women's Secretariat was created as a substitute for the Coordinating Committee, and in 2011, its budget was substantially expanded to address women's issues.

At the national level, a project by the civil organization CFEMEA (Feminist Center for Research and Advice) led to an annual analysis of the budget, which was conducted from 2002 to 2012. It systematically organized information on about 60 programs of the federal government to examine how public expenditures were addressing gender inequality, and it was called the Women's Budget (Coello, 2015). Information generated in the Women's Budget was used by civil society, feminist groups, and various groups and committees in the government to integrate gender perspectives into public policies and monitor resources for women's advancement.

Practical outcomes

The main success of these various gender budgeting initiatives in Brazil was that they strengthened civil society and brought together women to participate in citizens' activities. It is less clear how successful gender budgeting has been in Brazil, in bringing about fiscal policy changes and measurable improvements in social and economic outcomes.

As with Morocco and Mexico, conditional cash transfers could be better integrated into gender budgeting in Brazil. As we observed in Chapter 3, De Brauw et al. (2014) examined the effect of a Brazilian variant of a conditional cash transfer program called Bolsa Familia, on women's decision-making power. The power of female decision-making can be an important lever through which fiscal policies can effect change. Bolsa Familia was specifically designed with women as the recipient. Poor families received a combination of unconditional and conditional transfers on the basis of the conditions that pregnant women receive timely prenatal care, children ages zero to five receive timely vaccinations and growth monitoring, and all children ages six to 15 attend school. They found that Bolsa Familia had a significant impact on women's decision-making but had heterogeneous effects across households, and the main positive effects were in urban areas. They concluded that where the program led to benefits, both in spheres related to child-rearing and women's own welfare, it led to greater equity.

Argentina

Although its own gender budgeting initiatives were not sustained, in the last few years, Argentina has adopted far-reaching laws and programs with gender-related implications, including conditional cash transfers.[13] These efforts have produced practical results as reviewed next, even in the absence of well-developed gender budgeting procedures being implemented at the government level.

Examples of initiatives with gender-related implications and practical outcomes

The Universal Child Allowance, implemented at the end of 2009, and the Pregnancy Benefit, added in 2011, were intended to assist low-income women. These benefits were specifically aimed at the unemployed or those working in the informal economy and/or in unregistered domestic service, who have minor children and who must meet their children's health requirements to attend school. The Universal Child Allowance is paid to the mother, except when the father can demonstrate that he has custody of the child, and funded by the to Argentina's Social Security Administration. This policy has been perceived to have made a significant difference in supporting the income of low-income women and their households.

The Social Security Inclusion Plan and the 2007 Law on Early Retirement and Social Contribution Moratorium were intended to address poverty among older people. These measures provided access under the social security system to over two million women who did not have sufficient contributions registered for a social security benefit, thereby significantly expanding the rate of coverage.

The PROGRESAR program provides a stipend to young people for secondary education. It is estimated that 60 percent of the beneficiaries were women. The Work and Social Income Program—Argentina Trabaja—includes a component program called Ellas Hacen (Women in Action), engaging 100,000 female participants, which provides money for women to organize in cooperatives to provide services (mostly social services at the local level) or to manufacture small products (e.g., baked goods, candles, etc.). More than 60 percent of the participants in the National Foundation for Microcredit are female.

Conclusions from the Argentine experience

Over the past 15 years, Argentina has instituted a number of programs and policies and although not specifically designated as "women" or "gender-equality" initiatives, the results of these programs seem to have significantly and positively affected the lives of millions of women at different stages of life. Helping young women seeking to obtain an education, helping women with children searching for child care so that they may enter the labor force, or helping older women requiring income support are all examples of initiatives undertaken by the government through budget expenditure. Yet none of these programs required a separate gender budgeting exercise or rationale.

Chile

Similar to Argentina, Chile has not found success through a formal gender budgeting initiative. Nonetheless, early on, there were civil society organizations that examined budgets from a gender-equality perspective. Over time, the government has adopted policies that have gender-specific implications and have benefited women and gender equality, including with conditional cash transfers.

One notable achievement was in a program of public financial management reform, called Program for Improvement of Management (PMG) (Chile, Directorate of the Budget, 2014). This initiative was designed to promote a cross-cutting gender focus. The PMG, dating back to 1998 and lasting until 2014, paid bonuses to civil servants, both male and female, up to 4 percent of their salaries if their institution achieved agreed-on management objectives.[14] The early objectives were not gender related, but subsequently, these were added in areas of management of public service provision.

Guerrero Caviedes (2005) concludes that adding gender-related objectives to the PMG has been positive in two ways. First, it led to the development of a series of measures that have represented a step forward in gender equality, including the dissemination of information broken down by sex and the production of specific studies with a gender focus.[15] Such studies include programs providing health services to adolescents and assessments on how traffic solutions impact women and men differently.

Chile has also enacted some public policies that directly contributed to improving women's lives and gender equality. Among these is a program for early child care services (salas cunas), targeting the vulnerable population within the program with Chile Crece Contigo. This program targets children under age 12 living in households in vulnerable social conditions. It includes a variety of components, among which access to early child care services is one of the most important, not only for improving children's human capital but also for contributing to their mothers' work–life balance. These programs are thought to have had a beneficial impact on women's ability to enter or stay in the labor market.

Chile Solidario is another example of such a fiscal policy. Implemented in 2002, it involves support to the poorest—both male and female—who are assisted through a package of interventions that combine a moderate cash transfer for health, education, and employment services, as well as social and psychological counseling. The employment component of the program provides three types of support to foster adult participation in the labor market (Scarlato, D'Agostino, and Capparucci, 2016):

1 Job placement assistance programs, mainly job training and wage subsidies;
2 Self-employment programs and support for microenterprises, based on a combination of technical assistance and funding for inputs and startup capital;
3 Employability programs, ranging from adult education to soft-skills training.

Overall, the impact of this program in fostering adult economic participation has been positive. The program is viewed as successful in removing structural barriers to women's participation that are linked to child care access and assistance with caregiving within the household (Henriquez and Reca, 2005; Scarlato, D'Agostino, and Capparucci, 2016).

III. Conclusions

Country-specific outcomes

As this chapter has shown, the experience of gender budgeting and, more broadly, creating fiscal policies and management practices that are oriented toward achieving gender equality vary considerably across middle-income countries. In some countries, policies and programs have been instituted explicitly under the banner of gender budgeting and equality. In other countries, notably Argentina and Chile, successful policies have been carried out in response to a clear social need without labeling the policy or program as a "gender-related" initiative.

The case study on Morocco shows how a structured budget process can raise awareness about using budget programming to achieve gender equality in a society that is still traditional in its mores and family life. However, it has been difficult to discern how much real success has occurred in closing gender gaps, which remain substantial in Morocco, more so than in most middle-income countries and certainly in those outside North Africa and the Middle East.

Ukraine provides another example of a country where gender-equality practices are being institutionalized in budgeting, at both national and subnational levels, with a promise to build on an egalitarianism inherited from communist institutions of the past that are still in transition. Gender gaps in Ukraine are not as substantial as in Morocco, but the country faces many challenges in making effective use of the labor market potential of women and addressing other areas in which women remain at a disadvantage.

In Latin America, Mexico and Brazil represent examples of countries still trying to grapple with fundamental issues of underdevelopment. These issues include gender gaps in health-care access, education for low-income children, and safe transportation for women in the workforce. Some of these issues have been addressed through initiatives at the budget level or at the level of practical implementation, but in many cases, laws promoting or requiring gender equality are not translated into effective policies or programs. Argentina and Chile are more-developed countries similar to those in Europe and North America (albeit with lower incomes), and we see fiscal policies outside of gender budgeting frameworks addressing issues such as poverty alleviation, elderly women without strong work histories, and support for child care. In the absence of explicit gender budgeting initiatives and explicit laws on gender equality, these two countries have implemented programs that provide needed social services to women.

Overall outcomes for these emerging market and developing countries

Generally, we see in these countries that have already made the transition to emerging market and middle-income economies a change in the nature of women's needs, relative to those in poorer developing countries. In most of the economies discussed in this chapter, women comprise a substantial percentage

Table 7.1 Gender-Related Problems Increasingly Common in Emerging Market and Developing Countries

Circumstance Causing the Problem	*Social or Economic Problem Produced*
Young women want or need to work while rearing children	Lack of child care
Growth in proportion of women who are divorced or have children out of wedlock	Poverty and social problems caused by single mothers with children and low income
Older women without a well-developed or sufficient work history	Insufficient pension income

Source: Author.

of formal, paid employment. The gender-related challenges listed in Table 7.1 start to appear in countries that reach middle-income status with highly urbanized populations and near-universal literacy for both men and women and where traditional family life and mores have already started to erode.

The problems that women face in the more developed of these societies (e.g., Ukraine, Argentina, and Chile) reflect a combination of historical patterns of gender-based discrimination common in traditional societies and increasingly reflect gender-related concerns resulting from changing patterns of work, longer life spans, changing mores regarding marriage, and the decline of extended family and communal support systems. All of these factors make it more difficult for women, vis-à-vis men, to balance the demands of work life with child-rearing and other caregiving responsibilities. In addition, due to truncated and often-less-developed careers, women do not have the opportunity to earn the same pension income as men do and may face old age being single with financial burdens after retirement.

These are the problems of the developed world (see Chapter 8), but they now appear already in countries such as those in this chapter that are not yet fully developed.

Notes

1 This case study has benefited from Kolovich and Shibuya (2016).
2 Morocco's initiative was also part of UNIFEM's Global Gender-Responsive Budgeting Program, which was in effect between 2002 and 2008 (UN Women, 2009).
3 This case study has benefited from Quinn (2016).
4 Barba and Coello (2017, pp. 121–126).
5 This section largely drew from Pérez Fragoso and Rodríguez Enríquez (2016).
6 In Mexico, the track record on expenditures being spent on their intended purpose is weak, and therefore, earmarking makes it more likely that expenditures will be spent as intended.
7 INMUJERES' answer to the IMF questionnaire, unpublished, 2015.
8 INMUJERES DF (2010).
9 Ibid.
10 INMUJERES DF (2016).
11 The Municipality of Santo Andre developed during 1997–2000 a budget using racial and gender disaggregation as an analytical tool (UNIFEM, 2008).

12 Coello (2015) and UN Women in their answer to the IMF survey, unpublished (2015).
13 Government of Argentina response to IMF survey, unpublished (2015).
14 *Programas de Mejoramiento de la Gestión PMG: Evolución 2011–2014 y Desafíos Futuros* (Chile, Directorate of the Budget, 2014), as well as the information on the PMG presented on the web page of the Directorate of the Budget: www.dipres.gob.cl/594/w3-article-37413.html.
15 Examples include a study of the impact of a program of provision of electricity in rural areas, conducted by the National Commission for Energy, a study on preferred working areas for women in fisheries, conducted by the Undersecretariat for Fisheries, and a study on labor norms related to occupational diseases, conducted by the Undersecretariat for Social Welfare.

References

Attanasio, Orazio P., Costas Meghir, and Ana Santiago, 2011, "Education Choice in Mexico: Using a Structural Model and a Randomized Experiment to Evaluate PROGRESA," *Review of Economic Studies*, Vol. 79, pp. 37–66.

Barba, Lorena, and Raquel Coello, 2017, "Gender-Responsive Budgeting in Latin America: Regional Learning to Advance Financing for Gender Equality," in Zohra Khan and Nalini Burn, eds., *Financing for Gender Equality: Realising Women's Rights through Gender Responsive Budgeting* (London: Palgrave Macmillan), pp. 105–140.

Benhassine, Najy, Florencia Devoto, Esther Duflo, Pascaline Dupas, and Victor Pouliquen, 2015, "Turning a Shove Into a Nudge? A 'Labeled Cash Transfer' for Education," *American Economic Journal: Economic Policy*, Vol. 7, pp. 86–125.

Chafiki, Mohamed, and Zineb Touimi-Benjelloun, 2007, "Gender Responsive Budgets in Morocco: Illustration of the Paris Declaration Alignment and Ownership Principles," UNICEF. Available at: www.unicef.org/policyanalysis/files/Morocco_GR_budgets.pdf.

Chile, Directorate of the Budget, 2014, *Programas de Mejoramiento de la Gestión: PMG Evolución 2011–2014 y Desafíos Futuros* (*Programs to Improve Management: PMG Evolution 2011–2014 and Future Challenges*) (Santiago: Government of Chile).

Coello, Raquel, 2015, *Presupuestos con Perspectiva de Género en América Latina: una Mirada desde la Economía Institucionalista y Feminista* (*Budgets with a Gender Perspective in Latin America: A Look from the Institutional and Feminist Economy*). Tesis. Doctoral. Universidad Complutense de Madrid (Madrid).

Constitute Project, 2012, "Morocco's Constitution of 2011," Available at: www.constituteproject.org/constitution/Morocco_2011.pdf.

de Brauw, Alan, Daniel O. Gilligan, John Hoddinott, and Shalini Roy, 2014, "The Impact of Bolsa Familia on Women's Decision-Making Power," *World Development*, Vol. 59, pp. 487–504.

El Bouazzaoui, Ahmed, Abdessalam Fazouane, Hind Jalal, and Salama Saidi, 2010, "Gender Equality and Taxation in Morocco," in Caren Grown and Imraan Valodia, eds., *Taxation and Gender Equality: A Comparative Analysis of Direct and Indirect Taxes in Developing and Developed Countries* (New York: Routledge and IDRC), pp. 179–205.

Guerrero Caviedes, Elizabeth, 2005, *Transversalización de la Perspectiva de Género en Chile: En la Búsqueda de la Equidad* (*Cross-Cutting of the Gender Perspective in Chile: The Quest for Equity*), Tenth Congress of the Latin American Center for Development, Santiago de Chile, October.

Henriquez, H., and I. Reca, 2005, "Propuestas Para Fortalecer los Componentes de Genero en el Sistema de Protección en Chile Solidario (Proposals for Strengthening the Components of Gender in the System of Protection in Chile Solidario)," in Veronica Riquelme and Maria Elena Valenzuela, eds., *Chile Solidario y los Desafíos de la Igualdad: Proyecto Genero, Pobreza y Empleo* (*Chile Solidario and the Challenges of Equality: Gender Projects, Poverty, and Employment*) (Chile: ILO and UNDP), pp. 77–156.

INMUJERES DF, 2010, *Guía Básica para la Elaboración de Políticas, Programas y Presupuestos desde la Perspectiva de Género* (*Basic Guide for the Preparation of Policies, Programs, and Budgets from a Gender Perspective*) (Mexico: INMUJERES).

INMUJERES DF, 2013, *Programa General de Igualdad de Oportunidades y No Discriminación hacia las Mujeres en la Ciudad de México 2013–2018* (*General Program for Equality of Opportunity and Nondiscrimination against Women in Mexico City 2013–2018*) (Mexico: INMUJERES).

INMUJERES DF, 2016, *Análisis de Presupuesto 2008–2015, documento interno* (*Budget Analysis 2008–2015, Internal Document*) (Mexico: INMUJERES).

INMUJERES-UN Women, 2015, *Presupuestos con Perspectiva de Género en el Nivel Federal y Estatal en México* (*Budgets with a Gender Perspective at the Federal and State Level in Mexico*) (Mexico: INMUJERES-UN Women).

Kolovich, Lisa, and Sakina Shibuya, 2016, "Middle East and Central Asia: A Survey of Gender Budgeting Efforts," IMF Working Paper 16/151 (Washington, DC: IMF).

Morocco, Ministry of Economy and Finances, 2013, *Governmental Plan for Gender Equality (2012–2016) [PowerPoint slides]*. Available at: www.slideshare.net/Gobernabilidad/2-presentation-marocco-eng.

Morocco, Ministry of Economy and Finances, 2015, *Summary of the Gender Report 2015*. Unpublished. English.

Pérez Fragoso, Lucia, and Rosalio L. Rangel Cranado, 2004, *Guía para la Formulación de Presupuestos Públicos con Enfoque de Género en el Sector Salud* (*Guide for the Formulation of Public Budgets with a Gender Focus in the Health Sector*), Secretariat of Health; Fundar, Centro de Análisis e Investigación (Fundar, Center for Analysis and Research); Foro Nacional de Mujeres y Políticas de Población (National Forum for Women and Population Policies); Equidad de Género (Gender Equity): Citizenship, Work, and Family AC (Mexico: UNIFEM).

Pérez Fragoso, Lucia, and Corina Rodríguez Enríquez, 2016, "Western Hemisphere: A Survey of Gender Budgeting Efforts," IMF Working Paper 16/153 (Washington, DC: IMF).

Quinn, Sheila, 2016, "Europe: A Survey of Gender Budgeting Efforts," IMF Working Paper 16/155 (Washington, DC: IMF).

Scarlato, Margherita, Giorgio D'Agostino, and Francesca Capparucci, 2016, "Evaluating CCTs from a Gender Perspective: The Impact of Chile Solidario on Women's Employment Prospects," *Journal of International Development*, Vol. 28, pp. 177–197.

Schmitz, Catharina, 2019, "Budgeting for Gender Equality," Available at: www.niras.com/development-consulting/projects/gender-responsive-budgeting-in-ukraine/.

Ukraine, 2014, "National Review of Implementation of the Beijing Declaration and Platform for Action (1995) and the Outcomes of the Twenty-Third Special Session of the General Assembly (2000) in the Context of the Twentieth Anniversary of the Fourth World Conference on Women and the Adoption of the Beijing Declaration and Platform for Action (2015)," Available at: www.unece.org/fileadmin/DAM/Gender/publications_and_papers/NV111.07_att1_att2_att3_merged.pdf.

Ukraine, Ministry of Finance, 2016, "Summary of Gender Budget Analysis of Programs Financed by the State and Local Budgets in Ukraine in 2016," Available at: grbproject.org/wp-content/uploads/2017/04/Summary-email-eng.pdf.

UNIFEM, 2007, *Highlights of Best Practice from Morocco* (New York: UNIFEM).

UNIFEM, 2008, *Aportes a los Presupuestos Sensibles al Género. Experiencias de Argentina, Brasil, Chile y Uruguay* (*Contributions to Gender Responsive Budgets: Experiences of Argentina, Brazil, Chile, and Uruguay*) (Brazil: Cuadernos de Diálogos).

United Nations Economic Commission for Latin America and the Caribbean (ECLAC), 2013, *El Gasto Etiquetado para las Mujeres y la Igualdad de Género en México. Un Avance para Garantizar la Autonomía de las Mujeres* (*Earmarked Expenditure for Women and Gender Equality in Mexico: Progress to Guarantee the Autonomy of Women*) (New York: United Nations).

UN Women, 2009, *Evaluation Report: UNIFEM's Work on Gender-Responsive Budgeting Gender-Responsive Budgeting Programme: Morocco* (New York: UNIFEM).

UN Women, 2014a, "Morocco's Successful Case in Implementing Gender Responsive Budget" (New York: UN Women).

UN Women, 2014b, "Budgets Respond to the Needs of Women in Morocco" (New York: UN Women).

UN Women, 2014c, *GRB Regional Centers of Excellence: Knowledge Hubs on Gender Responsive Planning and Budgeting* (New York: UN Women).

World Bank, 2015a, *Morocco Mind The Gap: Empowering Women for a More Open, Inclusive and Prosperous Society* (Washington, DC: World Bank).

World Bank, 2015b, *Women, Business and the Law 2016: Getting to Equal* (Washington, DC: World Bank).

World Bank, 2019, *Women, Business and the Law 2019: A Decade of Reform* (Washington, DC: World Bank).

8 Developed countries

A survey of gender budgeting efforts[1]

I. Introduction

Gender budgeting originated in Australia, before spreading to the rest of the world (Sharp and Broomhill, 2002). But it has most readily been adopted in Europe. Some countries, such as Austria, have incorporated gender budgeting into the constitution. This chapter summarizes a few examples of the development of gender budgeting in developed countries, in order to provide a range of experiences that demonstrate useful role models for other countries. This chapter is not a comprehensive overview but draws on examples from three continents, demonstrating the breadth of efforts to promote gender budgeting or other pathways to gender equality in developed economies. O'Hagan and Klatzer (2018) and Quinn (2016) provide excellent overviews with case studies from Europe. Downes, von Trapp, and Nicol (2017) provide an analysis of an Organization for Economic Co-operation and Development (OECD) survey of member countries on gender budgeting efforts. In this chapter, we focus on Canada, Austria, Belgium, Sweden, and the Republic of Korea (Korea).

Austria is a world leader in gender budgeting, setting an example for developed countries. Its own experience demonstrates the importance of strong legislative backing and performance-based budgeting as factors in institutionalizing gender budgeting at the policy level. However, even in this case, where a strong gender budgeting framework exists, it has not been sufficient to generate strong results. Some suggestions on improving the process are offered, drawn from the Austrian experience. In the case of Canada, we also find some new developments.

Figures 8.1 and 8.2 present some summary indicators of progress of these countries relative to their peers in the same income group in both the GDI and the female-to-male employment ratio, respectively. We can see that all the countries improved their GDI score, especially Austria and Korea. With respect to the employment ratio, again, all the countries improved, most notably Austria and Belgium.

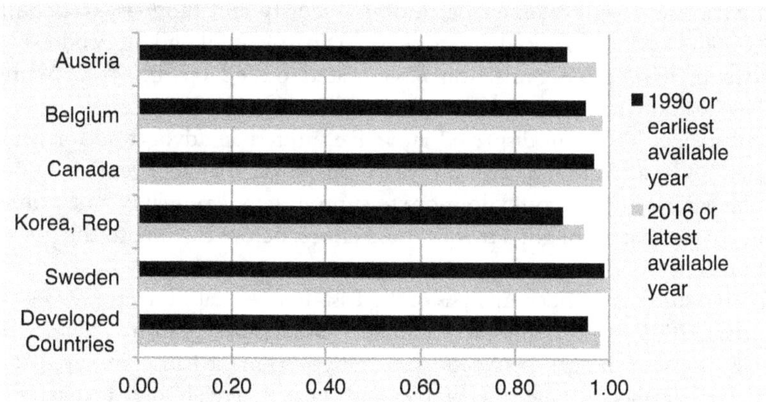

Figure 8.1 GDI, Time-Consistent Version

Sources: World Bank, World Development Indicators database; and authors' estimates.

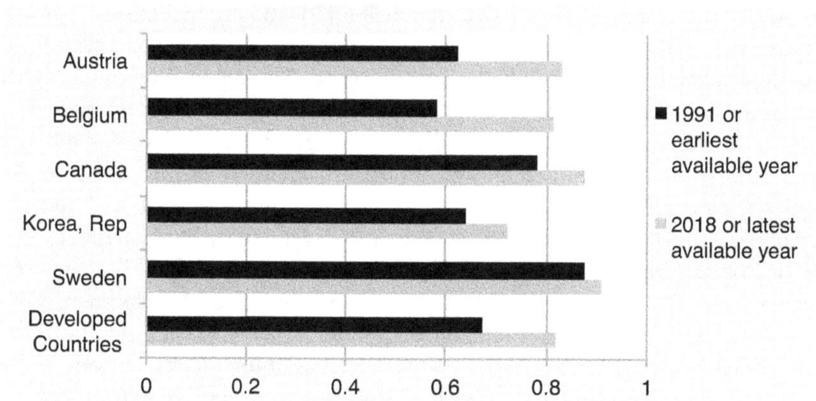

Figure 8.2 Employment (female-to-male ratio)

Sources: World Bank, World Development Indicators database; and authors' estimates.

II. Country case studies

Canada

Canada has long had formal mechanisms within the government for promoting the equality of women, although it has only recently enhanced the status of these efforts through the adoption of a formal gender budgeting initiative in the 2018 budget. The organization Status of Women Canada, established in 1971, served as an advocate for gender equality within the government, with priority attached to improving women's economic security and prosperity, encouraging women's leadership and democratic participation, and ending gender-based violence. In 2018, this organization was elevated to the Department for Women and Gender Equality.

Civil society also long displayed an active interest in advocating for gender equality in Canada and has, over the years, produced several cogent analyses on how the federal budget could do more to support gender equality and women's advancement. We highlight a few of these efforts before turning to the government's recent initiative.

An early study, A Gender Analysis of the Last Ten Federal Budgets (1995–2004) (Yalnizyan, 2005), was the first to examine Canada's budget from a gender perspective, assessing the gap between what the government had committed to do for gender equality through the budget and what it actually did. It divides this period into 1995–1997, called the deficit era, and 1998–2004, the surplus era. It concluded that the budget cuts of the deficit period were not offset by catch-up during the surplus period. The report cites the government for failing to support the most vulnerable through budget programs, during this 10-year period. A few tax measures, introduced from 1998, were helpful to women, including tax credits for caregivers and increased tax deductions for expenses on child care, but these benefited women only if they had taxable income. The report advocated higher spending to provide room in the budget to address health, post-secondary education, child care, social assistance, and other needs viewed as critical to women. The report also recommended that the government strengthen its analysis of benefit incidence by gender, to analyze the gender-differentiated impact of the budget.

Another initiative, the Alternative Federal Budget, led by the Canadian Centre for Policy Alternatives, provides regular analysis of the federal budget from a gender-equality perspective (Canadian Centre for Policy Alternatives, various years).[2] The 2015 report's chapter on gender equality highlighted both the gains of women in Canada and the continued areas of inequality. On one hand, there is a high level of post-secondary education and a high life expectancy for women, but there are also large gaps in these metrics for indigenous women. The report noted that women remain underrepresented in leadership roles, and women's poverty level remains consistently higher than men's poverty level. Violence against women remains high, and the burden of unpaid work has shifted only slightly toward men. Unpaid work at home limits the ability of women to participate in paid work, where rates of pay remain unequal. The report recommended concerted actions to address violence against women and investment in social infrastructure, including child care and other ways to increase women's access to jobs in growth sectors. It suggested changes to the tax code as well, providing a more level playing field for female income earners.[3]

Canada's new commitment to formal gender budgeting

More recently, the government has dedicated itself to comprehensive analysis and action on gender equality, including through a specific commitment to gender budgeting (Canada, 2019). In terms of fiscal policies and public financial management, the government's commitment entails including a gender statement in the federal budget to examine the gender impact of budget measures; increasing women in STEM fields, skilled trade, and other well-paying fields; investing in women-led businesses; launching a new parental sharing benefit to support a more equitable distribution of child care within the home; addressing the gender wage gap; strengthening the Canada Child Benefit so that it helps the most needy families; and investing in the National Housing Strategy, with at least 25 percent supporting women, girls, and their families. Other commitments include reducing gender-based violence, gender equality for LGBTQ2, and participating actively in efforts to support gender equality in various international forums in which Canada participates. Finally, it entails a commitment to increasing women's leadership in the civil service and corporate governance and increasing the budget of Status of Women Canada.

Scott (2019) assessed these efforts as significant and commends the 2019 budget for building on initiatives and targeting areas to advance gender equality, including increasing government funding. However, she still rates these efforts as falling short on investments in child care, pay equity, and poverty reduction. She commends the government's Gender Report and its budget documentation, for its effort to identify those women expected to benefit from government policy.

In the Canadian experience, a high GDI and a high female-to-male employment ratio were achieved throughout the study period (1990 to 2018) even without any formal gender budgeting commitment by the national government. Such a commitment was made only in 2018, starting with the 2019 budget cycle. This outcome demonstrates that there is a high gender-equality consciousness in the broader Canadian culture, backed by strong civil society organizations constantly advocating for women's needs. This seems to have been the key factor that has led to the positive gender-equality results shown in the charts.

Austria

Austria is a global leader in establishing gender budgeting as an integral part of the overall framework of government budgets. Its most notable feature is the constitutional and legislative underpinnings for gender budgeting, its integration into Austria's performance-budgeting framework, and the strong support for these efforts by top officials in the Ministry of Finance (Schratzenstaller, 2014). Austria introduced the concept of "effective" equality between men and women and required that all new laws, regulations and directives, as well as other large government projects, be assessed for their gender impact (Schratzenstaller, 2014). The comprehensiveness of this gender budgeting in Austria should in principle make it institutionally robust and effective.

History of gender budgeting in Austria

Klatzer, Brait, and Schlager (2018), Quinn (2016), Fritz (2011), and Frey and Kohnen (2012) provide the history of Austrian gender budgeting. Gender budgeting acquired formal standing in March 2004, when the Ministry of Finance issued guidelines announcing the goal of applying gender mainstreaming to all budgetary measures and requesting all government departments to nominate pilot projects. The resultant analysis was included in the budget documentation and in the legislative texts relating to the federal Finance Acts for the budgets 2005/2006 and 2007/2008 (Frey and Kohnen, 2012). In 2006, the federal Ministry of Finance introduced a regulation to give legal basis to this new instrument, referred to as gender audits (Fritz, 2011).

The federal budget reform process incorporated gender budgeting formally through new legislation and a constitutional amendment (Box 8.1). Constitutional changes included a mandate to target equality between women and men through budget management. The provision applies to all levels of government. Austria has incorporated gender budgeting specifically within the organic budget law. It was introduced as part of the performance-based budgeting framework, and the provisions require each chapter within the Annual Budget Statement to have outcome objectives, with at least one objective directly addressing gender equality (Downes, Trapp, and Nicol, 2017). Notably, in Austria, the objectives include those benefiting both women and men. Sample objectives for women include higher female participation in the labor market and a reduction in the gender pay gap, and for men, they include improvements in the state of health of men aged above 50 and improvements in road security for men and boys aged under 25.

Box 8.1 Austria: The Constitutional Requirement for Gender Budgeting in Austria

Austria's constitution has included gender budgeting as a requirement for all levels of government since 2009. The relevant provisions state the following:

- Article 13, Paragraph 3: "Federation, States and Communes are to strive for the effective equality of men and women in their budget management."
- Article 51, Paragraph 8: "In the Budget Management of the Federation the fundamental principles of impact orientations, especially under consideration of the objectives of the effective equality of men and women, transparency, efficiency and the most faithfully possible representation of the financial situation of the Federation are to be observed."
- Article 51, Paragraph 9: "The particularities . . . are to be fixed by Federal Laws . . . in accord with the provisions of Paragraph 8."

Source: Downes, von Trapp, and Nicol (2017, p. 11).

One of the strengths of Austria's approach to gender budgeting is that the government is required to undertake an ex ante assessment of the impact on gender equality for any regulation (Downes, von Trapp, and Nicol, 2017). The new impact assessment process, introduced in 2013 for all laws and ordinances (Wirkungsorientierte Folgenabschätzung), contains an explicit set of rules for assessing the impact of new regulations on gender equality, and it is combined with a new handbook and training for users and a mandatory ex post evaluation.

One drawback of Austria's approach is that is has not been clear how much money has been allocated in the budget specifically for the achievement of gender-related goals, and in an OECD survey of gender budgeting in OECD countries, Austria's self-assessment was that its initiative was "not significant" in influencing policy development and resource allocation (Downes, von Trapp, and Nicol, 2017, p. 20). This highlights the critical anomaly between formalizing the legal trappings of gender budgeting as required by legislation and actually institutionalizing gender-related objectives through meaningful budget allocations, outputs, and outcomes.

The Austrian government's draft budget for 2013 included 123 outcome objectives, of which 28 were gender-equality objectives, each with an average of two to three indicators. The defined gender-equality objectives and measures addressed important policy areas, such as the gender pay gap, balancing of work and family life, education and professional careers, and representation of women in the boardroom (Schratzenstaller, 2014). Also included were measures to improve the gender database in a number of key ministries as well as in the Court of Audit. Parliamentary debate on the draft budget focused on the broad range of performance-related information, in particular on the gender-related information. Similarly, the Parliamentary budget committee paid significant attention to outcome objectives and their ambitiousness, indicators, and measures (Ibid.).

Hammerschmid and Grunwald (2014) also touch on gender budgeting in their evaluation of the budget process and how to improve it through reforms. The evaluation, based on interviews with budget officials, finds that the majority of respondents were positive about the integration of gender equality, but many questioned its prominence as one of at most five outcome objectives. Respondents believed that, at this early stage in the reform process, it was unrealistic to give the same weight to gender equality as to other dimensions of reform. They also believed that gender equality was not being well served in this respect. The evaluation drew attention to the poorly specified gender-equality targets that did not reflect the complexity of the subject. As an example, the evaluation indicated that the idea that women should constitute 50 percent of any given target group is a poorly conceived gender-equality objective. Thus, the reviewers concluded that the gender-equality goals were not sufficiently ambitious, and a lack of data meant that the gender-equality objectives were not being subject to evaluation.

An Austrian government blogpost of the 2018 and 2019 budget observed that it takes account of 36 gender-equality objectives, in which almost 80 percent have an "external social impact," as required by the law.[4] These objectives cover the balancing of work and family life, improving the distribution of gainful employment, raising the awareness of gender equality, and improving the reintegration of women into the labor market as well as their share in research, innovation, and technology-related areas of work. Eight objectives apply to public administration. However, the blogpost notes that an analysis by the Austria Parliamentary Budget Office finds that although gender equality is a cross-cutting issue, neither the budget document nor strategy report present the objectives in a comprehensive way or embed them into a concise inter-ministerial strategy.

Klatzer, Brait, and Schlager (2018) critique the results of Austria's experience so far with gender budgeting and suggest ways to improve the results. Although noting a strength is the comprehensive legal basis, the practice lacks some key elements.[5] They note that gender budgeting was implemented through Austria's performance-budgeting system but that public institutions lacked the knowledge to integrate gender into the performance metrics, which was also noted by Quinn (2016). Moreover, because the gender-related objectives need only be included in a subset of components of the budget, they are not mainstreamed throughout. Finally, there lacks a clear link of gender-related objectives to funded allocations in the budget. Consequently, it is not possible to track the expenditure of money in different budget categories to gender-equality objectives. This would obviously be a serious flaw in any gender budgeting effort.

Klatzer, Brait, and Schlager (2018) make some recommendations for strengthening the process of building effective gender budgeting. First, they propose introducing a steering or coordinating mechanism across government involving the joint leadership of the Ministry of Finance and the Performance Controlling Department at the Federal Chancellery. Key public administration institutions, such as the Ministry of Women's Affairs and Court of Auditors, and parliamentarians, researchers, and civil society would all be included in this steering mechanism. An important task would be coordinating gender-equality performance planning and adequate budgeting and regularly evaluating success. Second, they propose enhancing the institutionalization of gender budgeting in public administration through better-trained staff, with adequate resources devoted to this task. This would include strengthening the independent role of parliament in this regard.

Third, they propose establishing binding requirements and accountability for ministries, especially as part of a coherent set of medium-term strategic objectives across government. They advocate the regular use of sex-disaggregated data and the integration of the analysis into the broader macroeconomic framework, a point often missed in gender budgeting discussions. Further, a better integration across various levels of government is advocated. Fourth, they propose that the government undertake high-quality gender impact assessments to provide evidence for policymaking. Fifth, they support the introduction of an annual gender budget report, to enhance transparency and accountability.

Sixth, they suggest creating an independent gender budgeting and fiscal policy body. Finally, they advocate the institutionalization of feminist economic policy research.

In summary, Austria has a strong history of interest in the procedures surrounding gender budgeting and has demonstrated a significant improvement in its GDI since 1990, when it was below the average for developed countries. Nonetheless, it does not seem to have approached the subject of gender budgeting with a serious intent to fund and accomplish substantive goals. This may be because the level of gender equality is already high, and there does not seem to be much urgency on the part of the political class to address the issues that disproportionately affect women in developed countries (such as caregiving, glass ceilings in employment, wage gaps, and inadequate pensions).

Belgium

Belgium's gender budgeting initiative, like Austria's, is underpinned by law (Downes, von Trapp, and Nicol, 2017; Quinn, 2016). Notably, Belgium's law mandates the following (Quinn, 2016):

1 Specific methods and processes to accommodate gender equality's integration into all budgetary processes;
2 The collection and management of gender-relevant data;
3 The specification of gender-equality objectives in line with the Beijing Platform for Action (BPfA);
4 Applying gender budgeting to government procurement.

A strength of Belgium's initiative is the alignment of its gender-equality objectives with the BPfA, a framework that encompasses all aspects of gender equality relevant to government policy. The implementation of Belgium's multifaceted and institutionally robust gender budgeting program has been hampered somewhat by political discontinuities during the past decade.

Quinn (2016) summarizes the history of Belgium's gender budgeting efforts. After cohosting a conference on the topic, in 2001, titled "Strengthening Economic and Financial Governance: Toward Gender-Responsive Budgeting," Belgium launched a pilot project to explore the feasibility of applying gender budgeting to all federal government services and activities (Holvoet, 2007). The research element of the pilot was to explore how budgetary decisions were being taken in relation to existing gender mainstreaming provisions.

The pilot, which studied gender mainstreaming more broadly, paved the way for legislation in 2007 that would effectively institutionalize gender budgeting. The purpose was "to structurally integrate the gender dimension into all federal policies" (Ibid., p. 3). Belgium at this time had begun to move toward performance-based budgeting.

The law mandates specific gender budgeting processes and responsibilities. In the first instance, the government is required at the beginning of its term of office to identify gender-equality objectives. The linking of these objectives with a budget allocation is achieved by preparing a gender note, quantifying the budgetary allocations of each ministry for each objective to be attained. The gender note, which is to be attached to each draft of the general expense budget, is effectively an accounting instrument, allowing for the calculation of aggregate budgetary spending targeted toward gender equality.

In addition to the gender note, the law stipulates the application of a "gender test": an assessment of the potential differential impact on women and men of all government legislative and regulatory measures presented to the Council of Ministers. An important element of the law is the mandate to collect and manage sex-disaggregated data and to develop gender-specific indicators.

In 2010, the Minister for Equal Opportunities issued a specific circular on gender budgeting, which elaborated on a method. This was supplemented with a manual in 2011. From 2010 on, the annual budgetary circular of the Federal Public Service Budget and Management Control also mentions the obligation of applying the gender budgeting method and refers to the specific circular on gender budgeting.

The Federal Plan on gender mainstreaming (2015–2019) renews the government's commitment to gender budgeting and gives details of the commitments that each member of government must make to integrate the gender perspective into their policies. For example, the Minister of Finance must commit to redressing any gender imbalances in relation to personal income tax, business expense deductibles, and incentives toward pension savings. The Minister of Civil Service must commit to both integrating a gender perspective into the review of pay scales, recruitment, and training procedures and developing new forms of working, including teleworking and flexible and temporary work arrangements. And finally, the Minister of Justice must commit to integrate a gender dimension into the development of prison policy, including the treatment of prisoners. It also must commit to take the gender perspective into account in the planned reform of the matrimonial and inheritance law.

In its evaluation of the application of a gender budgeting method, the Institute reported that the percentage of budgetary allocations not categorized appropriately by this method rose from 1.2 percent in 2013 to 8.5 percent in 2015, mostly consisting of allocations of the newly installed government.

An OECD survey found that Belgium assessed its own effort as "significant" in influencing policy development and resource allocation in specific sectors (Downes, von Trapp, and Nicol, 2017, p. 20). However, no information was provided regarding which specific areas were cited in this claim.

The situation in Belgium regarding gender budgeting seems similar to that in Austria; much effort has been expended in devising methods and processes for incorporating gender budgeting into the overall government budget framework. However, there does not seem to be much urgency felt to achieve programmatic results. Belgium has a high GDI, comparable to Canada, and this may account for the lack of interest in producing effective programs.

Sweden

Quinn (2016) summarizes the experience of Sweden. The Nordic countries were among the pioneers of gender budgeting in Europe, which is not surprising given their leading role in achieving gender equality in general. The Nordic Co-operation[6] provided the framework for the early initiatives in the region. A joint project was launched in 2004, with Finland, Iceland, Norway, Denmark, and Sweden[7] all undertaking pilot projects over the course of a two-year period.

Following this, each country has charted its own course. In Denmark, notwithstanding its stated commitment to gender budgeting, some commentators report that there is little evidence of a gender policy process. In Iceland, there is now a legal mandate in the Organic Budget Law.[8] In Sweden, the government has reinvigorated its long-standing commitment to gender budgeting.

Sweden has for many years been seen as a model for gender-equality policy and practice. It is known for its public provision of child care and other public policies that promote women's economic participation and help to promote a more equitable division of domestic responsibilities for men. Sweden has also led the way in capacity building for government officials, the development of methods and tools of gender budgeting, and the production and management of sex-disaggregated data. Other countries, both inside and outside of Europe, have adopted a number of the analytic and process tools developed in Sweden.

Following elections in September 2014, the government declared itself a feminist government. Among other gender-equality commitments, it outlined its intention to institute gender budgeting in the program for government presented to Parliament by the Prime Minister (Sweden, 2014).[9]

Women in Sweden have enjoyed the benefits of individual or separate income tax assessment since 1971. The Equal Opportunities Law, designed to combat discrimination in the workplace, came into force in 1980. Efforts to incorporate a gender-equality perspective in Sweden's economic policy date back to the late 1980s, and in 1988, a special appendix was introduced into the Budget Bill to show the distribution of economic resources between women and men. Since 2003, this appendix has been attached to the Budget Statement. Statistics Sweden has had a gender equality unit since 1982, and since 1984, it has published *Women and Men in Sweden, Facts and Figures* at regular intervals. In 1994, the Ordinance on Official Statistics mandated that all official statistics related to individuals are to be disaggregated by sex. Nonetheless, a review of the Budget Bill in 2006 found that the use of sex-disaggregated data needed improvement. At the request of the government, Statistics Sweden produced guidance on how to collect and use sex-disaggregated data and provided illustrations of its importance to government policy. The government's objective was to ensure that all tables and graphs related to individuals should be based on sex-disaggregated data in the 2007 Budget Bill (Sweden, Government Offices of, 2006).

Gender mainstreaming in the budget has been in operation in Sweden since 1994, initiated by the Ministry of Finance. Gender budgeting was subsumed into the new Plan for Gender Mainstreaming, 2004–2009, signaling that gender budgeting was to become part of the regular work of gender mainstreaming. A central goal of this plan was to integrate a gender analysis into the "two central decision-making processes in the Government Offices—the legislative process and the budget process" (Sweden, Government Offices, 2006, p. 7). This renewed focus led to the development of a range of methods, overseen by the JamStod Committee,[10] for which Sweden has become renowned and which has been influential across Europe and beyond. A 2006 government bill resulted in the drafting of new national gender-equality objectives, and in 2007, the new Ministry of Integration and Gender Equality was established (Bjorklund, 2007). Again in 2012, the government produced the five-part Gender Mainstreaming Plan.

From 2016, the annual budget circular includes instructions on the application of gender budgeting throughout the budget process. Among the requirements set out in the circular is that gender impact analysis be carried out at the early stage of new budget proposals. In addition, sex-disaggregated data and gender-equality indicators have been adopted. The government initiative is seen as strengthening gender mainstreaming in the budgetary process by improving the mechanisms for internal management and control, an improved method (JamKas), and better use of sex-disaggregated data.[11]

Republic of Korea (Korea)

Gender budgeting in Korea dates back to around 2002, when female parliamentarians took up the cause and lobbied to ensure that gender budgeting would be incorporated into national finance legislation (UN Women, 2016; Chakraborty, 2016). Since those initial efforts, gender budgeting has been incorporated into budget call circulars, and the government has adopted gender budget statements, gender impact assessment tools, and a national plan with a framework on gender equality. There is also engagement at subnational levels. The main actors have been the Ministry of Economy and Finance and the Korean Women's Development Institute (KWDI).

The first major achievement was the incorporation of gender budgeting into the 2006 National Finance Act (Box 8.2). Korea remains one of the few countries in Asia to have a legal basis for gender budgeting in its budget law.

Box 8.2 Korea: Key Gender Budget-Related Articles in the 2006 National Finance Act

- Article 16 (Budgeting Principles): The Government shall comply with the following principles for formulation and execution of its budget: <Amended by Act No. 10288, 17 May 2010; Act No. 11614, 1 Jan. 2013> . . .

  (5) The Government shall evaluate the impacts of the budget on both men and women and shall strive to reflect the results thereof in the formulation of its budget.

- Article 26 (Preparation of Gender-Sensitive Budget): The Government shall prepare a report on analysis conducted in advance on the impact that the budget is likely to have on women and men, alike (hereinafter referred to as "gender-sensitive budget").

  (9) The gender-sensitive budget;

- Article 57 (Preparation of Gender-Sensitive Settlement of Accounts) (1) The Government shall prepare a statement to evaluate whether women and men have equally benefited from the budget and whether the budget has been executed toward addressing gender discrimination (hereinafter referred to as "gender-sensitive settlement of accounts").

  (2) The gender-sensitive settlement of accounts shall include results of execution, effect analysis on and evaluation of gender equality, etc. <Newly Inserted by Act No. 10288, 17 May 2010>

Source: Korean Women's Development Institute, 2018. Brochure. Available at http://gb.kwdi.re.kr/en/contents/publish/etc_list.jsp.

Article 16 incorporates in the very principles of the budget into the mandate to evaluate the impact of the budget on both men and women and to reflect the results of that analysis in the formulation of the budget. Article 26 requires the preparation of a report conducted in advance of the budget on this differential impact (called the gender-sensitive budget).

Article 57 requires that the government prepare, for the settlement accounts, a statement as to whether women and men have equally benefited from the budget and whether the budget has attempted to address discrimination. Korea has passed other legislation that supports gender budgeting, including that related to local finances, which parallels the national legislation.

Since the 2006–2007 fiscal year, the Ministry of Finance has issued a budget circular that instructs the line ministries of the national government to report on allocations developed to promote gender equality and also includes templates for reporting in the gender budget statement (UN Women, 2016; Elson et al., 2009). In 2009 (2010 fiscal year), the first gender budget statement and performance report were produced for the national government. The report covered projects with the specific objective of promoting gender equality and general projects that could be analyzed from a gender perspective. A gender impact analysis framework was applied to projects in the latter category. However, initially, a small fraction of the budget was allocated to either of these categories (Kim, 2008). Over time, the share of the budget covered by programs in the gender budgeting statement has increased and had risen to 7 percent of the budget by 2015 (UN Women, 2016). The gender performance report reflects the performance outcome and is expected to explain whether goals were met, and if not, why. In 2012 (2013 fiscal year), the first gender budget statement and performance report for local governments were produced.

An example of the format of the gender budgeting statement is given in Box 8.3.

Box 8.3 Korea: Format of a Gender Budget Statement

Ministry of Health, Welfare and Family Affairs

1) Goals of gender-equality policies and direction of fiscal management
2) Table of all projects
3) Explanation by project

   a Title
   b Budget
   c Project objectives
   d Target population of the project
   e Characteristics or description of the project
   f Gender-equality goals
   g Beneficiary analysis
   h Performance objectives
   i Performance indicators

Sources: UN Women (2016) and www.unescap.org/sites/default/files/16.%20Republic%20of%20Korea.pdf.

From the perspective of the full budget cycle, Korea has been successful in integrating gender budgeting at each stage. At the stage of budget development, the submission of budget requests and deliberation are supposed to be undertaken with gender-equality goals in mind and supported by analysis disaggregated by gender (Cho et al., 2014a, 2014b; Kim et al., 2015). At the stage of budget implementation, projects intended to address gender-equality objectives are funded and monitored. A process is in place to audit and evaluate on a gender-sensitive basis. In addition, Korea builds gender-related goals into its medium-term planning (Cho et al., 2014a, 2014b). In principle, then, Korea should be well placed to progress on its gender-related goals.

It is difficult to discern, however, what the specific accomplishments of Korea's gender budgeting have been. Although there has been a growth in funding over time, the total remains small relative to the overall budget. In terms of specific policies, Kim (2010) noted that one achievement of gender budgeting was to identify unmet gender-specific needs for hygienic facilities, which led to increased construction of restrooms to accommodate more women. Other substantive results relate to the funding of programs to reduce women's unpaid care in the home to facilitate their greater labor force participation, which is a critical government objective in Korea, with its rapidly aging workforce and low level of women's participation (Kim, Lee, and Shin, 2016). It is not clear how much impact this latter program has had on the actual problem of worker shortages in the country, and Figure 8.2 shows that Korea has the lowest ratio of female-to-male employment among the developed countries surveyed.

In its own assessment, the KWDI's Gender Budget Research Center has identified what it sees as the weaknesses of Korea's gender budgeting efforts:

1 It is not adequately integrated into the performance-based budgeting system of the government. There are weak incentives to fully implement gender budgeting over a wider range of government activities and programs. There is a lack of coordination among line ministries, the Ministry of Economy and Finance, and the Ministry of Gender Equality and Family. There is too much focus on activities and a lack of influence on long-term goals in the medium-term expenditure framework. It generates an additional workload for line ministries that is actively resisted.
2 There is a relatively limited role played by civil society. The KWDI proposes better integration of gender budgeting to the wider public finance management system, strengthening the review and monitoring roles of the National Congress, and institutionalizing the participation of civil society groups.

III. Conclusions

This brief overview of gender budgeting efforts in a number of developed countries from different parts of the world illustrates that such efforts can be accomplished through legislation either in the constitution, as in Austria, or in the budget, as in Austria, Belgium, Canada, and elsewhere. However, legislation for gender budgeting is clearly insufficient to actually produce real programs that achieve social, economic, or political goals and can be monitored each year as part of a budget process.

It is difficult to point to specific gender-equality achievements in any of these countries that have resulted due to gender budgeting efforts. This is, in part, because these are all countries that have already achieved a fairly high degree of gender equality in most aspects of life. For instance, in the case of Sweden, as noted earlier, we see that some of the key goals of gender-equality advocates were achieved already in the 1980s. These goals include an equal opportunity law in the workplace, data disaggregation by sex to show how economic resources were distributed, and the public provision of child care. Accordingly, until 2014, the Swedish government did not feel the need to formally declare its intention to institute gender budgeting. The gender-equality policies and programs described in Sweden also exist in other Nordic countries, yet in Denmark, we noted that there is little evidence of any formal gender policy process as of the present time. Hence, there may not be any sense of urgency felt by political and civic leaders in these advanced and egalitarian countries to establish a specific gender budgeting framework in the national government budget process.

Even where governments in these countries have identified areas in which they would like to see improvement, such as in reducing women's unpaid care burdens or increasing women's workforce participation, it is difficult to isolate the contribution of the many factors that might lead to accomplishing these goals, beyond just the fiscal ones. Pilot projects with carefully designed activities, goals, and incentives, and clear ways of measuring success, are lacking. Nonetheless, they are needed in developed countries, just as in underdeveloped ones, to serve as examples of how gender budgeting can actually have a tangible impact on the life of society rather than to serve as a source of lip service to an ideology. The latter is the role that gender budgeting seems to be playing now in the developed countries.

All of the countries in this chapter demonstrate how gender budgeting was implemented in fiscal policy and budgeting practices. These ways provide practical mechanisms that can be used by developing and developed countries in designing their own gender budgeting efforts. Nevertheless, the historical record shows that great improvements in women's status have occurred in all of the countries discussed without well-developed gender budgeting policies or programs or effective government-led execution of the same. At present, we might conclude that it would be helpful to find a well-defined role for gender budgeting and gender-related fiscal policies that address the existing unmet needs in developed countries that have been discussed in Chapters 7 and 8. This would highlight the value of gender budgeting as an effective tool in promoting gender equality more generally.

Notes

1. This chapter has benefited from Quinn (2016) for European nations, from Chakraborty (2016) for Korea, and from Pérez Fragoso and Rodríguez Enríquez (2016) for Canada. It also draws on IMF (2017), principally drafted by Stotsky.
2. Canada Centre for Policy Alternatives (various years).
3. Canada Centre for Policy Alternatives (2015).
4. Federal Ministry for Women, Families, and Youth (2018): Available at: blog.imag-gendermainstreaming.at/index.php/en/category/austria/.
5. Klatzer, Brait, and Schlager (2018, pp. 143–157).
6. The Nordic Co-operation brings together Denmark, Finland, Iceland, Norway, Sweden, the Faroe Islands, Greenland, and Åland Islands to collaborate on numerous regional issues. Its work on gender equality dates to 1974 (Nordic Council of Ministers, 2015).
7. Sweden had already begun its own pilot projects in 2003, focusing on programs within the transport, regional development, and social sectors (Schmitz, 2006).
8. The five-year plan was adopted by Parliament in the summer of 2015 and the Organic Budget Law in December 2015.
9. Statement of Government Policy, available at www.government.se/information-material/2014/10/statement-of-government-policy-3-october-2014/.
10. JämStöd, the Swedish Gender Mainstreaming Support Committee, was set up in 2005 to support gender mainstreaming within government offices and agencies. It has overseen the development of many tools and methods, which have been adapted internationally.
11. Sweden, Government Offices of (2006).

References

Bjorklund, Erika, 2007, *Issue Histories Sweden: Series of Timelines of Policy Debates, Quality in Gender and Equality Policies* (Vienna: Institute for Human Sciences).

Canada, 2019, *Status of Women Canada* (Ottawa: Government of Canada). Available at: https://cfc-swc.gc.ca/index-en.html.

Canadian Centre for Policy Alternatives, various years, *Alternative Federal Budget* (Ottawa: Canadian Centre for Policy Alternatives).

Chakraborty, Lekha, 2016, "Asia: A Survey of Gender Budgeting Efforts," IMF Working Paper 16/150 (Washington, DC: IMF).

Cho, Sun-Joo et al., 2014a, *Analysis and Evaluation on Gender Budgeting in Korea (III)* (Seoul: Korean Women's Development Institute).

Cho, Sun-Joo et al., 2014b, *Analysis and Evaluation on Gender Budgeting in Korea (IV)* (Seoul: Korean Women's Development Institute).

Downes, Ronnie, Lisa von Trapp, and Scherie Nicol, 2017, "Gender Budgeting in OECD Countries," *OECD Journal on Budgeting*, Vol. 2016/3, pp. 1–37.

Elson, Diane, Rhonda Sharp, Reina Ichii, Sanjugta Vas Dev, and Monica Costa, 2009, *Gender Responsive Budgeting in the Asia Pacific Region: The Republic of South Korea* (Australia: UNISA).

Frey, Regina, and Manfred Kohnen, 2012, *Guidance on Gender Budgeting in Public Administration* (Vienna: Federal Chancellery).

Fritz, Elfriede, 2011, "Gender Budgeting: From Theory to Practice: The Role of the Ministry of Finance," paper given at the Council of Europe Conference in Yerevan.

Hammerschmid, Gerhard, and Alexander Grunwald, 2014, *Einführung der Wirkungsorientierten Verwaltungssteuerung: Erfolge—Potentiale—Perspektiven (Introduction of Results-Based Management Control: Success, Potential, Perspectives)* (Vienna: Federal Chancellery).

Holvoet, Nathalie, 2007, "Gender Budgeting in Belgium: Findings from a Pilot Project," *European Societies*, Vol. 9, pp. 275–300.

International Monetary Fund (IMF), 2017, *Gender Budgeting in G7 Countries* (Washington, DC: IMF).

Kim, Jinyoung, Jong-Wha Lee, and Kwanho Shin, 2016, "Impact of Gender Inequality on the Republic of Korea's Long-Term Economic Growth: An Application of the Theoretical Model of Gender Inequality and Economic Growth," Asian Development Bank Working Paper Series No. 473 (Manilla: Asian Development Bank).

Kim, Kyung-Hee et al., 2015, *Strategy to Improve Specific Gender Impact and Assessment and Analysis* (Seoul: Ministry of Gender Equality and Family).

Kim, Young-Ock, 2008, "Institutionalizing Gender Budgeting in Korea," *Gender Studies and Policy Review*, Vol. 1, pp. 13–24.

Kim, Young-Ock, 2010, *Institutionalizing Gender Budgeting: The Experience of Korea* (Seoul: Korean Women's Development Institute).

Klatzer, Elisabeth, Romana Brait, and Christie Schlager, 2018, "The Case of Austria: Reflections on Strengthening the Potential of Gender Budgeting for Substantial Change," in Angela O'Hagan and Elisabeth Klatzer, eds., *Gender Budgeting in Europe: Developments and Challenges* (Cham, Switzerland: Palgrave Macmillan), pp. 137–157.

Korean Women's Development Institute, Center for Gender Budget Research, 2018, *Gender Budgeting in Korea 2018* (Seoul: Korean Women's Development Institute).

Nordic Council of Ministers, 2015, *Together for Gender Equality: A Stronger Nordic Region: Nordic Co-operation Programme on Gender Equality, 2015–2018.*

O'Hagan, Angela, and Elisabeth Klatzer, eds., 2018, *Gender Budgeting in Europe: Developments and Challenges* (Cham, Switzerland: Palgrave Macmillan).

Pérez Fragoso, Lucia, and Corina Rodríguez Enríquez, 2016, "Western Hemisphere: A Survey of Gender Budgeting Efforts," IMF Working Paper 16/153 (Washington, DC: IMF).

Quinn, Sheila, 2016, "Europe: A Survey of Gender Budgeting Efforts," IMF Working Paper 16/155 (Washington, DC: IMF).

Sharp, Rhonda, and Ray Broomhill, 2002, "Budgeting for Equality: The Australian Experience," *Feminist Economics*, Vol. 8, pp. 25–47.

Schmitz, Catharina, 2006, "Now It's about the Money: Mainstreaming a Gender Equality Perspective Into Nordic National Budgets: Final Project Report 2004–2006," (Copenhagen: Nordic Council of Ministers).

Schratzenstaller, Margit, 2014, "Gender Impact Assessment," Exchange of Good Practices on Gender Equality Discussion Paper (Brussels: European Commission).

Scott, Katherine, 2019, "Budget 2019: A Win for the Women's Movement: But We Won't Get There without Child Care," (Ottawa: Canadian Centre for Policy Alternatives). Available at: behindthenumbers.ca/2019/03/21/budget-2019-investments-for-women/.

Sweden, Government Offices of, 2006, "Moving Ahead: Gender Budgeting in Sweden," Ministry of Integration and Gender Equality (Stockholm).

Sweden, 2014, Statement of Government Policy. Available at: www.government.se/information-material/2014/10/statement-of-government-policy-3-october-2014/.

UN Women, 2016, *Gender Responsive Budgeting in the Asia-Pacific Region: A Status Report* (New York: UN Women).

Yalnizyan, Armine, 2005, *Canada's Commitment to Equality: A Gender Analysis of the Last Ten Federal Budgets (1995–2004)* (Ottawa: Canadian Feminist Alliance for International Action).

9 The effect of gender budgeting and intergovernmental grants on gender equality in India

An empirical analysis[1]

I. Introduction

This chapter explores the impact of gender budgeting efforts and intergovernmental grants on the educational enrollment of girls and boys in Indian states. We are using educational enrollment as a surrogate for gender equality given that in almost all societies, a higher educational level for girls or women correlates with greater gender equality. Although gender budgeting efforts in the international context now date back several decades, there has been little effort to assess the results of these efforts in a quantitative manner. This study thus adds an important dimension to research on gender budgeting.

Gender budgeting at the state level in India offers a suitable empirical framework for assessing its effectiveness because 16 out of 29 states have adopted and sustained gender budgeting initiatives. Indian states introduced gender budgeting at various times over the past 20 years, with varying degrees of intensity, complementing a central (or Union) government initiative.

A few existing studies have tried to analyze the impact of gender budgeting on gender-equality outcomes and found a positive link between the two. In principle, gender budgeting should lead to more spending on, or more effective, public programs and policies geared toward promoting gender equality. Stotsky and Zaman (2016) examined gender budgeting in the context of state governments in India and found a positive effect of gender budgeting on female enrollment relative to males.[2] This chapter advances the Stotsky and Zaman (2016) methodology one step further by taking a more detailed look at Indian central government grants to individual states, in the context of gender budgeting. We have analyzed how gender budgeting and other key factors influence gender equality, as measured by the educational enrollment of boys and girls at the primary and secondary school levels.

This chapter is organized as follows. Section II looks at the existing literature on the topic. Section III presents data collected for the independent and dependent variables in the econometric model. Section IV explains the econometric model and presents and interprets the results. In the final section, we present our conclusions.

II. Review of the theoretical and empirical literature

Gender budgeting was first adopted by the central government of India, in 2000, and it was subsequently adopted by individual states (Chapter 6). The central government initiative was institutionalized by assigning responsibilities to each government ministry to identify gender-related goals and then devise ways to achieve these goals through budgetary spending (Figure 9.1). Drawing on the central government framework, states began to adopt gender budgeting, starting with Odisha in 2004. Since then, another 15 states have adopted gender budgeting efforts as well, such that more than half of Indian states now have accepted the principle of gender budgeting.

Several recent studies provide an overview and assessment of the effect of gender budgeting efforts at the state level in India, though none of these studies has undertaken a formal econometric evaluation.[3] These studies indicated that state governments have implemented gender budgeting by using a variety of approaches. The focus of most gender budgeting initiatives has generally been on identifying critical goals to improve girls' and women's education, health, and welfare and to build state infrastructure essential to achieving these objectives, eventually leading to women's economic empowerment. Among the approaches that states have pursued, these include setting up nodal departments or groups for gender budgeting; establishing committees for oversight; improving gender data; and training staff on the analytical methods that can be used to incorporate gender-related goals into the budget.

Stotsky and Zaman (2016) summarized gender budgeting initiatives in Indian states, as drawn from this literature. The studies in the literature drew mixed conclusions on the effectiveness of gender budgeting efforts. In India, the Ministry of Women and Child Development (2015) found that many states, including Karnataka, Kerala, Gujarat, Rajasthan, Madhya Pradesh, Chhattisgarh, and others, had institutionalized gender budgeting. The results of these gender budgeting efforts are now briefly summarized.

In Karnataka, gender budgeting was adopted in 2006/2007 and the Gender Budget Cell was established within the Finance Department to collaborate with the Women and Child Development Department to promote gender budgeting

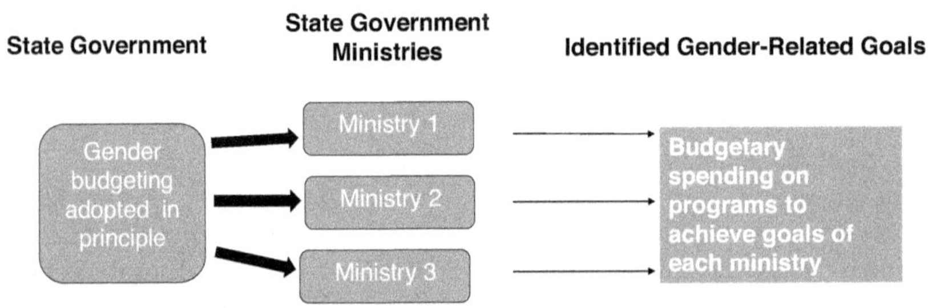

Figure 9.1 India: Graphical View of Institutionalization of Gender Budgeting

Source: Author.

activities. The initiative led to the institution of gender budget statements in the annual budget process with an accompanying circular asking state departments to indicate which programs had a substantial component devoted to goals for women and girls. A report on gender budgeting indicating allocations to relevant programs has been published since 2010 in the state finance accounts. One key program was the Karnataka Mahila Abhivruddhi Yojana scheme. This was intended to allocate one-third of the resources in labor-intensive schemes of the government across all areas of government spending, with a focus on education and skills training for jobs as well as social welfare and infrastructure programs.[4]

In Kerala, gender budgeting was adopted in 2008/2009, and a gender budget statement was also introduced. Some specific programs adopted as part of the initiative were programs for protecting women against domestic violence; school programs geared to training women for specific job skills; health and sanitation spending; and a transportation-related scheme to address female-related goals. The report noted, however, that a lack of sex-disaggregated data was one principal hindrance to more-effective gender budgeting efforts at the state level.

Joshi (2013) evaluated gender budgeting efforts in six states: Madhya Pradesh, Rajasthan, Andhra Pradesh, Gujarat, Jharkhand, and Odisha. She concluded that some states' efforts have focused mainly on pro forma, rather than substantive, actions. The Centre for Budget and Governance Accountability (2012) also evaluated state-level gender budgeting efforts. Focusing on Bihar, Karnataka, Kerala, and Madhya Pradesh, it concluded that Kerala and Madhya Pradesh had made the most substantive efforts that had led to meaningful change in fiscal policies for the purpose of addressing gender-related goals.

Our empirical analysis draws on two distinct strands of research. One examines the cause-and-effect relationships between gender inequality and economic efficiency, productivity, and growth. A World Bank (2011, Box 0.1, p. 49) study has highlighted the difficulties in empirically assessing the causal relationship between gender inequality and economic growth. Many variables influence other variables simultaneously, and it is not always clear what factors are causing which outcomes. For instance, improvements in technology can lead to economic growth, which creates jobs requiring cognitive skills. This may create more opportunities for women in the workforce, given their relatively higher educational achievement than that of men, in recent years. However, better public services accompanying economic growth may also improve gender equality in education, such that the real cause of improved women's status may stem more from better education than from more job opportunities. Moreover, there are factors such as improvements in health care that may independently lead to both greater growth and greater gender equality. Empirical studies have used a variety of approaches to assess the interconnectedness of these relationships. Some of these approaches involve models derived explicitly from theory or simulations. Meanwhile, others use reduced form (i.e., not derived explicitly from theory) statistical structures incorporating multiple potentially causative variables such as income and other economic, demographic, and political factors.

A second strand draws on the literature regarding modeling of public spending and revenue decisions. Some approaches in this area look at the importance of collective choice processes in which the government seeks to maximize utility or social welfare, and demand for spending emerges from addressing these challenges. Other alternative theories see government motivations stemming from political economy and institutional considerations.[5] A related topic examines the effect of intergovernmental grants on fiscal decisions. The normative theories of fiscal federalism posit that intergovernmental funding transfers can help achieve efficiency and equity goals in a fiscal system composed of a central government and other secondary layers of government (Bradford and Oates, 1971; Bird and Smart, 2002; Boadway and Shah, 2007). A sizeable literature has examined empirically the effect of intergovernmental grants on fiscal decisions (Hines and Thaler, 1995).[6]

Our empirical approach is "reduced form" in that we do not specify a social welfare function from which we derive specific demand equations. Nor do we posit a more general model assuming a direct impact of gender budgeting leading to a reduction in gender inequality. Instead, we rely on the frameworks described earlier to analyze certain key determinants of gender inequality, which is consistent with an underlying social welfare–based theory.

Our approach to gender budgeting presumes that higher spending on fiscal objectives, such as education and health, should lead to better gender-equality outcomes. Relatively few studies have examined the efficiency of public social sector spending in India. Kaur and Misra (2003) examined the relationship between social sector spending and gender-related outcomes in India over the 1985/1986–2000/2001 period. They concluded that public spending on education was productive, though more so at the primary than the secondary level, and more decisively in poorer states. The relationship between public spending on health and gender-related health outcomes was weaker, reflecting inadequate, rather than ineffective, spending. They also found that state spending on education was more instrumental in narrowing gender disparities than state spending on health. Consequently, Chakraborty (2010) suggested investigating gender-equity goals in school enrollment as a function of the intergovernmental grants process.

One can measure gender inequality in several ways. For the dependent variable, we use the female-to-male school enrollment ratio. We focus on school enrollment ratios because it is one of the most critical indicators of equality, as mentioned above. The labor force participation of women compared to men is another important indicator. Khera (2016) examined the impact of gender-related policies on relative rates of labor force participation. She found that government policies that increase education for women, social spending, and labor market flexibility raise women's labor force participation. We did not examine this issue in our study, because relevant labor market data are not available to determine how fiscal spending influences gender equality concerning this variable.

One shortcoming of the work by Stotsky and Zaman (2016) on gender budgeting in India was that it did not separate intergovernmental grants into their two components of conditional and unconditional grants. Intergovernmental grants to states are critical in India given the asymmetry between state revenues and expenditures. These grants account for more than half of revenues in Indian states. Looking at intergovernmental grants in a disaggregated form by splitting them into their two key components should provide a more realistic view of subnational decision-making in India. For conditional grants, we examined the specific impact of the Sarbha Siksha Abhiyan (SSA), which is a grant designed to universalize primary education. It accounted for about 12 percent of conditional grants in the period that we studied. We examined its historical performance up through 2018, after which it was consolidated with other education grants.

III. Describing the institutional setting and the data

Institutional setting and intergovernmental grants to states

India consists of 29 states and seven Union territories. Two Union territories, Delhi and Pondicherry, have their own elected governments, while the remaining are administered by officials appointed by the Union government. State governments have their own elected officials. State governments are further divided into urban and rural local governments. Rural local government consists of district, block, and village panchayats (elected councils).

Chakraborty et al. (2018), Isaac, Mohan, and Chakraborty (2019), and Reddy and Reddy (2019) describe intergovernmental grants in India, considering the various components and channels of these transfers. Intergovernmental grants can be broadly categorized into unconditional and conditional grants. Unconditional grants consist mainly of formula-linked automatic tax transfers from the central government's revenues. Conditional grants consist mainly of transfers from the central government that are designed for specific purposes.

In India, the Finance Commission, the Planning Commission (abolished in 2014 and replaced with the Niti Aayog or Organization for Policy), and line ministries of the central government are responsible for determining intergovernmental grants. India has had 15 finance commissions since independence. The Finance Commission's recommendations in India have so far been conclusively accepted by the National Parliament. The Finance Commission's unconditional grants to the states, as per their formula, have become mandatory, and these transfers are also therefore referred to as statutory fiscal transfers. The unconditional grants are essentially general-purpose transfers of funding. Until recently, a substantial flow of intergovernmental grants has been transferred through the former Planning Commission. In contrast, the non-statutory transfers of funding are channeled through the line ministries mostly as conditional grants for specific purposes. These conditional grants are also referred to as centrally sponsored schemes.

Fiscal data and calculated gender-equity index

The data examined cover 1991–2015. They were obtained from the following sources: the IMF database on gender created in 2016, the State Finance Accounts (budgeted unconditional transfers),[7] central government ministry websites (budgeted conditional transfers), and the Ministry of Women and Child Development (MWCD) gender budgeting information.[8] Table 9.1 provides the descriptive statistics.

Table 9.1 shows the variation in the gender-equality index calculated from school enrollment ratios at primary and secondary levels, plus other key variables describing the fiscal environment of these states, such as population, GDP, structural components of the economy, state revenues, and state expenditures by type of spending.

Between 1991 and 2015, 16 of the 29 states adopted gender budgeting. We do not include central government territories, because they have limited fiscal autonomy. The primary and secondary school gender-equality indices are constructed as follows: the number of female or male students enrolled at the relevant schooling level, regardless of age, is divided by the population of the relevant age group. Then the ratio of female-to-male ratios is taken.[9] All spending and revenue variables and income are measured in real per capita terms.

The samples of data for primary education encompass the period before gender budgeting was in place for any state and, for most, at least several years afterwards. However, the sample for secondary education is available only for a period following the start of gender budgeting in some states. The total population in the 16 states analyzed was 280 million for the sample period in primary school and 168 million in secondary school.

Although most states are close to parity in the female-to-male ratio in lower primary school enrollment, there are still a few that lag behind, and the ratios worsen at each successive level of education. The populations of Indian states, income per capita, and gross state domestic product vary widely. Services are the predominant source of state income, though agriculture and manufacturing are also important contributors. Education and infrastructure spending are higher than health spending, which is notably low. Shared central government taxes are a little less than half of state taxes, and central government grants are more than half of state nontax revenues.

IV. Econometric model and results

Our goal was to analyze econometrically the effects of gender budgeting and intergovernmental grants on educational enrollment (as a proxy for gender equality) across the 16 states of India.

Table 9.1 India: Descriptive Statistics

Variable	*Description*	*N*	*Mean*	*Median*	*Std. Dev.*	*Min*	*Max*
Gender-Equality Index	Gender-equality index: lower primary school	280	0.98	0.98	0.06	0.75	1.18
	Gender-equality index: upper primary school	280	0.94	0.96	0.11	0.59	1.22
	Gender-equality index: lower secondary school	168	0.93	0.96	0.14	0.57	1.20
	Gender-equality index: upper secondary school	168	0.90	0.90	0.16	0.53	1.33
Population	Population (millions)	280	38.27	27.60	41.47	0.55	199.35
GDP	Per capita income (nominal, thousand Rs)	280	38.27	32.09	25.16	6.83	192.03
	Per capita income (real [2014 = 100], thousand Rs)	280	56.87	50.46	30.20	13.03	207.17
	Nominal GSDP (billion Rs)	280	1,267.4	799.3	1,535.7	11.4	10,491.5
	Real GSDP (billion Rs)	280	1,907.4	1,234.9	2,136.3	20.9	12,495.8
Sectoral Share	Agriculture (% of state GDP)	280	18.7	18.9	6.5	2.2	34.4
	Manufacturing (% of state GDP)	280	12.7	11.5	8.1	1.1	39.0
	Service (% of state GDP)	280	48.2	47.8	7.3	30.7	64.1
Revenues(real per capita terms)	Nontax revenues (thousand Rs)	280	8.26	12.15	0.36	3.05	63.91
	Tax revenues (thousand Rs)	280	5.55	3.08	1.04	4.71	17.13
	Total revenues (thousand Rs)	280	13.81	13.54	2.31	9.38	80.00
	Conditional transfers (thousand Rs)	280	5.66	8.01	0.23	1.37	38.34
	Unconditional transfers (thousand Rs)	280	2.10	1.57	0.35	1.77	11.19
Expenditures(real per capita terms)	Education expenditure (thousand Rs)	280	2.28	1.68	0.59	1.79	12.63
	Infrastructure expenditure (thousand Rs)	280	2.32	2.29	0.29	1.46	18.79
	Health expenditure (thousand Rs)	280	0.66	0.55	0.13	0.43	3.24
	Total expenditure (thousand Rs)	280	15.89	14.30	3.09	11.03	81.92

Sources: IMF database; finance accounts of state governments; and central government ministry websites.

The most difficult problem in this analysis is trying to characterize the spending and quantify the amount of spending that is included in what we would define as gender budgeting. Specifically targeted allocations for gender equality or women's development comprise less than 1 percent of the entire Indian budget. However, there is also spending within the remaining 99 percent of the budget linked to gender-related objectives. Unless we try to quantify this other spending, discussing targeted public spending on gender-equality goals is potentially misleading. Consequently, we avoid using this spending as a proxy for gender budgeting initiatives.

Another way of measuring the extent of gender budgeting in any state is to note in a qualitative sense whether it is mandatory or not. In India, gender budgeting is not legally mandated.

A final dimension in categorizing the extent of gender budgeting is by classifying it in one of four phases of gender budgeting implementation:

1 In an early phase of model building;
2 In a process of institutionalizing gender budget statements and other aspects of implementation in the Finance Ministry;
3 In a phase of capacity building for sectoral ministries to integrate gender budgeting into programs and policies;
4 In a phase of designing accountability mechanisms to assess its effects.

However, it is difficult to assess where the various Indian states are in the implementation of their gender budgeting initiatives. Therefore, we did not use these four phases in our econometric models as a way of measuring the degree of gender budgeting implementation.

Given the aforementioned limitations of the data, following Stotsky and Zaman (2016), we categorize states as either gender budgeting or non–gender budgeting states on the basis of the announcement by the government that it has initiated gender budgeting. We measure the effect of gender budgeting through the use of a dummy variable, where the variable takes a value of 1 if the state has a gender budgeting effort in place and 0 if the state does not. The gender budgeting regime dummies are also matched to the year when gender budgeting began. The year of implementation is used as a regime changing dummy because gender budgeting has not been rolled back where it has been initiated in Indian states.[10]

Although we treat gender budgeting as a discrete event, there may be programs and policies of the government adopted over time that comprise in substance a gender-equality element, even if the government does not formally implement gender budgeting. Unfortunately, it is difficult to assess the evolution of a government budget in this manner and to categorize its change in a discrete manner. We thus caution the reader to regard the gender budgeting dummy variable as meaningful in that it represents a formal commitment of the government to achieving gender equality through the budget, even though in substance, programs and policies may not precisely correspond to the timing of adopting gender budgeting.

Econometric model

We have constructed the following equations to econometrically measure the effect of gender budgeting and intergovernmental grants on educational enrollment outcomes:

$$GEit = \beta_1 GBit + \beta_2 IGit + \delta Xit + \eta i + \nu t + \varepsilon it$$

GEit is the dependent variable representing gender equality in state *i* in year *t*, measured as the ratio of the scaled female-to-male enrollment in primary and secondary schools. IG_{it} are the intergovernmental grants variables, and GBit is the gender budgeting dummy that indicates whether there is an ongoing gender budgeting effort in state *i* in year *t*. Xit is a vector of control variables representing other factors that might influence the dependent variable (gender equality). These factors include items such as state revenue-raising capacity and preferences toward gender equality; εit is the random error term; and β and δ are parameters to be estimated.

The model also includes state-fixed effects, ηi, to control for time-invariant characteristics of state *i*, and time-fixed effects, νt, to control for state-invariant characteristics of time t. The state-fixed effects might capture any of a number of systematic and invariant (at least over the period of the sample) differences across states, such as religious and cultural traditions. The following is one example of a state-fixed effect:

> Kerala is well known in India as a state with a strong matriarchal tradition, where property is inherited through the mother, while most states in India have strong patriarchal traditions, where fathers are the head of the extended family.
>
> (Stotsky and Zaman, 2016, p. 18)

As noted in Stotsky and Zaman (2016), ideally, we would like to include in our analysis other variables influencing gender equality in education beyond gender parity in enrollment index. However, unfortunately, the database does not provide any other gender equality outcome variables for education in Indian states across time. The paucity of data on religious affiliation across states, and the multiplicity of political parties in different states, also limit the usefulness of these factors in the present model as independent variables.

We examined the following variables that might affect gender equality: real income per capita and per capita grants from the central government, with the latter disaggregated into unconditional and conditional fiscal transfers, both measured as the natural log of real per capita amounts; population, measured in millions; and GDP from agriculture, manufacturing, and services, all measured as a ratio of total state GDP.

Population is used to control for economies of scale in providing public services and might also have an effect on gender equality through indirect means. For instance, states with larger populations might be more exposed to influences that would change the dynamic toward gender equality (Stotsky and Zaman, 2016). The impact of structural transformation of the economy is captured through the share of the state economy attributed to various types of economic activity, which could affect gender-equality outcomes by influencing how women participate in the economic life of the society (Figure 9.2).

We cannot capture the full richness of all the determinants of gender equality by the limited number of variables included in our model. Unfortunately, we do not have available a dataset with household data that would be required to examine this issue in more detail.

Statistical methodology

We used a panel data approach to examine the effect of gender budgeting and intergovernmental grants on gender-equality outcomes in education. For our econometric model, we used the Hausman test to choose whether the fixed effects or random effects specification is better to explain the behavior of the error term. The test statistics suggest that the fixed effects specifications are better. In addition to fixed effects models, we also tried the generalized method of moments (GMM) approach to account for a lagged dependent variable and to address the potential endogeneity of the independent variables. The lagged dependent variable captured in the GMM models can better measure the dynamic process by which gender-equality indicators evolve over time. The following sections report both the panel data results with fixed effects and the GMM specifications.

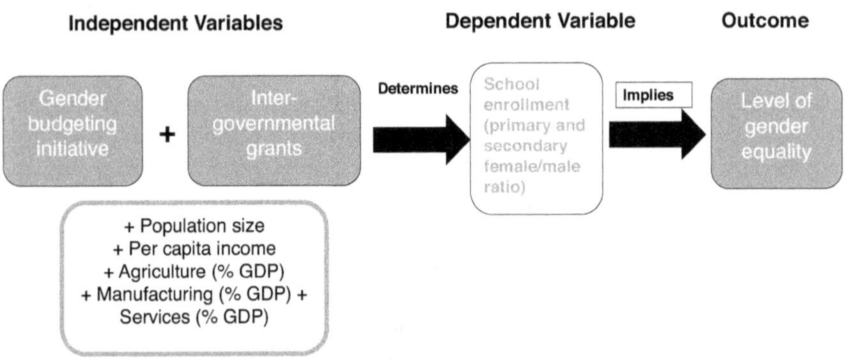

Figure 9.2 India: Fiscal and Economic Variables That Influence Gender Equality

Source: Author.

Fixed effect results

In our results (Tables 9.2 and 9.3), we present estimations with the gender-equality outcome variable measured in terms of enrollment in education, using fixed effects. We have used both one-way and two-way fixed effects. Stotsky and Zaman (2016) presented results based on probit analysis suggesting that the decision to adopt gender budgeting is not endogenous to economic decisions but rather is driven by political considerations, ruling out a potential complication.

In Table 9.2, we present the results of our analytical model, with the intergovernmental grants specified in aggregate form and gender budgeting specified as a contemporaneous dummy variable. The other variables in the model are real per capita income, log of population, agriculture GDP, manufacturing GDP, and services GDP, all measured as a ratio to state GDP. Time dummies have been suppressed, but complete results are available from the authors.

The first two columns of results (A and B) are for the dependent variable of gender equality in enrollment for lower primary school, with the one-way fixed effects reported in the first column and the two-way fixed effects reported in the second column. The fixed effects (one way and two way) for the gender-equality outcome for upper primary and lower and upper secondary school are reported in columns C through H. Our results show no significant relation of aggregate grants to gender equality in enrollment in the primary and secondary education sectors. The gender budgeting dummy is positive and significant only in the regression equations for lower and upper primary school for the one-way fixed effects models. These results provide limited evidence for the efficacy of gender budgeting in the 16 Indian states. One should note, though, that in many of these states, gender budgeting may have been initiated only a few years before enrollment data were collected, and therefore, its full effect is not yet visible in the statistics.

Real per capita income has significant and positive effects on gender-equality outcomes only for the one-way fixed effects model for lower and upper secondary enrollment ratios, suggesting that as income rises, gender equality improves. Population size is found positive and significant in influencing gender equality in the lower primary and lower secondary school equations of the one-way and two-way fixed effects models, suggesting some economies of scale. The sectoral shares of economic output do not have a significant impact, except for the services sector in the upper primary one-way fixed effects model. This suggests that the composition of state output does not have a strong impact on gender equality, at least measured by school enrollment.

These results provide support for the idea that rising income may lead to greater gender equality in education, measured by enrollment, and some limited support for the positive influence of gender budgeting but no support for grants and transfers. However, our concern is that the grants variable is measured in overly aggregate form and that we may be missing a crucial relationship. Our next approach was to disaggregate this grants variable into its two components of unconditional and conditional grants.

Table 9.2 India: Impact of Gender Budgeting and Intergovernmental Grants on Gender Equality with Aggregate Transfers, Fixed Effects Estimates

Variables	*Gender-Equality Index Lower Primary School (female-to-male ratio)*		*Gender-Equality Index Upper Primary School (female-to-male ratio)*		*Gender-Equality Index Lower Secondary School (female-to-male ratio)*		*Gender-Equality Index Upper Secondary School (female-to-male ratio)*	
	Panel One way	*Panel Two way*	*Panel One way*	*Panel Two way*	*Panel One way*	*Panel Two way*	*Panel One way*	*Panel Two way*
	A	*B*	*C*	*D*	*E*	*D*	*G*	*H*
Real per capita aggregate grants (log)	0. 013	-0.002	0.031	-0.001	0.010	-0.008	0.099	0.039
	(0.024)	(0.028)	(0.039)	(0.042)	(0.044)	(0.062)	(0.061)	(0.054)
Real per capita income (log)	0.018	-0.002	0.054	-0.059	0.156***	0.097	0.233***	-0.304
	(0.029)	(0.048)	(0.038)	(0.084)	(0.046)	(0.151)	(0.073)	(0.208)
Population (log)	0.002**	0.002*	0.003	0.002	0.010**	0.009*	−0.000	-0.005
	(0.001)	(0.001)	(0.002)	(0.002)	(0.005)	(0.005)	(0.005)	(0.005)
Agriculture GSDP(% of State GSDP)	0.001	-0.000	0.002	0.002	-0.002	-0.003	0.002	-0.000
	(0.001)	(0.002)	(0.002)	(0.002)	(0.003)	(0.004)	(0.005)	(0.005)
Manufacturing GSDP (% of State GSDP)	-0.000	-0.001	0.000	0.001	-0.001	-0.000	-0.002	0.002
	(0.001)	(0.002)	(0.002)	(0.002)	(0.003)	(0.003)	(0.003)	(0.004)
Services GSDP (% of State GSDP)	0.002	0.001	0.004*	0.002	0.002	0.001	0.001	-0.005
	(0.001)	(0.002)	(0.002)	(0.002)	(0.003)	(0.003)	(0.003)	(0.005)
Gender budgeting	0.024*	0.020	0.031*	0.029	0.005	0.002	-0.005	-0.024
	(0.012)	(0.013)	(0.018)	(0.018)	(0.021)	(0.023)	(0.025)	(0.027)
Constant	0.485*	0.911*	-0.222	1.297	-1.288**	-0.452	-2.58***	4.213*
	(0.275)	(0.470)	(0.337)	(0.878)	(0.525)	(1.931)	(0.594)	(2.461)
Observations	280	280	280	280	168	168	168	168
R-squared(within)	0.266	0.294	0.392	0.431	0.340	0.371	0.367	0.493
No. of states	28	28	28	28	28	28	28	28
State FE	Yes	Yes	Yes	Yes	Yes	Yes	Yes	Yes
Year FE		Yes		Yes		Yes		Yes

Sources: Our databases and estimates.

Notes: Robust standard error in parentheses

*** $p < 0.01$
** $p < 0.05$
* $p < 0.1$

Table 9.3 India: Impact of Gender Budgeting and Intergovernmental Grants on Gender Equality with Disaggregate Grants and Transfers Variables, Fixed Effects Estimates

Variables	*Gender-Equality Index Lower Primary School (female-to-male ratio)*		*Gender-Equality Index Upper Primary School (female-to-male ratio)*		*Gender-Equality Index Lower Secondary School (female-to-male ratio)*		*Gender-Equality Index Upper Secondary School (female-to-male ratio)*	
	Panel One way	*Panel Two way*	*Panel One way*	*Panel Two way*	*Panel One way*	*Panel Two way*	*Panel One way*	*Panel Two way*
Real per capita conditional grants (log)	0.004	-0.004	0.021	0.007	-0.018	-0.012	-0.003	0.005
	(.013)	(.014)	(0.026)	(0.025)	(0.033)	(0.033)	(0.033)	(0.035)
Real per capita unconditional grants (log)	0. 003	-0.016	-0.002	-0.050*	0.064*	0.027	0.168***	0.054
	(0.015)	(0.020)	(0.023)	(0.028)	(0.037)	(0.080)	(0.052)	(0.082)
Real income per capita (log)	0.025	0.003	0.069*	-0.043	0.132***	0.107	0.186**	-0.280
	(0.031)	(0.047)	(0.035)	(0.082)	(0.047)	(0.150)	(0.078)	(0.208)
Population (log)	0.002**	0.002	0.002	0.001	0.010**	0.010*	−0.000	-0.004
	(0.001)	(0.001)	(0.002)	(0.002)	(0.005)	(0.005)	(0.005)	(0.005)
Agriculture GSDP(% of State GSDP)	0.001	-0.000	0.002	0.001	-0.003	-0.003	0.001	-0.000
	(0.001)	(0.002)	(0.002)	(0.002)	(0.003)	(0.004)	(0.005)	(0.005)
Manufacturing GSDP (% of State GSDP)	-0.000	-0.001	0.000	0.001	-0.002	-0.001	-0.004	0.001
	(0.001)	(0.002)	(0.002)	(0.002)	(0.003)	(0.003)	(0.004)	(0.004)
Services GSDP(% of State GSDP)	0.002	0.001	0.004*	0.002	0.000	0.001	-0.002	-0.006
	(0.001)	(0.002)	(0.002)	(0.002)	(0.003)	(0.004)	(0.004)	(0.005)
Gender budgeting	0.024*	0.020	0.031*	0.028	0.002	0.002	-0.014	-0.023
	(0.012)	(0.013)	(0.018)	(0.018)	(0.021)	(0.023)	(0.025)	(0.027)
Constant	0.466	0.996**	-0.261	1.466	-1.189**	-0.716	-0.281***	3.860
	(0.288)	(0.468)	(0.347)	(0.900)	(0.510)	(2.064)	(0.646)	(2.617)
Observations	280	280	280	280	168	168	168	168
R-squared(within)	0.264	0.297	0.393	0.443	0.355	0.372	0.422	0.493
No. of states	28	28	28	28	28	28	28	28
State FE	Yes	Yes	Yes	Yes	Yes	Yes	Yes	Yes
Year FE		Yes		Yes		Yes		Yes

Sources: Our databases and estimates.

Notes: Robust standard error in parentheses

*** $p < 0.01$
** $p < 0.05$
* $p < 0.1$

In Table 9.3, we present the impact of gender budgeting and intergovernmental grants, but here we disaggregate the grants variables. We find that conditional grants have no significant relationship to gender equality. However, we also discover that in the upper primary school two-way fixed effects estimation, unconditional grants have an inverse and significant relationship with gender equality. In contrast, in the lower and upper secondary school one-way fixed effects results, we find that transfers have a positive and significant relationship. Gender budgeting has a positive and significant effect on gender equality in the one-way fixed effects estimations, as in the earlier analysis. Real per capita income has a significant effect on gender equality in the one-way fixed effects specifications for upper primary schooling and for lower and upper secondary schooling. Population size is positive and significant in lower primary and lower secondary education, and services are positive and significant again in only one estimation.

We explore further disaggregation of the conditional grants by separating SSA grants dedicated to education from other conditional grants and enter both variables linearly in the equation. This analysis relaxes the constraint that the SSA grants and other conditional grants have the same coefficient. Table 9.4 presents the results.

We find that SSA grants are positive and significant in the primary education estimations and one upper secondary estimation—an intuitively appealing result. Their significance seems to reduce the significance of the gender budgeting variables that we previously found significant in some estimations. This suggests that gender budgeting might have been picking up some of the effect of this grant program that was concealed by the aggregate specification. Whether gender budgeting contributed to the efficacy of the program or whether this is an incidental correlation is hard to discern from these aggregate data.

Generalized method of moments (GMM) results

A GMM specification, in contrast to the fixed effects estimations, may better account for the persistence of the indicator over time and also possible endogeneity of right-hand side variables. We explore a number of GMM estimators and present the system GMM as the best specification, after an examination of the test statistics.[11] Table 9.5 presents the results. In each column, we choose the set of endogenous variables by examining the difference-in-Sargan test on exogeneity of instrumental variables and use the minimal set of endogenous variables to satisfy the chi-squared test statistic for adequacy.

For all four dependent variables, the lagged dependent variable is positive and strongly significant, with a value above 0.6, suggesting strong persistence of the indicator over time. We also obtain that the grants variables and income and population are endogenous in all regressions. As with the fixed effects specification (using Table 9.3 results), we find that the conditional transfers are not

Table 9.4 India: Impact of Gender Budgeting and Intergovernmental Grants on Gender Equality with Disaggregated SSA and Grants Variables, Fixed Effects Estimates

Variables	*Gender-Equality Index Lower Primary School (female-to-male ratio)*		*Gender-Equality Index Upper Primary School (female-to-male ratio)*		*Gender-Equality Index Lower Secondary School (female-to-male ratio)*		*Gender-Equality Index Upper Secondary School (female-to-male ratio)*	
	Panel One way	*Panel Two way*	*Panel One way*	*Panel Two way*	*Panel One way*	*Panel Two way*	*Panel One way*	*Panel Two way*
Real per capita conditional grants minus SSA (log)	0.011	0.012	0.035	0.041	-0.007	-0.002	0.009	0.019
	(.010)	(.012)	(0.031)	(0.031)	(0.029)	(0.030)	(0.030)	(0.029)
Real per capita SSA (log)	0.009**	0.009**	0.012*	0.019**	0.000	0.006	0.006	0.013*
	(.004)	(0.004)	(0.007)	(0.009)	(0.009)	(0.010)	(0.009)	(0.007)
Real per capita unconditional grants (log)	0. 034	0.060	0.028	0.014	0.061	0.024	0.171***	0.057
	(0.027)	(0.042)	(0.026)	(0.075)	(0.037)	(0.081)	(0.053)	(0.082)
Real income per capita (log)	0.005	-0.001	0.073	0.038	0.122**	0.093	0.175**	-0.339
	(0.035)	(0.107)	(0.046)	(0.121)	(0.046)	(0.151)	(0.075)	(0.210)
Population (log)	0.006*	0.006*	0.005	0.005	0.010*	0.010*	−0.000	-0.005
	(0.003)	(0.003)	(0.004)	(0.004)	(0.005)	(0.005)	(0.005)	(0.005)
Agriculture GSDP(% of State GSDP)	0.001	0.001	0.002	0.001	-0.003	-0.003	0.001	0.001
	(0.002)	(0.002)	(0.003)	(0.004)	(0.004)	(0.004)	(0.005)	(0.005)
Manufacturing GSDP(% of State GSDP)	0.000	-0.000	-0.001	-0.001	-0.002	-0.000	-0.003	0.002
	(0.002)	(0.002)	(0.002)	(0.003)	(0.003)	(0.003)	(0.004)	(0.004)
Services GSDP(% of State GSDP)	0.001	0.000	0.002*	0.002	0.000	0.001	-0.002	-0.006
	(0.002)	(0.002)	(0.002)	(0.002)	(0.003)	(0.004)	(0.004)	(0.005)
Gender budgeting	0.009	0.011	0.020	0.024	0.002	0.003	-0.014	-0.022
	(0.010)	(0.012)	(0.018)	(0.017)	(0.021)	(0.022)	(0.025)	(0.026)
Constant	0.240	0.149**	-0.708	-0.269	-1.167**	-0.661	-2.334***	4.313
	(0.316)	(1.197)	(0.574)	(1.913)	(0.536)	(2.042)	(0.638)	(2.617)
Observations	167	167	167	167	168	168	168	168
R-squared(within)	0.282	0.288	0.369	0.399	0.351	0.371	0.425	0.507
No. of states	28	28	28	28	28	28	28	28
State FE	Yes	Yes	Yes	Yes	Yes	Yes	Yes	Yes
Year FE		Yes		Yes		Yes		Yes

Sources: Our databases and estimates.

Notes: Robust standard error in parentheses

*** $p < 0.01$
** $p < 0.05$
* $p < 0.1$

Table 9.5 India: Impact of Gender Budgeting and Intergovernmental Grants on Gender Equality, GMM Estimates

Variables	*Gender-Equality Index Lower Primary School (female-to-male ratio)*	*Gender-Equality Index Upper Primary School (female-to-male ratio)*	*Gender-Equality Index Lower Secondary School (female-to-male ratio)*	*Gender-Equality Index Upper Secondary School (female-to-male ratio)*
Lagged dependent variable	0.629***	0.739***	0.780***	0.831***
	(0.052)	(0.047)	(0.071)	(0.058)
Real per capita conditional grants (log)	0.003	0.003	-0.002	-0.005
	(0.004)	(0.006)	(0.010)	(0.010)
Real per capita unconditional grants (log)	-0.003	0.011	0.028*	0.038**
	(0.006)	(0.008)	(0.017)	(0.020)
Real income per capita (log)	0.022***	0.023**	0.002	0.001
	(0.008)	(0.010)	(0.022)	(0.021)
Population (log)	0.000	-0.000	-0.000	-0.000*
	(0.000)	(0.000)	(0.000)	(0.002)
Agriculture GSDP (% of State GSDP)	0.001**0.001)	0.002**	0.001	-0.004***
		(0.001)	(0.002)	(0.001)
Manufacturing GSDP(% of State GSDP)	0.001	0.001	0.001	-0.002
	(0.001)	(0.001)	(0.002)	(0.002)
Services GSDP(% of State GSDP)	0.001	0.001**	0.001	0.002
	(0.000)	(0.001)	(0.001)	(0.001)
Gender budgeting	0.008*	0.004	-0.018	-0.023**
	(0.005)	(0.006)	(0.012)	(0.011)
Constant	0.071	-0.194*	-0.077	-0.228
	(0.076)	(0.104)	(0.265)	(0.285)
Number of instruments	137	113	109	97
Difference-in-Sargan test on exogeneity of iv instruments (chi2 and prob > chi2)	5.53	6.68	0.63	4.00
	(0.237)	(0.245)	(0.427)	(0.135)
	4 degrees of freedom	5 degrees of freedom	1 degree of freedom	2 degrees of freedom

Sources: Our databases and estimates.

significant, while we find some limited significance of the unconditional transfers. For the two secondary school dependent variables, unconditional grants are positive and significant. We also find a positive effect of per capita income, here for primary school, while in the fixed income, it was mixed across primary and secondary school. Population has a negative and significant effect for upper secondary school, while it had a positive and significant effect in several of the fixed effects specifications. Agriculture has positive and significant effects for primary school and a negative effect for upper secondary school, in contrast to no significance for the fixed effects.

This finding is somewhat at variance with the expectation that the more agrarian states would be less gender equal in school enrollment. Services, as with the fixed effects specification, is positive and significant only for upper primary school. Some similarity is found with gender budgeting at the primary level, here only for lower primary school. Curiously, gender budgeting is found to have a negative and significant effect for upper secondary school, a result that demands further exploration at a more detailed level.

Altogether the results suggest some degree of correspondence with the fixed effects results, providing comfort with regard to the robustness of the analysis, the strong significance of the lagged dependent variable and extent of endogeneity of the explanatory variables weighs heavily in favor of the GMM analysis. The results suggest little impact of conditional grants overall, though some positive impact of unconditional grants and income, where unconditional grants are functioning largely as a form of income augmentation to the states. Gender budgeting's mixed effect is curious.

We also examine the disaggregate results where, as in Table 9.4, we disaggregate conditional grants by removing SSA grants from the aggregate and include two variables, conditional grants without SSA grants and SSA grants alone, and using the same specification. The GMM results for this specification are presented in Table 9.6. Again, we use system GMM and varying endogenous right-hand variables, selected on the basis of the difference-in-Sargan test of exogeneity. We see that the lagged dependent variable is still positive and strongly significant and that conditional grants without SSA grants are not significant. Interestingly, SSA grants are no longer significant at all, in contrast to the fixed effects outcome, where they were significant for primary education and upper secondary school for the two-way fixed effects. Unconditional grants are significant for secondary school, showing some correspondence with the result for fixed effects, where they were for the upper secondary school one-way fixed effects estimation. Also, interestingly, income is not significant and population is negative and significant only for upper secondary school. Agriculture is again significant for primary school, as in Table 9.5, whereas manufacturing and services show some mixed positive effects. Gender budgeting is again negative and significant only for upper secondary school—again, a surprising finding.

Table 9.6 India: Impact of Gender Budgeting and Intergovernmental Grants on Gender Equality with Separate SSA and Grants Variables, GMM Estimates

Variables	*Gender-Equality Index Lower Primary School (female-to-male ratio)*	*Gender-Equality Index Upper Primary School (female-to-male ratio)*	*Gender-Equality Index Lower Secondary School (female-to-male ratio)*	*Gender-Equality Index Upper Secondary School (female-to-male ratio)*
Lagged dependent variable	0.521***	0.734***	0.741***	0.828***
	(0.061)	(0.057)	(0.072)	(0.060)
Real per capita conditional grants minus SSA (log)	0.004	-0.000	-0.001	-0.001
	(0.005)	(0.007)	(0.010)	(0.009)
Real per capita SSA (log)	0.003	0.000	-0.007	-0.006
	(0.004)	(0.005)	(0.008)	(0.008)
Real per capita unconditional grants (log)	-0.005	0.028	0.038**	0.031*
	(0.009)	(0.011)	(0.018)	(0.018)
Real income per capita (log)	0.003	0.009	0.000	-0.008
	(0.011)	(0.015)	(0.022)	(0.021)
Population (log)	0.000	-0.000	-0.000	-0.000*
	(0.000)	(0.000)	(0.000)	(0.000)
Agriculture GSDP (% of State GSDP)	0.002**	0.002**	0.003	-0.002
	(0.001)	(0.001)	(0.002)	(0.002)
Manufacturing GSDP(% of State GSDP)	0.002**	0.001	0.002	0.003
	(0.001)	(0.001)	(0.002)	(0.002)
Services GSDP(% of State GSDP)	0.001	0.002**	0.002*	0.002
	(0.001)	(0.001)	(0.001)	(0.001)
Gender budgeting	0.003	-0.001	-0.017	-0.023**
	(0.005)	(0.007)	(0.012)	(0.011)
Constant	0.355	-0.177	-0.154	-0.069
	(0.121)	(0.182)	(0.296)	(0.292)
Number of instruments	89	89	98	98
Difference-in-Sargan test on exogeneity of iv instruments (chi2 and prob > chi2)	5.60	5.19	2.36	3.57
	(0.348)	(0.393)	(0.500)	(0.312)
	5 degrees of freedom	5 degrees of freedom	3 degrees of freedom	3 degrees of freedom

Sources: Our databases and estimates.

V. Conclusion

Our results suggest that intergovernmental grants from the federal government to states do not have a strong impact in promoting gender equality in enrollment in primary and secondary education in India. There is some evidence that unconditional grants have a positive effect on gender-equality outcomes, but there is little evidence to suggest conditional grants, even those falling within an educational grants program, SSA, have had a strong influence on outcomes. Real per capita income is shown to have some effect, but again, it is not as strong and consistent as one might have expected.

Gender budgeting also surprisingly shows a mixed effect, with a small effect on primary school enrollment in the fixed effects model but a little to negative effect in the GMM models. The precise mechanism through which gender-related programs may be working to influence educational parity deserves greater attention. A higher degree of data granularity might allow for more accurate measurements about the extent of gender budgeting in each state; and with better data, this type of analysis might offer more consistent and stronger correlations between gender budgeting and female school enrollment. Finally, it might be worth doing this analysis, with the outcome variable being *tertiary* enrollment ratios rather than primary and secondary. Table 9.1 shows that the female-to-male enrollment ratios are all greater than or equal to 0.90 in the 16 states surveyed. This means there isn't much improvement that can be achieved, even if gender budgeting and governmental grants are effective. However, Figure 6.8 in Chapter 6 shows that recent tertiary enrollment ratios in India were below 0.80. This could be an analysis worth investigating to further clarify the impact of gender budgeting and government transfers on gender equality measured in this way.

For policymakers, the results suggest that integrating gender criteria in intergovernmental grants could strengthen the positive impact on gender equality. Another important conclusion from this analysis is that income gains do not seem sufficient by themselves to generate a significant change in equality of enrollment. Thus, even as income in India rises due to economic growth, government interventions to reduce gender inequality via policies and budgeting priorities will still be necessary.

Gender budgeting efforts at subnational government levels have not been sufficient to promote gender equality in educational enrollment at the primary and secondary levels. Further investigation with more detailed fiscal and demographic data and at a finer level of disaggregation of transfer programs is called for.

Notes

1 This chapter draws on previously published work: Stotsky and Zaman (2016) and Stotsky, Chakraborty, and Gandhi (2019). I thank Manuk Ghazanchyan and Li Tang for expert assistance with the statistical work and several referees for useful comments.

2 See also Chakraborty, Ingrams, and Singh (2017).

3 See the Centre for Budget and Governance Accountability (2012), Joshi (2013), and India's Ministry of Women and Child Development (2015).
4 See Karnataka, Department of Women and Child Development web page.
5 Hindriks and Myles (2006) provides a useful overview of different approaches.
6 Dahlberg et al. (2008) found, using data from Sweden, that grants from the central government increased local spending and that taking into account the endogeneity of grants was critical in accurately assessing the marginal impact of grants on local fiscal decisions.
7 In India, there may be a significant discrepancy between budgeted and actual expenditures.
8 Details on the compilation of the data are available from the author.
9 Lower primary school roughly encompasses ages six to ten and upper primary school ages 11 to 13. Lower secondary school roughly encompasses ages 14 to 16 and upper secondary school, higher ages. It is possible to have female-to-male ratios above 1 because of repeating students or enrollment of students above the typical age.
10 In the Asia Pacific context, Chakraborty, Ingrams, and Singh (2017) use budget call circulars as given in a 2017 UN Women survey to categorize the countries into gender budgeting and non–gender budgeting countries.
11 Our GMM specification makes use of STATA's Xtbond2 routine. For lower primary school, all variables up to population are treated as endogenous. For upper primary school, population is treated as exogenous. Although the results are relatively stable with other assumptions on exogeneity, this specification for the explanatory variables yields appropriate chi-squared statistics on the Sargan difference tests of the exogeneity of instrumental variables instruments. Full results are available from the authors.

References

Bird, Richard M., and Michael Smart, 2002, "Intergovernmental Fiscal Transfers: International Lessons for Developing Countries," *World Development*, Vol. 30, pp. 899–212.

Boadway, Robin W., and Anwar Shah, 2007, *Intergovernmental Fiscal Transfers: Principles and Practice* (Washington, DC: The World Bank).

Bradford, David, and Wallace E. Oates, 1971, "Towards a Predictive Theory of Intergovernmental Grants," *American Economic Review*, Vol. 61, pp. 440–448.

Centre for Budget and Governance Accountability, 2012, "Recognizing Gender Biases, Rethinking Budgets," CBGA Report supported by UN Women (New Delhi: CBGA).

Chakraborty, Lekha S., 2010, "Determining Gender Equity in Fiscal Federalism: Analytical Issues and Empirical Evidence from India," Working Paper 590 (New York: The Levy Economics Institute of Bard College).

Chakraborty, Lekha S., Marian Ingrams, and Yadawendra Singh, 2017, "Effectiveness of Gender Budgeting on Gender Equality Outcomes and Fiscal Space: Evidence from Asia Pacific," GRoW Research Paper WP 2017–09 (Montreal: McGill University).

Chakraborty, Pinaki, Lekha S. Chakraborty, Manish Gupta, Amandeep Kaur, Shatakshi Garg, and Azharuddin Khan, 2018, "A Study of Intergovernmental Fiscal Transfers in India," NIPFP-IDRC Report (New Delhi: NIPFP).

Dahlberg, Matz, Eva Mörk, Jorn Rattsø, and Hanna Ågren, 2008, "Using a Discontinuous Grant Rule to Identify the Effect of Grants on Local Taxes and Spending," *Journal of Public Economics*, Vol. 92, pp. 2320–2335.

Hindriks, Jean, and Gareth D. Myles, 2006, *Intermediate Public Economics* (Cambridge, MA: MIT Press).

Hines, James R., and Richard H. Thaler, 1995, "Anomalies: The Flypaper Effect," *Journal of Economic Perspectives*, Vol. 9, pp. 217–226.

India, Ministry of Women and Child Development, 2015, *Gender Budgeting Handbook* (New Delhi: Government of India).

Isaac, Thomas T.M., R. Mohan, and Lekha Chakraborty, 2019, *Challenges to Indian Fiscal Federalism* (New Delhi: Leftward Books).

Joshi, Swapna B., 2013, *Assessing Gender Equality Investments: A Multi-State Perspective* (New Delhi: UN Women and National Foundation for India).

Kaur, Balbir, and Sangita Misra, 2003, "Social Sector Expenditure and Attainments: An Analysis of Indian States," Reserve Bank of India Occasional Papers 24 (New Delhi: Reserve Bank of India).

Khera, Purva, 2016, "Macroeconomic Impacts of Gender Inequality and Informality in India," International Monetary Fund Working Paper, Vol. 16 (Washington, DC: IMF).

Reddy, Y. V. and G. R. Reddy, 2019, *Indian Fiscal Federalism* (New Delhi: Oxford University Press).

Stotsky, Janet G., and Asad Zaman, 2016, "The Influence of Gender Budgeting in Indian States on Gender Inequality and Fiscal Spending," IMF Working Paper 16/227 (Washington, DC: IMF).

Stotsky, Janet G., Lekha Chakraborty, and Piyush Gandhi, "Impact of Intergovernmental Fiscal Transfers on Gender Equality in India: An Empirical Analysis," McGill University and IDRC, GRoW Working Paper Series, GWP-2019–22 (Montreal: IDRC).

World Bank, 2011, *World Development Report 2012: Gender Equality and Development* (Washington, DC: World Bank).

10 General summary, recommendations, and conclusions

I. Introduction

Since its inception about 30 years ago, gender budgeting has spread to over 80 countries in the world and has been recognized as an important, if inadequately implemented, tool in improving women's and girls' access to education, health care, and the labor force, and in empowering them economically and politically. Gender budgeting also calls attention to the role that fiscal policies and public financial management can play in promoting gender equality, even when ingrained cultural influences and traditional practices present countervailing pressures.

Early interest in gender budgeting arose mostly in developed countries, perhaps as an outcome of the women's movements in the 1960s and 1970s, accompanied by large growth in female political participation in these countries. The research evidence that we have presented in this book, however, clearly shows that the greater need to elevate equality for women is in the developing world where gender disparities in fundamental areas, such as education, health-care access, paid workforce participation, and legal inheritance, still prevail in many countries.

Developing regions of the world with pronounced gender inequality, such as the Middle East, South Asia, and sub-Saharan Africa, have experienced a significant increase in female political participation in recent decades, but usually without comparable gains in economic equality. Our review of developing regions shows, though, that both increased political participation *and* economic equality are needed to significantly improve the welfare of women and their societies, as a whole. Figure 2.1 in Chapter 2 shows that as GDP increases, typically the GDI rises. However, the results of our econometric analysis in Chapter 9 demonstrates that modest rises in income in a developing country like India do not necessarily translate into sufficient increases in school enrollment to close all gender gaps. Specific policies are needed to ensure that gender equality is achieved in the near future.

There are wealthy countries in the Middle East where women have high income (as part of household income) but few political and social rights. There are also developing countries like Rwanda and Ethiopia in which women are now gaining more equal political rights compared to men but have not yet achieved wage parity or equivalent economic opportunities. Gender budgeting efforts should be focused on both of these dimensions—the economic and the political or social—and in model programs, such as that in Rwanda, this is happening.

However, the successes of Rwanda and Ethiopia in recent years in reaching parity between men/boys and women/girls in important variables such as secondary school enrollments (as one example), are not the real end goals. Table 10.1 (with data taken from Appendix A in Chapter 5) shows three African countries, specifically their female-to-male ratios in secondary school enrollments and their absolute level of female enrollment.

With secondary school enrollments at such a low level, even with gender parity, a country will advance only so far. The goal of gender budgeting, therefore, should be to achieve gender equality but also to raise the level of well-being for both genders and the society as a whole.

Looking at various strategies to improve girls' education in the developing countries of Asia and Africa, it appears that programs designed to increase school enrollment that were gender-neutral (in other words, targeted at all children regardless of gender) on average achieved the same results as those that were directed specifically at girls (discussed in Chapter 3). Hence, gender budgeting need not always mean programming directed solely at girls or women but rather programs that raise the level of girls and boys or women and men, if applicable. In order to demonstrate this, of course, outcomes data must be disaggregated by sex.

II. Overall global summary assessment of gender budgeting efforts from a fiscal policy perspective

- In some countries, gender budgeting has led to changes in fiscal policies in such key areas as school enrollment and health care and contributed to achieving specific gender-related goals.
- In some countries, gender budgeting has led to improvements in transportation, utilities, and economic infrastructure and has contributed to greater participation of women and girls in economic and political life.

Table 10.1 Relative Female-to-Male Secondary School Enrollments and Absolute Levels of Female Enrollment

Country	*Relative Female-to-Male Enrollment Ratio (as a percentage)*	*Absolute Level of Female Secondary School Enrollment (as a percentage)*
Ethiopia	96	34
Rwanda	110	38
Uganda	83	25

Source: Author.

- Gender budgeting efforts seem to have led to meaningful fiscal policy changes only when they had the public support of top political leadership making fiscal decisions, such as the prime minister (or president) and the minister of finance.
- Incorporating gender budgeting into budget laws and public financial management practices is an important element to ensure that these efforts are long-lasting and lead to sustained reforms in policies and programs.

Adequately funding policies or programs derived from gender budgeting efforts and monitoring actual implementation are just as important parts of gender budgeting as declarations about policy intent and passing laws by a legislature or government. This point is demonstrated by comparing two African countries, Rwanda and Uganda, both of which incorporated gender-related concerns into their development budgets and introduced gender budgeting at national and local levels. The improved outcomes in Rwanda versus the less successful outcomes in Uganda (discussed in Chapter 5) demonstrate that establishing gender budgeting processes is not sufficient to produce progress. The critical factor favoring Rwanda was adequate funding, implementation, follow-through, and monitoring the results. All of these were more successfully executed in Rwanda than in Uganda.

III. Overall summary assessment of gender budgeting efforts from a public financial management perspective

Budgeting requirements

- In some countries, gender budgeting has led to improved systems for the public financial management of spending for gender-related purposes, even though most countries have so far not fully integrated gender-related objectives into public financial management systems.
- The use of gender budget statements, budget circulars, and monitoring the spending (and revenue) of institutions is a vital part of the institutionalization of gender budgeting.
- Adapting a budget classification system and an associated chart of accounts to incorporate a tracking of gender-related objectives facilitates the more-effective implementation and institutionalization of gender budgeting initiatives.
- A few countries have successfully incorporated gender budgeting into performance-based or program-based budgeting, which is a natural fit because of the thematic and cross-cutting nature of gender budgeting. Two examples of successful countries are Austria and Rwanda.
- Even without explicit program-based gender budgeting, a government should strive to integrate gender-related goals across the relevant government.
- Systematically integrating sex-disaggregated data into analysis of government programs and policies would allow for better monitoring of the success or failure of gender-related or gender-neutral programs.

- Effective gender budgeting efforts rely on the ability of governments to improve their policies and programs over time and to monitor the results across the agencies and departments of government. Only a few countries have elevated the monitoring function to the level and quality expected of government oversight and audit offices (e.g., Rwanda and some OECD countries).

Leadership requirements

- Within the executive branch of government, the leadership of the minister of finance is essential to driving fiscal policy and public financial management changes to support the goals of gender budgeting. The leadership of a prime minister or president is even more important in galvanizing support and follow-through (e.g., Ethiopia and Rwanda).
- The full participation of relevant spending and administrative ministries (such as health, education, infrastructure, and justice) into gender budgeting efforts has also been essential in ensuring that gender budgeting efforts were institutionalized in all areas of government spending and responsibility.
- Parliamentarians, parliamentary committees, and women's ministries (or advocacy groups) are important supports of the executive branch and have sometimes been catalytic in establishing gender budgeting processes (e.g., India, Indonesia, and the Philippines).
- Nongovernmental organizations, academic research and scholarship, and advocacy can at times play an essential role in gender budgeting efforts and in informing fiscal policies. Some gender budgeting initiatives remained alive only because of the persistent support of entities outside of government. But without the government as a full participant, gender budgeting efforts ultimately wane.
- International organizations and donors provide important technical assistance and financial support. Key external supporters of gender budgeting are UN Women, the United Nations Development Programme, and government foreign aid agencies.
- In most countries, subnational governments play a critical role in the provision of essential public services, such as education, health care, and infrastructure, and gender budgeting efforts should extend to these governments as well (e.g., case studies and econometric analysis of Indian states).

IV. Recommendations for low-income developing countries and some emerging market and developing countries

- Align gender budgeting efforts with the goals outlined in national development plans, including those related to the Sustainable Development Goals. This way, countries can ensure that their gender-related objectives fit into both the existing budget process and the overall national development schemes that have broad support.
- Ensure that girls have equal access to all levels of education, including their participation in science, technology, and math education. Gender equality

in education is universally correlated with a higher level of national development and income.

- Keep gender-related health goals as priorities. These goals include reducing high rates of maternal mortality and sexually transmitted diseases, including HIV/AIDS, and providing contraception services.
- Use cash transfer programs as a means to improve women's and children's access to education and health care, as a complement to essential state services.
- Improve the supply of electricity and water to households as well as cooking technologies to reduce girls' and women's time demands for domestic work; these demands often prevent women and girls from accessing educational resources and engaging in work experiences.
- Assess key sectors of the economy and educational system in which women could participate more productively; identify the constraints to their participation, including issues such as poor hygienic conditions and unsafe transportation; and develop fiscal policies to help address these constraints.
- Extend fiscal incentives, such as subsidies or reduced tax rates, to individuals, employers, and financial institutions, to encourage greater participation from women in economic activities.
- Ensure that subsistence agriculture remains a focus of fiscal policies and programs (e.g., Rwanda, Ethiopia, and Uganda), including through enhanced training for farmers in sub-Saharan Africa and other regions where women continue to play a predominant role.
- Adapt the chart of accounts and program budgeting to incorporate gender-related objectives over medium-term economic frameworks, not just short-term ones.
- Eliminate gender-based inequalities in tax, financial, civil, and other laws, and ensure that women's rights to ownership and control of property are equal to men's rights.

Strengthening support for gender budgeting goals in developing countries

Meaningful gender budgeting requires informational tools such as gender budgeting statements (discussed in Chapter 4) and disaggregating public expenditure into male and female categories, in order to measure existing gaps and improvements that result from new policies and programs. Many gender budgeting advocates believe that practical efforts should initially focus on limited areas of the budget that relate to specific female development concerns—such as education and health care—and expand later, after initial successes in implementation in the entire budget.

The problem with this approach is that governments can easily make proclamations about the importance of gender equality, establish a limited number of high-profile projects in education and health care, and then abandon interest in the more challenging areas. This seems to have been what has happened in India at the national level and in Korea (discussed in Chapters 7 and 8, respectively). In contrast, the Indian state of Kerala has implemented a gender budgeting approach throughout the entire budget and has produced impressive changes in many gender-related dimensions. Of participants in local citizens' forums that make governing decisions, 50 percent are women (discussed in Chapter 7). Three schemes in areas not traditionally seen as "women related" have been instituted: gender-friendly infrastructure, an income support scheme for women, and a food security scheme for women. Similarly, in Rwanda, gender budgeting has been applied across broad areas of the budget since 2010/2011. Half of the national cabinet is now female, and girls' secondary school enrollment presently surpasses that of boys.

The Rwanda model

We have consistently noted throughout this book that Rwanda's gender budgeting policies and programs could be considered a model for sub-Saharan Africa and elsewhere. A quick review of how the Rwandan government developed its gender budgeting framework demonstrates the sort of process that other developing countries could emulate (discussed in Chapter 5).

1 Rwanda's constitution of 2003 mandated at least 30 percent of decision-making positions in government (among other institutions) must be held by women. A gender monitoring office issues periodic reports on the implementation of gender budgeting and how many women hold positions in key economic and political sectors.
2 A first attempt in Rwanda to institutionalize gender budgeting failed because of both a lack of central involvement from the Minister of Finance and an overreliance on outside experts rather than building local capacity. These shortcomings were later rectified.
3 Pilot programs were set up across many sectors of the budget, not just the obvious gender-related ones such as health care and education but also areas such as social services, economic development, and infrastructure.
4 The gender monitoring office ensures follow-through on developing, funding, and executing programs.
5 Matching the format of gender budgeting to a program-based budgeting approach, rather than a line-item one, helps to keep track of the progress of programs and allows cost-benefit calculations to be made regarding program value once outcomes data are collected.
6 Strong and consistent support from the president for gender-equality goals has no doubt been a factor in the improvement of key gender-equality indicators for Rwanda.

V. Recommendations for emerging market and developing and developed countries

Gender-related inequality concerns in emerging markets and developed countries are in many ways different from those in low-income developing countries.

In most of the more-developed countries, girls' enrollment in secondary and tertiary education now surpasses that of boys. Women work in occupations that were once held mostly by men, although wage rates in all job categories still favor men for similar work performed. The main gender-specific concerns of women in developed countries center on the burdens of caregiving, child-rearing, and insufficient pensions that are unique to women trying to balance work and family obligations. Hence, our recommendations concerning gender-related policies and programs focus on this set of issues.

- Identify structures in income tax systems that lead to a higher effective tax rate on secondary workers in the household, which may discourage women's participation in the labor force. The move to individual-based income tax systems is one means to reduce this problem. Even within income tax systems that impose a joint income tax on the household, structure the income tax to reduce the higher effective tax rate on secondary earners.
- Use fiscal incentives or public spending to support child and dependent care to ease the burden of unpaid labor in the home, including dependent care, which still falls disproportionately on women.
- Restructure low-income assistance programs to ensure that the specific needs of women and single woman–headed families are met, and these families are treated equitably with two-parent families.
- Ensure income security for elderly women by reforming fiscal policies directed toward pensions and social security–type payments in old age.

VI. Final thoughts

Well-structured fiscal policies and sound public financial management practices have the potential to improve gender equality and aid in the healthy development of women and girls. This can be seen in the case studies that we have outlined in various country experiences of gender budgeting. Nonetheless, evaluated objectively, our review has shown that explicit gender budgeting efforts have generally achieved modest results so far in the developing world. Furthermore, most of the countries in the developed world that have the highest level of gender equality have not implemented gender budgeting at all or have only started to move in this direction in the past few years.

Meanwhile, in developing countries in Africa and Asia, as we have noted in Chapters 5 and 6, many countries have put into place an assortment of gender budgeting proclamations, policies, and accounting methodologies without producing significant, measurable, or meaningful outcomes. As our comparison of Rwanda and Uganda earlier in the chapter demonstrated, it is not the idea or even the process of enacting gender budgeting that matters most but instead the conscientious implementation of well-designed programs and policies and then the application of successful programs on a larger scale that really matters.

In both developing countries and developed countries, we see, then, that improvements in the status of women and caring for their special needs can be accomplished regardless of whether an initiative is called gender budgeting or not. But programs must be incorporated into the government budget to have an effect. However, gender budgeting helps inculcate a gender-related consciousness and attentiveness to ingrained biases against women that existed in almost all societies until recently, and still exist to a great extent in the developing world, when developing policies and programs through government budgeting. If discussions about gender budgeting and training of government officials in gender budgeting techniques strengthens this consciousness, then good policies will undoubtedly result, even without an official gender budgeting framework.

From the national experiences and data regarding gender equality presented in this book, we conclude that the level of urgency to implement gender budgeting and women-related reforms through changing government fiscal policies and financial management tools is much greater in the developing world than in the developed one. In most developing countries, gender-related reforms face strong headwinds from traditional cultural attitudes and practices that favor men. Therefore, well thought-out gender-related initiatives can serve as a counterweight to traditional attitudes, when they are undertaken and monitored for effective implementation, with support from national leaders. That is where the energy and the focus of gender budgeting advocates should be for the foreseeable future.

Glossary

Budget call circular

A budget call circular is a document, issued by the ministry of finance or office of budget, that instructs the spending ministries and other agencies of government how to formulate proposals for the areas of the budget falling under their ministries' or agencies' jurisdictions.

Chart of accounts

The chart of accounts of a government provides an organized approach to classifying the accounts of the government used to record transactions.

Convention on the Elimination of All Forms of Discrimination Against Women (CEDAW)

A Convention, adopted by the United Nations General Assembly in 1979, that emphasizes the importance of gender equality and women's and girls' development, to strengthen prosperity, and as a matter of basic human rights.

Gender budgeting

An approach to budgeting that uses fiscal policy and management to promote gender equality and women's and girls' development.

Gender budget statement

A document prepared by a ministry of finance or agency of government responsible for gender-related objectives that lays out the government's objectives, programs, and policies with respect to gender.

Gender equality audit

An analysis of the effectiveness or impact of a government program or policy or specific aspects of it, often undertaken with respect to legal or regulatory aspects of implementation.

Gender equality impact analysis

This is similar to a benefit incidence analysis, but it is more general in that it may focus not only on the incidence but on the full range of effects that might result from government programs and policies.

Millennium Development Goals (MDGs)

MDGs set targets for countries to achieve by 2015 in eight areas, including gender equality and empowering women, achieving universal primary education, and improving maternal health.

Program budgeting

An approach to budgeting that relies on a programmatic classification of expenditures (and possibly other components of the budget) and generally entails the systematic use of performance information to inform decisions about budgetary priorities.

Sustainable Development Goals (SDGs)

The SDGs, approved by the United Nations in 2015, set objectives for the international community for the next 15 years.

Index

Note: Page numbers in *italics* indicate figures and page numbers in **bold** indicate tables on the corresponding pages.

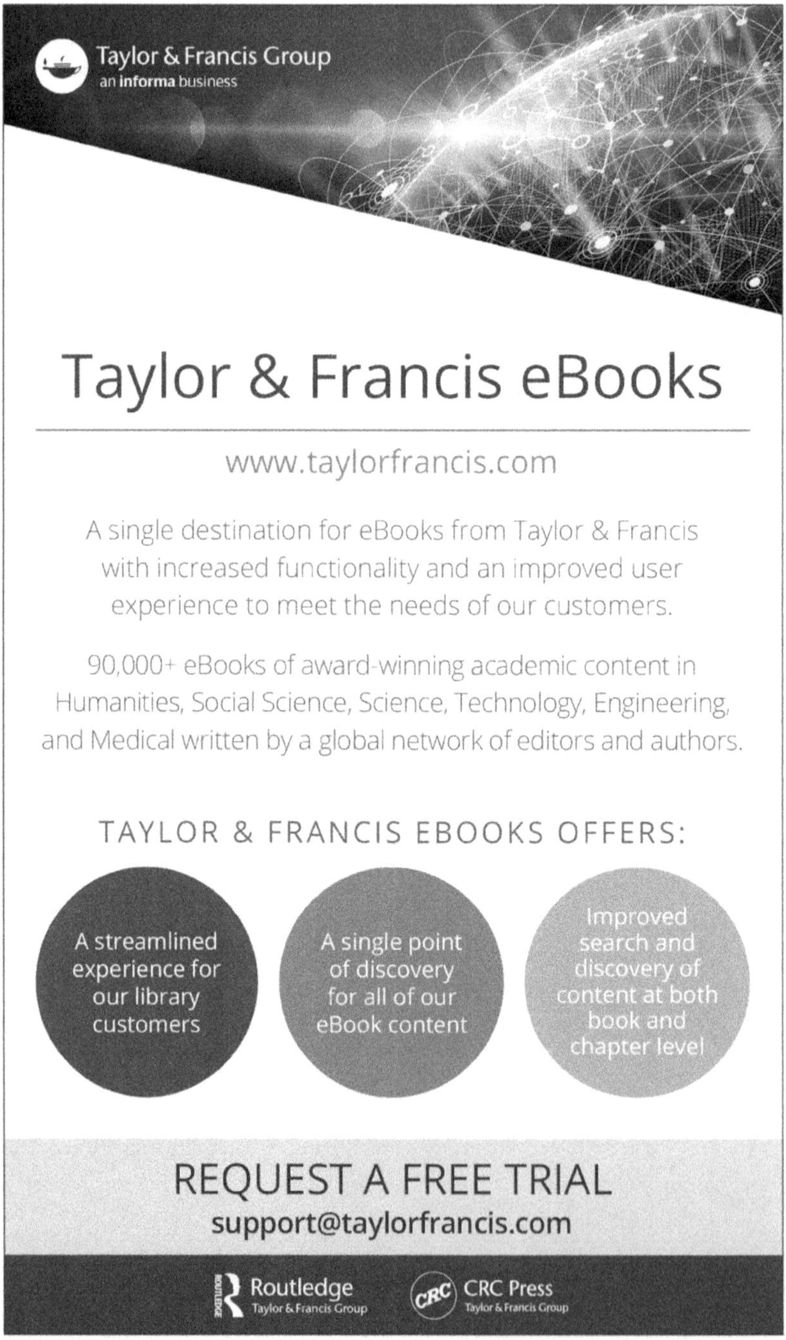
Taylor & Francis Group
an informa business
Taylor & Francis eBooks
www.taylorfrancis.com
A single destination for eBooks from Taylor & Francis with increased functionality and an improved user experience to meet the needs of our customers.
90,000+ eBooks of award-winning academic content in Humanities, Social Science, Science, Technology, Engineering, and Medical written by a global network of editors and authors.
TAYLOR & FRANCIS EBOOKS OFFERS:
A streamlined experience for our library customers
A single point of discovery for all of our eBook content
Improved search and discovery of content at both book and chapter level
REQUEST A FREE TRIAL
support@taylorfrancis.com
Routledge
Taylor & Francis Group
CRC Press
Taylor & Francis Group

For Product Safety Concerns and Information please contact our EU representative GPSR@taylorandfrancis.com
Taylor & Francis Verlag GmbH, Kaufingerstraße 24, 80331 München, Germany

www.ingramcontent.com/pod-product-compliance
Lightning Source LLC
LaVergne TN
LVHW011128300926
849160LV00008B/559
9781032175416